Traci Lords
Underneath It All

THERS FIELD.

REMEMBER that day. I WAS EXCITED. N
'D BEEN RAKING my FATHER'S FIELD. W
stupid little DRESS. ROCKiN' out. R
SorT of SWEATing. FEELiNG GOOD. I WAS
MAKiNG big angels. I WAS FEELiNG kind
grass   like
FELT   hen a
Don't   All
SEEiNG   Star
Right   ER b
cuz   lips
i coul   my fac
tickli   wer
I WAS   WARM
hot   ot it
Just   hru
Raking it up. I'D never REALLY
me like that before aside from my r
there was something wrong but
i Kinda liked it . it was sorta
like amazing. HE COULD HAVE b
on top of me for an hour

TRACI LORDS

Underneath
It All

Traci Elizabeth Lords

 HarperEntertainment
An Imprint of HarperCollins*Publishers*

FIRST EDITION

Designed by Elliott Beard

Printed on acid-free paper

Library of Congress Cataloging-in-Publication Data has been applied for.

ISBN 0-06-050820-5

03 04 05 06 07 ❖/RRD 10 9 8 7 6 5 4 3 2 1

Certain names have been changed to protect the guilty. My attorneys say it has to be that way. Funny how life works.

For the children of the night

Contents

Acknowledgments

Special thanks to Juliet Green, my true soul sister. This book would not have been possible without you.

I would also like to thank my dear husband, Jeffery Lee.

For their help and support on this journey, my appreciation goes to Josh Behar, Andrea Cagan, and Stephen LaManna.

To the following lifesavers, my gratitude: Leslie Abramson, Kenneth Beck, Alan G. Dowling, Robert Edwards, Vincent Fauci, Howard Fine, Joanne Jacobs, Lorraine, Pat Moran, Danna Rutherford, Donna Stocker, John Tierney, and Cynthia Watson.

I would also like to thank the following artists and photographers for their contributions to this project and my life: Kent Belden, Brendan Burke, Dennis Ferrara, Greg Gorman, Jeff House, Gary Kurfirst, Michelle Laurita, Cynthia Levine, Sam Maxwell, Jeff Pitterelli, Elisabetta Rogiani, Mike Ruiz, Liz Smith, Gilles Toucas, Raúl Vega, John Waters, and Albert and Elizabeth Watson.

And for their continued inspiration, Dr. Lois Lee and Children of the Night (www.childrenofthenight.org), a non-profit organization dedicated to working with children between the ages of eleven and seventeen who are victims of the sex industry.

My love to all my fans and friends who have supported me throughout my career. I welcome your comments at www.tracilords.com.

TRACI LORDS
Underneath It All

I

The Ohio Valley

grew up in a dirty little steel town called Steubenville, in eastern Ohio. It was one of those places where everyone was old, or just plain seemed like it. Even the kids felt the times, and the times were tough.

The streets were narrow and filled with men in Levi's with metal lunch boxes coming and going to the mills and the coal mines. It seemed like there was a railroad crossing on every other street, where coils of steel were piled up high along the tracks like giant gleaming snakes resting in the sun. It got real hot in the summertime and the dust from the mills wrapped around the people and held them firmly in their places, and the echo of coughing miners was so common you just didn't hear it.

The local bar, Lou Anne's, was always hopping. It wasn't odd to see your neighbor howling at the moon, and every now and then some of the miners would wander down for a cold one and tie their horses to the stop sign. Drinking was a hobby in that little town, and as in a lot of small towns, everyone knew everyone else's business. Women had not quite yet been liberated. Husbands ruled the house, women cleaned it, and any strong female opinion was often rewarded with a fat lip. But no one thought much about that.

At seventeen years old, all my mother, Patricia, ever wanted was to escape. She was born in Pennsylvania in the late 1940s, and her dad took off to California and left her and her mother alone. They moved around from place to place, and after a while she had a new stepdad and two half brothers and sisters. Never fully welcomed into this second family, she found comfort and a home at her grandmother's house.

My great-grandma Harris was a little redheaded Irish woman who loved sugar-toast and drank tea all day long, no matter how hot it was. She combined a fierce sense of social justice with an almost patrician gentleness that was unusual to find in the government housing project where she lived.

The projects were cockroach-ridden matchbox-shaped dwellings inhabited by desperately poor black families who barely survived on meager monthly public assistance checks. It was a place where hungry children played in the gutters of potholed streets while munching on sandwiches of Wonder bread and mayonnaise they dubbed "welfare burgers."

My mother, Patricia, holds me, 1968.

Just a pebble's throw away down the hill was the University of Ohio, where professors drove their shiny new cars to garden fund-raisers on the campus lawn. I remember catching glimpses of white tablecloths blowing in the afternoon breeze while ladies in crisp white dresses sipped drinks from tall glasses. Every once in a while a burst of applause from the appreciative anthill of university people would enter our world. My mouth watered at the scent of cooking barbecue meat, and I longed to race down the hill and devour the mountain of food on the huge banquet tables.

But my mother explained that "people like us" don't mix with "people like those." "People like what?" I demanded, meeting the weary look of my mother, who said it was a matter of "social class." I was five years old at the time and didn't understand why I wasn't one of the chosen few who could receive hot meals and pretty dresses. I only knew that some people had food and others didn't, and I was on the wrong side of the fence. I'd gather crab apples from my great-granny's yard and hurl them in protest toward the happy people down the hill. Although my targets were never struck, I felt justice had been served.

Great-grandma Harris lived in the first brick building at the beginning of the housing projects. There must have been fifty other little red houses, winding around like a figure eight, each one containing four units. Grandma was known by her neighbors as "the crazy white witch" because she was something of a mind reader who had a reputation for being very accurate. People didn't always like what they were told, but their fear kept Grandma safe in a very dodgy neighborhood where racism was a sickening fact of life. Despite it all, my great-grandma was always light, gentle, and seemingly unaffected by her status and the people around her. My mother got a lot of love in that house, and ultimately so did I.

In 1965 the Vietnam War had cast a spell over the people of Steubenville, inspiring in them a patriotic fervor. My mother was a beautiful redheaded teenager with piercing green eyes and a peaches-and-cream complexion. Though she was smart and ambitious, she found herself stuck, working in a jewelry store in a town that celebrated everything she loathed. She thought the war was immoral and said so to anyone who would listen.

An independent thinker, she didn't buy the "be a virgin, go to church, follow the establishment" routine that a lot of her friends were falling into. She liked to dance, listened to the Stones and Bob Dylan, and filled her private notebooks with poems. She played the guitar, made out with boys at the drive-in, and went roller-skating on Saturday nights. She lived her life fully but was always hungry for a bigger bite.

The war weighed heavily on my mother's heart because it touched her as it inevitably touched everyone. She watched as her friends' brothers marched off to a foreign land, and cried like everyone else did when they didn't come back. She ached to have a voice, to make a difference, and to be seen and valued. But she was dead broke and depressed at her lack of opportunities, and no matter which way she looked at it, her future appeared grim. Though she desperately wanted to go to college, she had only managed to get a GED and a crappy part-time job. Her father, who lived in San Diego and hadn't seen her since she was a young child, promised her a place to stay if she came out west, but he did nothing to help her realize her dreams.

My father's family, the Kuzmas, left the Ukraine in the 1930s and settled in Weirton, West Virginia. I suppose my grandfather wanted the same thing all immigrants do, a better life for himself and his family, so he bought a little house by a creek in Weirton and raised three sons and a daughter there.

My grandfather John had a thick Russian accent and a fierce work ethic that he drilled into his boys. His wife, Mary, was a stout five-footer who drank Pabst Blue Ribbon out of a big blue bowl and sang Russian songs at the top of her lungs while cooking up batches of pierogi and borscht.

My father, Louis, was born with double pneumonia and spent the first weeks of his existence in the hospital fighting for his life. He grew into a young man who dreamed of California and loathed the war. Rejected from the draft because of the scar tissue on his lungs left from the pneumonia, he ended up doing time at the steel mill instead. He also started to study biology at Morgantown College in Pennsylvania but found it difficult to

work at the mill and get an education at the same time. Overwhelmed and exhausted, he dropped out and went home to live
with his parents.

I'm told it was a gorgeous summer day when Louis Kuzma
first spied my mom standing on a corner waiting for the light to
change in downtown Steubenville. Patricia was on her way to
work and had neither time nor patience for the handsome
stranger who was trying to
pick her up. But he followed
her for several blocks, rambling on about the weather
and how it was so nice to see
her "again." He acted like she
already belonged to him. She
was about a second away from
telling him to take a flying
leap, but something stopped
her. He was a real looker, my
dad, with his baby blue Clint
Eastwood eyes, honey-dipped
skin, and a thick head of
sandy blond hair. It wasn't just
his looks that got to her, however. It was the kindred spirit
she saw in him.

When I was a baby.

They started to spend
hours together—walking and
talking about the war, their families, and their mutual longing
for California. They shared their dreams of a more exciting life
together. And they fell in love.

My parents eventually had a common-law marriage. It was
the mid-1960s and the thought of a church wedding seemed
ridiculous to Patricia. She always swore she'd pass out if she
had to stand up and promise to love someone forever while
everyone was staring at her. At eighteen that thought was just
too scary for her. Instead, they found a small house about three

miles from his parents' place, walked in the front door, announced themselves as husband and wife, and that was that.

The following year my older sister, Lorraine, was born.

I was conceived at the end of the Summer of Love and born in the wee hours of the morning on May 7, 1968. I was huge at nearly nine pounds and entered this world totally silent. People say I had the temperament of a baby Buddha with an uncanny resemblance to Clark Gable thanks to thick jet-black hair that gave my fair-haired father a bit of a shock.

My baby sisters trailed closely behind. Rachel arrived twenty-three months after me and Grace was hot on her heels, completing the tribe known as the Kuzma Girls.

My father was horrified that he had four daughters with no sons to protect them, and although he loved the idea of kids, he had little patience for the nasty reality of the diapers, whining, and constant chatter the four of us enveloped him in. After a while he started coming home later and later, often leaving us with his parents with whom we'd temporarily moved in so we could save money while my parents looked for a new house.

My mother had an odd look on her face the day my dad announced he'd found the perfect home to buy, right up the hill from his parents. There were twenty-two steps from our yard to theirs, and even though we now had our own home, Dad still parked the car in his parents' driveway and walked up the hill through a big field, down the steps, and onto our porch. My mother said Dad would never really leave his parents and she seemed to be right. But we all loved that house so much that nothing more was ever said about it.

My happiest childhood memories are of times in our backyard. My mother had an old clothesline that hung out in front. It seemed like it stretched a mile long, and I loved sitting in the sun while she hung clothes. She always twisted her hair into a soft knot on top of her head and wore a white cotton dress I loved. There was nothing but miles of green fields in front of our house, thick woods behind it, and a big winding driveway that was never used. On the outside, things looked wonderful, but inside it was a different story. My mom didn't have a car or a phone, and after a while she felt like a prisoner in her own palace. Dad was always at work or out at a bar somewhere, and at twenty-four, Mom resented the burden of tending to four little girls by herself.

The situation was tense and got worse as my mother realized she was now just a housewife, and started to resist her confinement. Dad came home drunk some nights. When he did, he became angry and wild, accusing Mom of having a lover hidden in the house somewhere. The fights were loud and unrelenting, and after a while they escalated to blows. She hated it when he drank, and told him so. Then the screaming began, every night after *The Lone Ranger*. I started retreating to the nearest closet before the program ended to secure the breathing corner, since I hated being stuck in the back with the spiders. Grandma Kuzma thought my hiding adventures indicated I was a smart girl, told me that what I was doing was called "proper planning." All my sisters coveted the spot too, and when they beat me to it I'd start to panic, running down the hallway imagining a monster at my heels. After a while it became like a game, with my father as the monster brandishing big teeth and several heads.

I wondered if he'd really eat us if we were caught, or just chew on us and spit us out as he seemed to do with Mom. She looked like a rag doll when he shook her, and I always prayed she wouldn't break. It was hard to look in her eyes after the fights. I felt guilty about not being able to help her. I really wanted to make him stop, but he was so big that I was afraid. I started studying westerns on TV, wanting to become brave like Clint Eastwood, but it didn't work, and I felt like a great big scaredy-cat instead.

I couldn't understand what Dad was so angry about. What had we done wrong? Was it because we were girls? My mom always said he wanted a son, and I wondered if things would be different if we were boys. Would that make everything better? What was the difference between boys and girls anyway? Sports? Did he want someone to play baseball with? Oh no! I couldn't play baseball! I hated tiny hard balls being thrown at me and never mastered the clobbering technique of batting that the boys in the neighborhood had. And I never wore pants. I preferred Lorraine's hand-me-down baby-doll dresses. Why did he want silly boys anyway? What was wrong with being a girl? Was it really a man's world like my mom said? And if so, where did that leave us?

The reality of the ugliness and turmoil at home eventually took its toll on our mother. One morning while we were eating our breakfast of Fruit Loops and peanut butter, she finally snapped. She'd been trying to quiet us down, but we were rowdy and she was totally overwhelmed. She picked up a shoe and hurled it across the room at my sister Lorraine. It hit her square in the forehead and sent us all to the emergency room to have my sister's forehead sewn back up. I've never seen my mother cry so much. Beside herself with guilt at harming her own child, she became determined to make some changes.

I was seven years old when we left our father. Mom said they were getting a divorce, and I immediately searched the dictionary for the word. I'd heard other children use it, but I wanted to be absolutely sure of its definition. Webster's dictionary informed me that it meant "to cut off" or "separate," and while the idea of being separated from our daddy made me sad, I couldn't ignore the relief I felt when I imagined how quiet our home would now be.

During that time, my siblings were my best friends. I belonged to Lorraine because she and I were the older girls, and Rachel hung around with Grace. We believed in democracy, and after Mom told us we were leaving our father, we huddled together in our closet courtroom for an emergency meeting. I informed the community of sisters of my findings in the dictionary and we debated whether we should stay and fight or go. There were, after all, four of us plus Mom against Dad. Lorraine thought we could take him, but I was less certain, secretly fearing those big teeth coming after me.

My little sisters didn't really understand what leaving Dad meant. They thought we were going on vacation, and Lorraine and I let them think that. We just didn't want them to be sad. I cast my vote for Mom and agreed to go along willingly, since she needed us more than he seemed to, and the meeting of the Kuzma Clan was adjourned. Just like in the meetings on TV, order was restored. Satisfied, we filed out of the closet and marched off to an unknown fate.

My father was furious when he arrived home to an empty house. We were holed up at my great-grandma's house in the

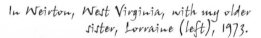

In Weirton, West Virginia, with my older sister, Lorraine (left), 1973.

projects and he called there, blaming Mom for their marital problems and demanding that she "get her ass home at once." But Mom decided we would stay, even though my sisters and I weren't welcome in this new black neighborhood, and the local girls made sure we knew it every single day. Maybe Mom thought it was safer than going back to Dad, but for us kids it was just a new battlefield. After school we always rode the bus home and the moment our feet hit concrete the war was on.

Great-granny's house was only sixty-three steps away from where the bus left us, but as close as we were to the safety zone, we were still sixty-two steps shy of getting away. We were never bothered until we reached our stop on Parkview Circle, where we would be out of parental sight and alone. Lorraine and I plotted our escape route every day on the tense ride home. We tried everything to befriend these girls but nothing worked. I offered sweets and Lorraine tried reasoning. When that failed, we prayed for the front seat closest to the doors to get a head start on them. But the angry gang of ten-year-old girls who enjoyed beating the crap out of us was not to be denied.

The white bus driver turned a blind eye, letting these kids beat on us while he sat safely in his school bus. Like so many people I'd encountered in my young life, he didn't want to get involved. I promised myself I'd never be like him and punished him with spitballs to the back of his head while he drove.

I didn't understand why the neighborhood girls hated us so much. We were all in the same boat. We lived seconds from one another, but apparently the color of our skin set us a world apart. And it was hard not to hate them back, since they made my life such a living hell.

These battles after school went on for weeks until finally we spilled the beans and told Mom, who started showing up at the bus stop to collect us. Lorraine and I were mortified that our mom was now picking us up. It was even more ammunition for ridicule in the schoolyard.

The day after Mom started showing up to collect us from the bus stop, the mothers of all the little black girls started showing up too, screaming about how "no white woman" better tell their kids how to act. My mother ignored them, leading us away and explaining that those girls were just doing what they'd been taught. Somehow that made sense. Maybe one day they would discover democracy, I thought, and rule more fairly. Still, I knew it wasn't going to happen anytime soon and I hoped Mom's presence had scared them off. Otherwise we might have to run away. We decided to give it a little more time, but I started hoarding my milk money just in case.

During this time, Dad seemed to enjoy Mom's struggles to make ends meet and deal with the gang of us on her own. I guess he figured that if things got hard enough she'd come back to him. But he was wrong. Mom enrolled in college at the University of Ohio down the street and she also landed a part-time job with a lung-study program. I remember she was studying the air and people's lungs to see if there was a connection between the two. She was very proud of this, but I thought it was really silly. I mean, anyone could see that the air in our town was brown and that couldn't be a good thing. I often felt like Pig Pen from *Charlie Brown* who was followed around by a dirty brown cloud that hung over his head wherever he went. But I didn't share these thoughts with Mom. She was happy being in school with her new job and I didn't want to spoil it.

Things were looking up. Mom bought an old Dodge—which I thought was the coolest car ever—she landed on the dean's list at school, and the neighborhood girls had grown bored of beating us up. But for my mother, the better she did, the more jealous my father became.

One afternoon he showed up after school. Granny answered the door and he told her he needed to speak to Mom. I watched my parents arguing as they walked across the street toward the park.

Later, I found out Dad had heard a rumor that Mom had a new boyfriend, a black man named Howard with whom she worked. Apparently one of Dad's buddies had seen them having coffee together and reported back. Dad was livid. From across the street, we saw him punch her in the face several times. The blood streamed down her neck as I stood screaming in Granny's bedroom window upstairs.

Granny grabbed a butcher knife, I got the broom, and the whole tribe of us tore across the street like banshees screaming our heads off. But before we got there my father took off in his red Ford truck, leaving Mom stunned and bleeding on the sidewalk. Rivers of blood streaked her beautiful white skin. I thought she was dead, and I was hysterical. My eighty-three-year-old granny tried to help her up. Mom was moving and I begged her not to die. She got up and headed for the preschool that sat on the corner where our school bus stopped. There through the window, I saw one of the teachers look at her, look at us, and then slowly close the blinds.

We waited anxiously while the doctors sewed up our mother. It took more than twenty stitches and she nearly lost her eye. Even at ten, I knew that my father's actions were nothing but cowardice. Boys weren't supposed to hit girls. My father had taught me that. The barely solid foundation beneath my feet—after the divorce and the move and the fights and separation—gave way. My whole life was turned upside down and it made me feel like God was somehow punishing me.

I thought my head would explode. My left eye twitched nervously and I couldn't stop blinking. Breathing heavily, I closed my eyes and tried to think of something else. My thoughts drifted to Saturday-morning cartoons. Images of the coyote and the Roadrunner filled my mind. I became the Roadrunner, running from the coyote. I attacked the coyote with dynamite and he blew up and I raced off into the sunset free again.

Dynamite! That's what I needed, something strong enough to stop all my enemies. I AM DYNAMITE! I thought. I AM DYNAMITE! The chant grew louder in my head as I shook in my chair, balling up my fists into tight knots of power and imagining blowing up my father's truck, orange flames dancing around me as I watched.

My mother emerged from the room with black zigzags all

over her face that held the skin together. Horrified, we raced to hug her. We were so small we ended up hugging her legs, sobbing until no tears would come.

We left town the next morning. My mom's brother picked us up and we drove and drove. We were on the run, to where I didn't know. We played the license plate game, counting them all the way to the Grand Canyon. We hiked around it, saying hello to all the geckos and other creatures that lived there. I was fascinated by that whopping hole in the ground. We stayed two days as Mom slept the hours away while our uncle watched us.

I idolized my mother's brother. He became a hero in my eyes for rescuing us from a bad place. He took us to eat at McDonald's and played hide-

An elementary school photo.

and-seek with us in the woods behind the motel. When Mom seemed a little better, we packed up our stuff and headed for Utah, where, she said, there were lots of jobs to be had.

As soon as we arrived she started looking for work, but it didn't go very well. I wondered if it was because of her face. The stitches had already come out, but the scars were still fresh. And her eyes were haunted. She was no longer the perky, happy woman people wanted to have as an employee.

The summer came and went and so did we. We were on our way back to Ohio.

I don't know why she went back, but she did, and the whole way there I was terrified of what was waiting for us. I started having frightening, vivid dreams about my father punching holes in us. I would wake in a sweat and be scared the entire day, but when I told my mother about the dreams, she simply said that Dad had done a bad thing, that he was going to be punished for it, and that we shouldn't be afraid because it was all going to be all right.

But it wasn't.

As soon as we got home, Mom was slapped with divorce papers. She was called a "kidnapper." Dad filed on the grounds of abandonment, and Mom's lawyer told her not to contest it or she would get stuck paying court costs. We attended court wearing our Sunday best and I tried to hide under the bench in the long hallway as my father arrived. We sat in the front row like evidence of their coupling. The judge turned bright red when he was handed my mom's hospital photos and immediately dismissed the kidnapping charges. Then he turned on my father: "If you ever show up in my courtroom again, it'll be a sad day indeed."

But his words meant nothing. Dad was only fined ten dollars, and he was even granted visitation rights.

Visitation rights? I jumped to my feet to protest, but Lorraine pulled me back down. I thought I must have heard him wrong. The judge was supposed to be on our side. We were the good guys. Dad was the bad guy. Mom said so. She said he was going to be punished. Why was everyone lying to me? I was indignant. We were going to be sent straight into the monster's den. That stupid man in the robe said we had to visit our father every weekend. No one asked us how we felt about that. He'd ruled without our vote. How could that happen? Didn't he see that we could be hurt? Even killed!

I was too young to die.

I no longer believed in democracy. Did that make me a Communist? My head was spinning. The monster was smiling and I wanted to smash my shoe right into his ugly face.

2

The Curse of the C Cups

A week had passed since the judge ordered us to visit our father, and my mom moved us into an apartment a few doors down from Granny. Being close to the university made it easier for her to get to class on time, but I didn't understand how every day Mom could walk down the very street where she'd lain bleeding only a few months before.

I guess being close to Granny was more important to her than I knew. Great-granny was like a mother to my mom, always there when her own mother was not.

Visiting day arrived and Dad's red truck rounded the corner, the horn blaring. He wasn't allowed to come up to the door, though, which was the only thing that dense judge had done right. When my sisters and I had discussed our impending doom, we decided not to bring up the horrible fight unless he did. I wanted to make it go away, and my only hope was that Dad would see he'd made a terrible mistake. But he never said he had, and although I slowly got over the idea that he was going to murder us, I was still pretty rattled by the fact that a crazy man would have control over us for a weekend.

Lorraine was the brave one. She volunteered to sit next to him on the way to his house. I was in awe of her fearlessness.

Mom watched us through the window as we walked toward the truck. I tried to stay calm. He would never get away with killing us all, I reasoned with myself. Besides, Mom wouldn't let us go if it wasn't all right, would she?

I felt my chest heaving as I watched my feet move along the walkway to the truck's door. Panicking when I saw his face, I commanded my feet to run away, but they defied me. Before I was able to force them into submission we were sitting in the long front seat of Dad's truck.

A row of eight little hands grasped the dashboard and I hoped my sisters wouldn't notice that my knuckles were the whitest. Silently, I cursed the idiot who'd invented trucks with no backseats.

As we rolled out of the driveway, country music played on the radio station, my dad laughed often, and he acted like nothing had happened. I felt like we had entered the Twilight Zone, and all we could do was sit quietly, not say a word, and speak only when spoken to.

From then on, we stayed with Dad every weekend.

What had been "our house" was now "Dad's house," and "visiting" it was weird. The pink piggy bank still lived in the corner by the front door, but that was the only thing that hadn't changed. There was a new carpet, a game room, and a brand-new pool table. The place was a mansion compared with Mom's one-bedroom apartment. At Daddy's, we each shared a bedroom with our designated sibling: Lorraine and I slept in the upstairs front bedroom and the little girls were down the hall. Dad's room was in the front, open to the stairway so there was no way downstairs except through his space.

Luckily, Dad slept like a log and his thunderous snores shook the whole house.

I loved prowling around that big house after everyone had gone to sleep. I fixed snacks in the kitchen and took strolls on the front lawn wearing the big boots that Dad always left by the door near the patio. My mom used to say, "Don't judge a person until you've walked a mile in his shoes," so I strolled the yard in Dad's boots, trying to feel like him. I wanted to understand what he had done and forgive him, but I couldn't get the image of Mom's bloody face out of my head.

For years I would replay our first evening back together, amazed at the things he never did or said. I just couldn't figure out how he could fix a barbecue as a special treat for us yet say nothing about the beating he gave our mother. Didn't he realize how frightening that was? I was sure he saw me eyeing him at supper, searching his face for signs of remorse, waiting for him to say he was sorry. The words never came out of his mouth, but I thought I saw regret in his eyes. I just didn't know what he regretted. Was he sorry he had beaten a woman? Or sorry we saw him do it? I couldn't read his mind. Where was Great-granny when I needed her? Maybe her mental powers could give me the answers I so desperately needed.

It was hard to hate my father He was my father and I needed him. I wanted to forget, so I made myself think of all the things I liked about him. He was the Julia Child of Weirton. A fabulous cook, he filled our weekend visits with homecooked pierogies, sweet cakes, and stews. The kitchen was the only place I ever felt at ease as a child. Food was like a tunnel straight to Dad's heart and he was kindest when covered in flour with a piecrust in his hand. Soon I was promoted to his assistant, since I spent so much time in the kitchen by his side. I loved rolling up the cabbage, and together we created the perfect blend of spicy-sweet cabbage rolls.

These good times would later confuse me, as it was always feast or famine for us girls. We were stuffed to the gills on the weekends and hungry the rest of the week. Dad seemed blind to the fact that Mom never had enough money to give us the things we needed, and seeing our father live comfortably while we struggled every day made me resent him.

Eventually the weekends blended together as time began to heal our wounds on the inside as well as the outside. Mom's face was glowing again. That horrible day at the hospital became a distant memory. Finally, it was as if the doors to our prison had been unlocked. We were pardoned, and I was allowed to be happy again.

We spent many Sunday afternoons digging in the huge garden Dad had planted in front of his house. We grew tomatoes, corn, lettuce, and radishes. My sisters and I picked the fresh vegetables to make big salads for dinner, and Dad gave us bags of tomatoes to take home. When it was hot, Dad took us swimming at his brother's house, where we played in Uncle Johnny's pool while the grown-ups drank beer under the sun. We rode our bikes, played cops and robbers by Granny Kuzma's creek, and I even snuck Granny a beer now and then.

Those are the early days I remember most fondly as a kid: hanging out on Granny's front porch, listening to crickets sing, and going about our business of growing up.

Lorraine and I developed early. We were nine and ten when Dad started talking about our "blossoming," and it turned him into a maniacal clipper of sex advice columns. His favorite was "Dear Abby," which we secretly nicknamed "Dear Old Daddy." It was embarrassing to be constantly greeted with clippings about young girls who get pregnant. Dad referred to these girls as "whores," "bad girls" who got what they deserved. I didn't understand why my father was so obsessed with this subject. Did he think I was in danger of becoming one of "those" girls? I became resentful of my ever-changing body. "Play and you're gonna pay," he'd ramble, or "only whores make out with boys" or "boys only want one thing." But I had no idea what the "one thing" was.

Word on the school playground was that if a boy gave a girl kisses "down there" a baby was made. I wondered what it would feel like to get kissed on my panties, and fantasized about my new friend, Ricky, doing the kissing. He was an older boy I'd met a few months earlier. I'd been walking to the birthday party of a girlfriend from school when he did a few laps around me on his ten-speed bike. I was ten, he was sixteen, and he was funny, making me laugh by pretending to fall from his bike.

When I arrived at the party I told all my girlfriends that I had a secret admirer. I didn't even know his name, but I was sure he liked me. It made me feel wanted, and as I walked home that evening, I heard the clicking of his bike behind me. He

Christmas in Mingo Junction, age ten.

stopped, got off, and pushed his bike as we walked together. He told me that his name was Ricky and that he saw me at the park up the street all the time. He liked the way I wore my hair. I'd never had a boy speak to me like that before and was flush with excitement. As we neared my house I got nervous that my sisters might see us together and report to Dad, so I told him I had to go as I raced off, promising to meet him on the swings in the park the following afternoon.

Ricky looked young for sixteen, and he wasn't much taller than I was. He had no guy friends and got teased constantly because of his height. He told me how the girls at school were constantly mean to him too, and how bad it made him feel, but none of that mattered anymore because now he had me.

I couldn't wait for the school bell to ring every day so I could see Ricky, and we had so much fun playing together. We wrestled in the tall grass and he always let me win, and we collected lightning bugs in a big jar. They were our candlelight, he said, and I thought that was so funny. When he pushed me on the swings, I soared so high I thought I was going to fly away. I screamed and laughed until tears ran down my face, and the pure exhilaration of it all set me free.

Through him, I was learning how to be fearless, just like my sister Lorraine.

I drew hearts all over my notebooks at school: I love Ricky. I love Ricky. I love Ricky. I couldn't wait to bring my new best friend to the upcoming school dance. My friends would be so jealous that my boyfriend was in high school! I was bursting to tell my sisters, but he made me promise to wait for a special time.

So I kept my secret.

I've always felt feline, enjoying the simple pleasures of a cat, like lying in the sun all stretched out, or feeling the grass tickling my limbs. It was sheer bliss for me. One lazy afternoon about three months after I met Ricky, I was lying in a field making big angels in the tall grass as I waited for him. We had a date. He was late, but I didn't care, content to soak up the rays of sunshine, peaceful and warm.

I must have fallen asleep because when I woke up, Ricky was stroking my hair. I purred quietly in pleasure, happy he was finally there. He was so beautiful with his sweet lips and long blond hair falling in his eyes. He kissed me softly as he'd done so many times before, and I cuddled closer to him. Lying on top of me, he pressed his body against mine, and I could feel the wetness in my panties as I wiggled under his weight.

He told me I was beautiful as he started unbuttoning my blouse. I was in a trance, but I blocked his fingers and told him to stop. My heart was racing. I'd never let anyone touch me under my shirt and it scared me.

A flash of anger passed over his face but just as quickly disappeared. He said he was sorry and changed the subject. He said he wanted to play the wedding game, which we'd played many times before. It was where we pretended to be married and he'd carry his new bride across the threshold into a new life. Only this time he said we'd be going on a honeymoon.

It was getting dark outside and I wasn't sure about his new game. I was still a little mad at him for messing with the buttons on my blouse. I wanted to go home. I tried to get up and he pushed me back down. Alarms were going off in my head. I was scared and I told him so, but he kept taking my clothes off. I tried to push him off me but he wouldn't budge. I felt so weak beneath my friend. Why was he doing this? I had never done anything mean to him. I started to cry and he put his hand over my mouth, telling me to be quiet.

"This is what you asked for," he whispered in my ear.

Those words stunned me as my thoughts drifted to my fantasy of him kissing me on my panties. *Oh my God*, I thought, what had I wished for? I heard myself sobbing, but it all became dreamlike. I felt like a part of me wasn't even there anymore as I struggled to free myself.

When he entered me, I screamed until I couldn't scream anymore, but he wouldn't stop. When it was over, he left me lying there all alone, bloody and naked in the dark.

My whole body ached and I tasted blood.

Huge sobs rocked my whole being. Terrified, I crawled around looking for my clothes, scared to death he'd come back.

I just couldn't believe what he'd done.

I didn't know how bad I was hurt, only that I felt like dying. Ricky and I were best friends. We were supposed to get married when we grew up. Now everything was ruined. What had I done? Was this the "one thing" boys wanted? Dad had tried to warn me, but I didn't understand. Maybe I was one of those bad girls from the "Dear Abby" column. Oh my God, was I going to be pregnant now?

It was my fault, all my fault.

I walked home in a daze, climbed in the back window to the bathroom, and stood in the shower until my skin was wrinkly. Everything ached. I thought I would cry forever. I loved Ricky so much and now I was losing him. When I stepped out of the shower, I still couldn't get his face out of my head, and I kept hearing my dad's voice, over and over again telling me that only whores kissed boys.

Then it had to be true. How could I deny it? I was a whore.

And I was only ten years old.

3

Hazy Days

It had been weeks since the attack in the field. I told no one . . . desperate to forget it even happened. I said nothing in my diary, afraid that if I wrote the words or dared utter them aloud I'd be found out. The thought of my father knowing a boy put his thing in me filled me with shame. I was certain his love would be gone forever, and at ten years old the thought of being hated by my daddy was unbearable. Silence was my only salvation. If no one knew, maybe I was innocent.

Forcing thoughts of Ricky out of my head, I pretended it was all a dream. But as the weeks dragged on, memories of that day haunted me. I couldn't shake it. Every blond boy at school became Ricky. His presence was *everywhere*, following me around like a ghost. I was afraid of my own shadow. I felt hollow inside . . . gutted and raw . . . left with nothing but an empty carcass to carry me to fourth grade. Deeply wounded, I turned my back on myself, refusing to meet my own eyes in the mirror when I dressed for school.

I wished I were someone else. I hated myself . . . everything about me . . . even my stupid name. Who names their daughter Nora anyway? Why couldn't I have a pretty, popular name like Lisa or Tina or Traci?

I started pretending to be other people, borrowing my identities straight from Saturday-morning television. I was a cowgirl with a big fat mustache who could shoot her enemies dead, a flying fairy dressed in pink, a mouse that stole cheese from a big cat named Tom.

I preferred my make-believe world, discovering a place where I had total control.

Months had passed since Ricky hurt me, but it still felt fresh. I was confused by what had happened. Was sex always violent? Was it supposed to be that way? I didn't know for sure. I only knew that I felt unbelievably sad . . . like I had been robbed. But was I part of it? Was I an accomplice in the theft of my own body? I went there. I waited for him . . . welcomed his sweet lips . . . even felt pleasure at first. What did that mean?

Was I guilty too?

I spoke to no one at school, ashamed of my swelling breasts and secret past. Hiding behind my long wheat-colored hair, I tried desperately to disappear. I became obsessed with understanding what I was going through, spending all my free time scanning books in the school library, certain there must be a book with answers to my questions. I discovered an author named Judy Blume, who wrote about young girls and sex, and was shocked to find some of the girls were just as curious to know about sex as I was! Maybe I wasn't a freak after all. What if everyone thought these things?

But how could that be? Why would my father say sex was the devil's work if it wasn't?

What was going on!

The more I read, the more confused I became. Passages on menstruation and pregnancy held me transfixed as I realized I couldn't have a baby—I didn't even have my period yet! But why hadn't anyone told me any of this? Was it true, or did books lie too?

I slammed the book closed and flung it across the table, suddenly aware of my public outburst when the school librarian told me to collect my things and "behave like a lady." Glaring at her, I stomped out and stared down my giggling classmates. My eyes screamed, Don't fuck with me . . .

Liars! Robbers! I was a runaway train, challenging everyone on the way home with an anger I couldn't even fathom. Come on, I was saying. Take me on!

Cutting through the Jewish cemetery as the crisp fall air stung my lungs, I hopped over the graves of dead people and muttered, "Excuse me," not wanting to disturb the resting souls and remembering what the minister at our United Methodist Church said about respecting the dead. Did one have to die to be respected?

By the time my feet sank in the marshy grass near the end of the cemetery, my mind was crystal clear. Blood was pumping through my veins and it felt good. Adrenaline, I thought, smiling to myself. I had discovered its release.

My mother was taping boxes together when I got home. I guess she couldn't pay the rent again, I thought, making my way toward the kitchen for some water. I slammed the refrigerator door for some acknowledgment. She said nothing and ignored me as she finished loading a box of dirty clothes. For the first time ever, I lashed out.

"*Mother!*" I screamed, startling her. "Where are we going this time?" I stood fuming in the kitchen doorway.

"Hey," she said firmly, "don't make a fuss. Your sisters will be home any time now and you need to help me pack up. We're moving this weekend to Mingo Junction. Don't worry, it's just until Mom gets back on her feet."

I stomped across the living room, making a huge display of flinging the bedroom door open, and locked myself inside. I didn't care about leaving this dump—I just wanted to be seen! Why was it always about my mother getting back on her feet? What about us? Sitting in the corner of the room, I could hear my sisters coming home. Lorraine pounded on the door and demanded entrance. I lifted myself from the floor and unlocked the door.

Maybe the next house would give me my own bedroom.

The following Saturday we moved again. This time it was

fifty miles down the Ohio River to a foul little town called Mingo Junction. We looked like a traveling circus with our bags strapped to the top of Mom's beat-up brown car.

Moving was nothing new to us girls. Mom dragged us from dump to dump at least once a year. We had no permanent home, but at least constant change was one thing I could count on in my life. Mom would run out of money, unpaid rent would add up, and sooner or later we'd have to leave and start all over again. We knew she felt bad about dragging us around, and maybe that's why we said so little about it. She was our mother and we loved her. Besides, what did four girls under twelve know anyway?

Maybe the change would be good for us this time. Maybe the move would help me forget about Ricky.

Driving up the steep hill toward our new residence, I felt safer already. I closed my eyes and thanked God, thinking of what I would say to him on Sunday—it was time for me to at least tell God what had happened. It was settled. When Daddy dropped us off at Sunday school, I would confide in the Lord. But wait a minute. Why did Daddy drop us off? Why didn't he ever come in? If God was as important as Dad said, why did he ignore Him? If Dad didn't trust God, maybe I shouldn't either. And why was God a Him? Is that why boys were better than girls?

I looked at my sisters to see if they were struggling too, but I saw no trace of worry on their faces. Why was I so tortured by these thoughts when they weren't? Was I the bad seed? Daddy said there was one in every family. Was he talking about me?

Good grief . . . would it ever end?

Lorraine hummed a song to herself, her golden hair resting on the backseat of Mom's car. She saw me staring at her and wrapped her arm around me. "Don't worry, sissy," she said, "it's not so bad." Yes it is! I wanted to cry. Tell her everything! But I couldn't speak. I could only stare at her in awe and hope that one day maybe I would be as peaceful and strong and pretty as she was.

Our next place was the smallest one yet: a one-bedroom apartment on the second floor of a weathered building at the top of a long and winding road. It was pouring outside, and the dark fall skies were a perfect backdrop to the stormy mood that had come over me during the ride. I pressed my face against the window in the backseat and watched my hot breath fog up the glass. Some people with cameras were making a movie called *The Deer Hunter* outside, and we had to wait for their car to come by before we could park and unload our stuff.

As I watched them shoot pictures of our new neighborhood, I wondered if the man in the movie hunted deer like our daddy. I thought of the deer's vacant eyes staring straight ahead as it swung from a rope in Dad's backyard. The memory made me feel sick and I was glad when Mom finally pulled into our new carport, leaving the film crew behind.

It was Saturday and normally we'd be at our father's house eating mountains of sweets by now. But we had to move boxes in the rain. As I climbed the stairs to our new apartment I thought of my father. I dreaded him picking us up the following day. We all knew he would be angry—he always was when we moved. I'm not sure if he was angry because he had to drive twenty minutes farther to collect us, or if he was disappointed that a day had been taken off his weekend visit.

I liked to believe the latter, but I wasn't sure if it was true.

Looking back on those times, I think he was just plain angry that his life hadn't turned out as he wanted it to. A divorced father who worked in a steel mill was a far cry from the ocean-ologist dream he shared with my mother when they first met. Perhaps my father felt robbed too.

Dubbed "the science experiment" by my father, my mother's new boyfriend really wasn't that far off from the description. Roger Hays was attending the University of Ohio at the same time as my mother, and they'd hit it right off the first day they met in history class. A seminary student from Fort Lauderdale,

Roger drove a big lime green van that reminded me of the Green Hornet. He was several years older than my mom and prematurely balding with a yellowish long beard he sometimes braided. My dad referred to him as "the fat hippie," but he wasn't really fat—he just had a bit of a paunch from eating too many Ho Hos.

Mom splurged on a brand-new dress for their first date. She was ready when he arrived, looking gorgeous in her pale peach taffy-colored outfit. She seemed embarrassed to have him see our dirty apartment and she rushed around quickly gathering her things to go.

Washing clothes in the kitchen sink and sneaking glances at the two of them, I got annoyed when he came over and exclaimed, "Lookeeeeeeee, she's showing me how she does her laundry!" like it was some kind of game for his benefit. No, bonehead, I thought, disgusted, I'm doing my laundry because my socks are standing up by themselves and Mom is too busy with you to care. I felt he was just another clueless grown-up and wrote him off immediately, ignoring him. Glad to see him leave, I finished my kitchen duties and took up my guard post in the living room, falling asleep by the TV as I waited for Mom to come home.

Roger and my mom became an item fast. Roger's father was an admiral in the navy and I guess he had a few extra bucks because he was always sending him money. Roger, in turn, spent some of it on us. He bought us lots of groceries and filled the apartment with junk food. Free goodies seemed to be his way of taking care of us while he monopolized our mother's time.

My sisters and I shared the one tiny bedroom that was filled with our bunk beds. We were like loaves of Wonder bread resting on shelves. It was so cramped in our room that we had to take turns getting in and out of bed to avoid a mass pileup. We each had our own corner of the room where we kept our clothes and schoolbooks. Our things rested in piles on the hardwood floor. Mom slept on the couch in the living room. But now that Roger was around, she spent less and less time at home, and more and more time in Roger's Green Hornet–mobile, conveniently parked alongside our house.

I was pissed that she had chosen him over us. Barely eleven, I was too young to be in charge of raising my eight- and nine-year-old sisters. And although twelve-year-old Lorraine really carried the weight of this responsibility, I still felt overwhelmed by my siblings' needs. What kind of mother leaves four young children alone in a house while she sleeps in her boyfriend's van? She even let him run a plug from our house to his "house on wheels" so that it stayed warm. Meanwhile, the long orange extension cord that ran down the icy sidewalk and poked under our front door brought a freezing draft with it.

How could she do this? None of the other mothers in the neighborhood did this and plenty of them were single too!

The old lady who lived next door pumped me for information about the goings-on in our place whenever she saw me. She was Daddy's information source too and was clearly offended by the orange cord. She'd follow it down the sidewalk and poke at it with her cane, swearing under her breath about property values.

Mom's hippie boyfriend quickly became the talk of the neighborhood and I was mortified. Dad was crankier than ever, making nasty comments every time he saw the "heathen mobile," and I was totally embarrassed, choosing back routes to our house so I didn't add to the public spectacle that was going on in the front. I even considered putting a bag over my head as I'd seen the Unknown Comic on *The Gong Show* do. That was one way to protect my identity.

It was impossible to ignore the disapproving stares of the neighborhood ladies as I left for school each morning. Although the change of residence had helped me forget Ricky, and had put a hold on the nightmares that had been haunting me for months, I now found myself ashamed of something new — my mother. I was truly mortified that she was acting so *unmotherly*. Wasn't it bad enough that in a new neighborhood we already had the ugliest car and lived in the dingiest building? Why did she have to make it even worse? Now there were rumors of her having sex in the driveway, which made me even hotter with anger.

Totally ashamed at the way we lived, I never brought any friends home from school and always kept to myself. My only real escape came from fantasy. I disappeared into a world of books, becoming obsessed with science fiction. I believed in other planets and races, searching the sky at night for stars, secretly hoping to be abducted and taken to a kinder planet. Maybe God had made a mistake sending me here, I thought. It was obvious I belonged somewhere else. Here I questioned everything, and nothing ever made sense.

It came as a surprise when Roger and my mom took us on their summer vacation to Key West. They made us swear we wouldn't tell our dad, but that was the last thing on my mind. I was just glad I didn't have to stay home baby-sitting my sisters.

For the trip, Roger had converted the van into a rolling motel. We had bunk beds and a Porta Potti hidden away in the closet and there was a tiny kitchen area with a little sink we could wash up in. Heading out on the road, we passed the time lounging in the back playing checkers or ticktacktoe for hours. We listened to the stereo, singing along to Air Supply and REO Speedwagon, and I took long naps in the bottom bunk closest to the front of the van while Mom and Roger hung out in the pilot and copilot seats up front. There was a curtain they pulled when they wanted to speak privately, and I just enjoyed cruising down the highway to destinations unknown.

At night we stayed at campgrounds and ate at restaurants serving all-you-can-eat smorgasbords. That's where Roger taught us how to steal food. Leaving the restaurant with our pockets bulging, we felt like we were really a part of something, like it was a special secret that only we shared.

During this first "family" vacation, I began to see Roger as a provider, which was something we all desperately needed. At eleven years old, I didn't realize teaching us how to steal was wrong. I was just glad he was there. And so, I slowly began to let down my guard and trust him.

It started on that long trip to the Keys, when I awoke from a deep sleep feeling cold.

I sat up, realizing my tube top was pulled all the way down, exposing my breasts. I didn't know what time it was, or where we were, but it was dark outside and I could just make out Roger standing near me.

My sisters were snoring under mounds of covers, the curtain up front was closed, and Roger was right over me, zipping up his pants. I was disoriented, confused. *Where am I? What's going on?* He just stood there, staring at my breasts.

After a moment, he turned away and opened the curtain. Mom was driving, and he moved into the copilot seat. He tried to make a joke about it to her, announcing loudly that my top fell down and "Hee hee hee, look at her little poached eggs!"

Hot with fury, I pulled up my top. Mom smiled in my direction and scolded Roger lightly with a "Behave now." It was all just a funny joke. She couldn't see what I was going through. How upset I was! I felt violated and had no idea why.

Again I doubted my instincts. Surely Mom would tell me if something was wrong. I had to believe that. She was my mom. So I got angry with myself, for not knowing the answers and for doubting the very people who loved me.

Settling back down, I listened intently to the songs on the radio. Someday I'd get away from all this. I sang along to the music, losing myself in the words and fantasizing about running away to join a band.

4

Route 66

Roger Hays did what my parents had always dreamed of: he moved to California.

Only days before we'd left for Florida, he and my mom were discussing whether he should accept a job as an engineer in El Segundo after graduation. Mom had put on a brave face, but I could see the thought of losing him really mattered to her. Roger just said they'd talk about it later.

When we returned from the Keys, we got the news. Mom sat us down and told us Roger was moving to California, and in two months' time, we'd be joining him. I was surprised at how quickly it was all happening. We'd moved a dozen times over the years but this was different. We were leaving for good.

A panic rose in my chest as I thought of my father. Dad would never let us go. What kind of trouble was she trying to start? I sat there sweating in my plastic chair, waiting for Mom to continue. "You'll love it! Palm trees, sun all year round, the ocean, and so many more opportunities to make money!"

The place Mom described sounded pretty great. I got excited as I imagined what it would be like. I hated our cramped little apartment, and certainly wasn't going to miss the cockroaches and freezing winters. But most of all I wasn't going to miss my father. I was tired of feeling scared all the time and sick of the way he would talk to us about our mom. I felt like I was being poisoned. We needed to get away.

I looked over at Lorraine and wondered if she was thinking about Dad too. She hadn't seen him for months. On our last visit, they'd argued about a red mark on her neck. He said it was a "love bite" and she insisted it wasn't. Then he slapped her in the face. She'd stormed out of the house while I trailed behind with the little girls. I was stunned. He'd attacked her without warning. Would I be next?

Mom warned us not to say a word about the move. It was two tense months away and I was as nervous as a cat in a room full of rocking chairs, convinced one of us would accidentally blurt out our escape plan.

It was so smoggy the morning we left Ohio that I could taste the air. People were pushing and shoving to get on the bus. My mother was trying to herd my sisters and me through the line. She was shaking so badly the suitcases kept falling out of her hands.

One by one we marched up the big black rubber steps onto the Greyhound bus. It had a logo of a running dog painted on the side. I liked that. It was a good sign, I thought. Freedom. I held my breath. "One, two, three, four," I counted to myself, looking down at my Mickey Mouse watch. My cheeks felt hot as I exhaled. *Hiccup.* I was so nervous I couldn't stop hiccuping. I could taste the IHOP breakfast we'd eaten hours earlier.

The bus driver was a friendly black man who instantly became my hero. I wanted to hug him, but I just smiled as I moved toward the back. I had to pee again but held it in favor of getting a window seat. I sat there holding hands with Lorraine, looking out the window, searching the parking lot. Was Dad going to appear suddenly?

I couldn't stand to look anymore so I slammed my eyes shut and tried not to breathe too loudly. "Come on, mister, pull this bus onto the highway," I prayed silently. I sneaked a peek at Mom. She was quiet and her eyes seemed glazed. I wondered if she'd been crying. My little sisters were playing a game of go fish and just as we were pulling out onto the highway, two police cruisers stopped our bus. I threw up all over my white mary janes.

My sister howled at our mother that I'd made a mess, it stunk, and she wanted a new seat. I hid my head between my legs and started to mop myself up as the cops boarded and walked right by us.

I felt guilty, though I didn't know why. I looked up in time to see the policemen take a young boy off the bus. He was carrying a yellow duffel bag with a big eagle on it and he looked very sad. He started to cry and I did too. I wondered if his dirty little house was as bad as ours. My body was tight. I thought of my favorite cartoon characters, Bugs and the Roadrunner, and became strong. I am dynamite, I told myself, clenching my fists. I can survive anything.

I closed my eyes and willed that bus onto the highway, leaving my father behind.

We drove for three days and three nights, stopping at rest stops and little diners along the way. My body ached from sitting and I developed a rash from the cloth seat. But I didn't care. I felt better every day. Safer. The distance gave me room to breathe.

I scribbled giant question marks in my notebook as I daydreamed, trying to imagine what my new bedroom would be like. It should be pale pink, I decided, with a beautiful vanity and a big mirror for Lorraine and me to share. We would brush each other's hair while listening to the Eagles' "Hotel California" on the radio our new stepdaddy would buy us. There would be a whole new group of friends at school and no one would tease me anymore. At lunchtime I wouldn't have to pretend not to be hungry to avoid the shame of my free-meal coupon.

My mom would have a whole closetful of pretty peach-colored dresses and she'd smile all the time. My little sisters would get the braces they needed and we'd all be happy. Our new family would be perfect. It was all going to be okay. The sun would shine every day and set every night over the swaying palm trees in our front yard.

I sat grinning all the way to California. I love palm trees, I thought, I love my mom . . . it's all okay. We're safe now.

5

Hollywood, California

Welcome to Hollywood, California, ladies and gentlemen. Please be sure to gather all your personal belongings before departing the bus. This is our final destination. Thank you for choosing Greyhound."

I sat bolt upright from a dead sleep. I was annoyed that I slept through our arrival, but who cared! We were here! Bouncing slightly in my seat, I pressed my face to the window to take in every new image. There, sitting in the parking lot, I spied it: the green van! "Roger's here, Mommy! Look, there he is!" My sisters and I started squealing with delight.

I didn't realize how much I'd missed him.

My mother's face flushed with anticipation. Though desperately trying to gather our things, round us up, and fix her hair all at the same time, she was beaming. I got lost in her beautiful eyes. She was so stunning and in control of everything in that moment, and I loved her more than ever. I wanted to tell her how proud I was of her, how brave I thought she was, that it would all be different now. But I didn't know those words then. I watched her, soaking her in. The fear of being wrong suddenly nagged at me. But how could I be wrong? She looked like she'd just won something, and I hadn't seen her smile in such a long time.

We were off the bus, in that van, and on our way to Redondo Beach faster than I could say "Book 'em Dano." I barely caught a glimpse of Hollywood Boulevard as we pulled onto the 101 freeway, but I still remember the way the stars lay along the sidewalk. I lost my breath for a moment, in awe of the palm-lined street. We drove off just as I had truly arrived. I knew then I'd be back.

I just didn't know why.

6

Two Butch Palms

We pulled into the driveway of a white-and-tan Spanish-style house in a typical middle-class neighborhood in Redondo Beach, California. Roger ruffled my hair as he pointed out the twin palms on the front lawn. "Those are our two 'butch palms.'" He laughed. We all giggled along with him, but I didn't have a clue what he meant.

Maybe it was California slang.

I couldn't help noticing all the cars parked in the driveway and wondered if they were for us. Maybe when we were bigger we'd all get to choose one. But until then they'd just sit there, pretty in the sun, waiting for us to grow up. My mother was getting close to the house and I had to be the first to touch the doorknob.

Racing up the steps, I threw open the front door, which was strangely unlocked. Maybe people are more relaxed in California, I reasoned with myself, bursting into the living room with my sisters right behind me. The first thing I saw was an extremely hairy fat man wearing boxer shorts, drinking a beer with one hand and smoking a really smelly cigarette with the other. I was pretty sure it was "reefer." I'd seen Roger smoking it before and knew Mother wouldn't be pleased. I wanted to punch this man in his jelly belly for ruining my perfect day. He was sitting on what I thought was supposed to be our couch. He smiled at me and said, "Hey, my name's Greg. You must be the Kuzmas. I'm your roommate."

I stood there, mouth gaping, staring at this bear of a man that would be living with us. Mother was behind me in the doorway. I thought she was going to cry as she scowled at Roger. The air was suddenly thick again.

7

Junior HIGH

Junior high is a place where young people get stoned," my pretty, tan pot-smoking thirteen-year-old next-door neighbor, Dee Dee, informed me on my first day of school in southern California. I was sitting under a palm tree on the campus of my new school, completely amazed that we actually had to leave the building to go from class to class. The schools back east were all enclosed. You entered the building at sunrise and didn't see light again until that afternoon, if at all.

I'd been eyeballing my watch all morning waiting for my least favorite time of the day to arrive: lunchtime. I had learned long ago how dangerous and humiliating something as simple as lunch could be. Having been the new kid a dozen times before, I knew what was coming. It was about pecking order. If you wanted any respect you had to fight for your place. I'd avoid insensitive teachers hunting me down announcing to the entire cafeteria that I'd forgotten my free-meal coupon, which would seal my doom with the title of "loser" forever. I was in a foul mood. Didn't any of these teachers ever think about what it must be like to be a poor kid in a rich world?

How could people so oblivious to reality teach me anything?

The vultures had been circling the playground waiting for me to make my move. They were all so . . . white, but that was where our similarities ended. I felt like I was from another planet with my Ohio look. A stranger in a strange land, I sat completely still on a bench looking for Lorraine, my partner in crime. I couldn't see her anywhere. My sister was usually close by, since she was only one grade ahead of me, but now I wondered if older classrooms had recess in another area. My thoughts drifted to Saturday-morning cartoons and I envisioned the Wonder Twins, who could disappear in times of trouble. I concentrated, thinking how cool it would be if it really worked, for once. But I was still here.

My mop of curly light brown hair and pale skin stuck out like a sore thumb. California girls didn't wear makeup, so I wiped the red gloss from my lips and crossed my arms over my breasts, hoping no one would notice me. Sitting on the bench counting pebbles, I watched shoes go by. I saw Vans, Reeboks, and a pair of hot pink thongs—a far cry from the winter snow boots of Ohio. I was glad I'd worn my red Christmas shoes. Mom had bought them for me last year and I'd been saving them for a special occasion. They twinkled prettily in the sun like Dorothy's in *The Wizard of Oz*. "You're a long way from Kansas, Dorothy," I giggled to myself.

I caught pieces of conversation that made no sense. I didn't have the California slang down yet. It was like another language, but I tried to relax and enjoy it. I told myself it was an adventure, pretending I was in a foreign country. I was daydreaming about France when these long golden-brown legs walked right up to me and demanded my attention. Hello, legs. The feet were bare, a no-no I had been told by the plump school administrator that very morning. The toenails were well groomed and painted slate-black with a silver thunderbolt on the big toes. Looking up, I saw the girl was wearing an AC/DC T-shirt with a thunderbolt on it. My favorite band! I was immediately in awe of her.

She stopped right in front of me and we stared each other

down, my eyes intense as I dared this rock chick to mess with one of Ozzy's own. But she just looked at me, snapped her gum, and said, "So, you just moved in with the freaks next door, huh?"

Before I could say anything, she was sitting next to me gathering pebbles into a pile. We talked about music and I was relieved to find one thing that hadn't changed. Kids everywhere liked heavy metal music. Ozzy was a god and Judas Priest reigned on high.

Dee Dee gave me an education, pointing out which teachers gave pop quizzes, which homework I should do, and what I didn't have to bother with. I found out beer drinking and pot smoking were common pastimes in junior high, and that Dee Dee often stole the butts of marijuana cigarettes out of her parents' ashtray and sold them for a buck apiece on the playground.

We were interrupted by a couple of boys walking by. One of them made a comment about "the new chick" and wham! Dee Dee hurled pebble after pebble at his naked ankles. I found myself grinning at her feistiness. Thump, bam . . . ooouch . . . quit it! They hightailed it across the playground lickety-split and she went back to her rock collecting. Her calm blue eyes seemed wise beyond their years and were burdened with experience. I wondered if she suffered from the same afflictions I did. She told me she lived in the house next door with a bunch of freaks she happened to be related to. She couldn't wait to grow up and move out of this dead-end place.

It hit me like a truck: Ohio or California, it wasn't the place—it was the life, being young and having seen things you couldn't just wish away.

The school bell rang and took me out of my trance. Lunch was over and I had a new partner in crime. She said she'd wait for me after school. Then she reached over and planted a kiss on the side of my mouth. I didn't know what to think. Was this the way people said good-bye in California? I'd never been kissed by a girl like that, but it was exciting. I breathed in the sweetness of her skin. She smelled of vanilla, and, strangely, I wanted to kiss her again.

I got up and quickly walked back to class, fearful she would guess what I was thinking. What does it mean? I thought, feeling weird that I was having lustful thoughts about a girl.

Dee Dee and I spent the remainder of the year hanging out together, trading homework and avoiding our parental units. I managed to squash my fantasies about her, but I still couldn't help but wonder if she'd ever try to kiss me again.

Mom and Roger were on the rocks.

They kept arguing about broken promises. She was livid we had to live with strangers and demanded he stop using drugs. I wondered if it was pot, or maybe something else. Everyone smoked pot, so I didn't think that was a big deal. And despite the fact that fat Greg and his friends were annoying, it was still a hell of a lot better living in California than in our crappy little hovel in Ohio. I wasn't going back there, and I certainly couldn't go back to my father. He had disappeared from my life. I didn't even get letters from him anymore. It hurt to see how quickly he'd forgotten us. Well, I'd forget him too!

I was fed up, sick of Mom's hasty decisions ruining my life. I wasn't going to let it happen again. I started taking Roger's side in the fights and decided then and there that I was better off on my own.

Music blared and parties were always raging in our living room. I took Dee Dee's advice for making a little money on the side and snagged roaches from the ashtray for resale later. It was impossible to get any homework done, though I somehow managed to pass all my classes anyway.

Sleep, on the other hand, was a whole other battle.

Roger was coming into my room at night. I no longer thought that I was imagining or making it up, but I still didn't know why he was there. I started pretending to be asleep when I wasn't, lying quietly in the dark waiting for something to happen. One night Lorraine was snoring across the room from me and I'd almost fallen asleep when, in my groggy state, I saw

Roger's face hovering above me. At first I thought I was dreaming, but when I sat up, I could feel his fingers inside me.

Before I could say a word he was out the door and down the hallway. I was left alone, knowing something had taken place but not knowing exactly what.

I couldn't wrap my brain around this incident. Did he really do this to me? Or was I going crazy? I thought of the road trips to Florida, and the way he and Mom laughed about my "poached eggs" when my top fell down. But if he was doing something wrong wouldn't my mother notice? It didn't make any sense. I needed time to think.

I started sleeping in layers of clothes in the sweltering heat of summer. My mother said something about my bedroom light always being on. She thought I was afraid of the monster under my bed. But actually I was afraid of the monster in hers.

By the end of the summer, things were quiet in our little house—for a change. But it was a scary kind of quiet—like the calm before a big storm. It had been a few weeks since Roger had come into my room and I was once again starting to doubt the whole thing. Roger was as sweet, kind, and helpful as always. He took us out for burgers after school, bought me new clothes, and was always willing to drive me where I needed to go. How could I think those things about him? I decided it was me. Something was wrong with *me*. Maybe my head was playing tricks on me because of what happened with Ricky. Maybe I was sick. Was I paranoid? It was maddening having these thoughts. I was edgy, annoyed all the time, and desperately needed to know the truth.

But that would have to wait.

Mom began drilling Roger. Apparently, she hadn't been talking about pot when she wanted him to stop using drugs. She was referring to cocaine, which Roger had started using and selling on a regular basis, all the while continuing to report for his job at the aerospace company. She wouldn't live with a "shifty-eyed speed freak" and wanted out.

Roger's friend Daniel came to her rescue. He'd come to visit Roger several times over the last few weeks, but it was really Mom he came to see. I could tell she liked him. They started seeing each other on the sly, but I was sure if Roger found out, my new California life would be ruined forever.

Why was my mother so damn reckless?

I confronted her: "Daniel is just another version of Roger. Can't you see that? Why go from the frying pan into the fire? At least with Roger we know the deal." She refused to listen, telling me I was too young to understand these things. Defeated, I vowed to stand my ground if she wanted to move again.

The fighting escalated, with Daniel feeding the flames. He was more than happy to volunteer his apartment as a temporary home to Mom and us. He wanted her to leave Roger and obviously didn't care about the other four lives it affected. Our house became a war zone.

Roger got wind of Dan and my mother's little tryst and threw tantrums that would have been funny in a movie but were absolutely terrifying in real life. The two grown men charged around each other hurling insults, trading punches, and bleeding on our floor. I couldn't help but think it would have been completely different if only she had waited. But she didn't. Maybe we could have put our heads together to find a better road to travel if she had.

Mom told us to pack our things. We were moving out.

I told her to forget it. I wasn't going along with her latest whim. Instead, I went to school, and when I came home she was gone. She'd taken my little sisters off to Dan's and left Lorraine and me there. I was devastated. I knew I was being defiant, but I never expected to be left behind. *How could my own mother leave me?* I waited for Lorraine to get home. I'd seen her only hours before at school so I knew she'd been dumped too. I hoped she'd be home soon. I needed her near me. I needed something to hold on to.

Several hours later my mother called. Roger told me I had to speak to her. I begrudgingly obeyed him. I knew Roger was sell-ing drugs, and I still had anxiety about being touched in my sleep, but I also knew he was all we had. He'd been taking care of Sissy and me for a while now and that was more than I could say for my mother.

We had no place else to go.

The weeks that followed were spent chasing my tail, as I was more confused than I'd ever been in my life. Sissy and I came and went as we pleased, only relying on each other, but in my head it was like a time bomb was ticking closer and closer to the end.

Mom and Daniel's love nest fell apart as quickly as it had begun. Not realizing the heavy demands of an instant family, he'd simply bit off more than he could chew and within a few weeks he'd thrown them out. Mom called us from a woman's shelter in Torrance relaying the whole sad story. She said she was apartment hunting, and that we'd all be under the same roof soon.

I was incredulous. I couldn't stand her pretending that everything happening to us was normal. My little sisters were living in a shelter! They had to be scared and embarrassed, and I was embarrassed too—for all of us. But there was nothing I could do. Slamming down the phone, I turned around and smashed my fist into a wall.

8

School Daze

My Walkman blared, pumping my brain full of Ozzy Osbourne. It was 7:25 in the morning and the city bus crawled along the ocean toward Redondo High, where I was just days into my freshman year of high school. The bus was packed with kids and grannies alike, but aside from my older sister, Lorraine, a sophomore, I didn't know anyone.

Stuck without a seat again, I hung on to a pole while we made our way across town. We'd worked out all the kinks in our class schedule. I now had two physical education classes and was able to pawn off the dreaded biology class on Lorraine, who had a much stronger stomach for frog dissection than I did. My sister and I had been swapping classes since the new school year had begun. We got the occasional odd look from our schoolmates, who were hip to our game, but the teachers didn't notice we weren't who we said we were, and I was spared the barbaric task of cutting up helpless creatures.

Imagining myself pole-vaulting in gym, I groaned. I was so tired that I was bound for disaster, but I laughed at the thought of it anyway. At least Maria would be there to identify the body. She was one of the two beach girls I hung with at the time — Maria Sanchez and Sherri Brady, my best friends. Like me, they both had major problems at home. Maria's parents had died a few years earlier in a car crash and her older sister, Anna, was raising her. Her family was Spanish and very religious, but she hated the Catholic Church and was thoroughly pissed at God for taking her parents away.

Sherri's mom was a drunk and never around. They lived in a trailer park a few blocks away from school and the rumor was her mom was a prostitute. Sherri was always getting into fights defending her mother's honor.

I really liked being on a campus so big anyone could get lost, and I blended in well after a few years in California. My hair was soft and sun-streaked. Our crowd's uniform was simple: jeans, OP sneakers, and concert T-shirts. The gang of us liked to smoke pot and to swim. Maria and I were on the swim team and the water was heaven to me. As my body cut through the water, my mind emptied itself of every thought. It was trance-like, taking me away from the chaotic and noisy apartment we now had.

I took the average required classes. My electives were interior design and advanced baking. Interior design was where I constructed my dreams, building my dream house with a magnificent open-space kitchen, a stacked double oven, and a refrigerator with an ice maker.

A few weeks after her split with Daniel, my mother forced us to move back in with her, threatening to call the cops if we didn't. *One minute she leaves us, the next she wants us back*. I was outraged at her selective parenting, and tired—tired of baby-sitting my younger sisters, tired of cooking tuna surprise for dinner, and sick to death of her promising that things would get better when they never did. How could she bring us all the way to California, only to live in poverty again? My little sisters were traumatized from living in the shelter while Mom hunted for an apartment. And Lorraine and I were fed up with the nonstop drama in our lives.

I started smoking Marlboro reds, ditching classes, and crashing out at Roger's when I was too wasted to go home. Lorraine had a new boyfriend and we were always going off some-where with him. He had a car and we'd take long rides up the coast to check out bands. We'd bake in the sun and drink beers in the alleys of Hermosa Beach.

Music was my only salvation. It made me feel like I was part of something, since so many of the songs seemed to tell my story and reflect my pain. I loved it all, from Journey to the Thompson Twins, from Ozzy to Blondie. I didn't discriminate. I wasn't a rock chick or a pop chick. It was about whatever gave me release, and I'd dig into the words and pick them apart for hidden messages, filling page after page of my spiral notebooks with words of my own that the music inspired.

At school I joined band, but it only lasted a few weeks. The instructor was an impatient man who was always leering at the girls, and I had enough of that going on in my life. He cornered me one day after practice and got right in my face, telling me how he noticed that I was always checking myself out in the mirror while I played the keyboards. He said he too appreciated my beauty. He offered to buy me dinner. I told him I wasn't hungry, and dropped out of band the next day. Once again I was left wondering what I'd done to attract this attention. It seemed like everywhere I went there was some older man trying to feel me up. The most confusing part was that while I ran away from it, and secretly it made me feel wanted, I longed for that attention.

My first love was Dean Weatherly. He was a surfer boy from Hermosa Beach and a senior at Redondo High. I'd seen him around school and noticed him mainly because he always seemed to notice me. He made my skin feel hot and I always made a hasty exit whenever he showed up. Boys made me nervous and this one scared me to death.

I loved the ocean and I had my regular spot on the beach. Lorraine and I would set up camp right by the wall that separated the sand from the bike path, and Dean started showing up more and more, often chatting up my sister. He'd come by on his Strand cruiser holding a brown bag, and they'd go off and drink. I stayed behind in favor of basking in the sun and grabbing a ride on the waves with his Boogie board. My sister said he often asked about me, wanting to know if I was always so quiet or if I just didn't like him. I thought that was funny because secretly I had a crush on him. Beer gave me courage one afternoon, so when he came by while I was a little tipsy, we drove off to score another pint. I was on his handlebars, leaning back into him, my bikini making me feel kind of sexy.

We ended up sitting under the pier drinking Mickey's big mouths and talking about music all afternoon. He told me he loved playing the guitar and was excited about the Us Festival coming up—a three- to four-day band gathering over the summer. All my favorite groups were going to be there and I decided I had to attend.

I fell for him fast. He liked all the things I did and we spent that entire summer drifting in the ocean, lying on the beach, listening to our boom box, singing along to Led Zeppelin, and hitchhiking to the Us Festival. The festival crowd was huge, and it was scorching hot that day, but I had a great perch on top of Dean's shoulders. I fantasized about being on that stage too, and let the music take me away.

The summer sunsets were awesome, with orange, yellow, and blue swirls in the sky. We stayed in the parks until long after dark and kissed for hours. But the closer we got, the more difficult our relationship became. All our friends were having sex except Dean and me. He was losing patience with my excuses, and I was worried I'd lose him. It wasn't that I didn't want to be with him. I could lie there for hours kissing and holding him. It was the next step that scared me. I'd be assaulted with images of Ricky in the field and my father's endless warnings. Memories of that pain and the guilt of letting someone touch me like that would tear through me, and I'd stop Dean from going further.

I just couldn't go there.

My sexuality confused me. The only way to stop the constant pounding in my head was to write, so I did, spending hours with my diary. I suspected my mom might be reading it because every once in a while she'd try to parent me, telling me that I needed to come home after school, that we should talk. But I ignored her. *She must be crazy trying to get to know me now!*

I hardly ever went home at this point and I wasn't the only one. Our little apartment on Vanderbilt Lane seemed like nothing but a pullout couch, all five of us females coming and going as we pleased. Mom had gone back to school again, and had a part-time job at the mall, so I'd literally go weeks without seeing her.

Dean and I dated throughout freshman year, over the summer, and on into the new school term. He was a seventeen-year-old senior and I was a fourteen-year-old sophomore when we started going all the way. The first time was on our one-year anniversary. After school he sat me down in his living room and presented me with a pretty package containing a white bikini I'd been eyeballing in a surf shop for a while. I squealed with delight, wrapping my arms around him. He kissed me sweetly and said it wasn't the only surprise he had for me. There was a treat waiting in his bedroom. I'd been in his room plenty of times, but we weren't allowed to close the door or his parents would come pounding. So when he asked me to wait in the bathroom I thought nothing of it. Then he came in with a bottle of champagne and turned on the shower to mask our conversation, even though no one knew I was there. I'd never had champagne before, and he said it was the good stuff. Tott's, it was called. The bubbles went right to my head and after a while I felt as light as a feather.

We had sex that afternoon and it wasn't nearly as awful as the first time. I was drunk enough to feel brave. He was gentle and it didn't go on for very long. Afterward, I wondered why I had made such a big deal out of it. It only hurt the first few times, and I wasn't worried about birth control because we had made a deal that he'd always pull out.

I found out I was pregnant just after my fifteenth birthday. Completely freaked out, I waited for Dean outside his shop class and broke the news to him there. Without saying one word to me, he turned around and walked away.

My heart sank. I played and now I was going to pay . . . just like my father always said.

Ditching class for the rest of the day to try to figure out what I was going to do, I ended up walking all the way across town to Roger's. He was the only adult I knew besides my mother, and I wasn't talking to her.

9

Porn Again

When I arrived on Dow Avenue I found Roger in the garage. He had converted it into a mini apartment. The entrance was through the backyard, and as I fought my way through the rosebushes, I bit my lip to hold back the tears I'd been swallowing all afternoon. I didn't know what I was going to say, but I knew whatever it was, Roger would understand.

Smiling with relief when he answered the door, I got a queen's welcome from a gang of attractive guys who were hanging out in his house. The mood was light and the pot smoke was thick as I made my way inside. The place had been transformed: the front had been partitioned off into a living room, where there was a big pullout couch, a mini fridge, a makeshift bar, and brightly colored Egyptian carpets depicting women in various stages of undress on the walls. I blushed at their naked breasts.

A few hours and several beers later, the party cleared out and I was left with Roger and a full-blown buzz that rendered me even more depressed than when I arrived. My story poured out. He listened and fixed me a cocktail. I told him what had happened with Dean, how he just blew me off, that I didn't want to have a baby, and how scared I was of becoming just like my mother—dead broke with kids to feed.

Roger helped me find a clinic where I could get an abortion without my mother's permission. It was set to take place two weeks later, and all I needed was a ride. I returned to school the next day. Racked with guilt, I sought out Dean at school, feeling that maybe I was making a mistake, and hoping he would say something to make it all better, but he avoided me completely. I was damaged goods—used and discarded by age fifteen. He stopped answering the phone at home. He'd see me coming and cross the street. He made me feel like I was a stalker.

I was overwhelmed with rage at my own stupidity. I had been tricked! How could I have ever been so stupid? After what had happened with Ricky, I knew better! I'd learned this fucking lesson already. Why had I allowed myself to believe in love again? I am such a fuck-up! I wanted to punch Dean's face in, make him pay for not loving me. Once again my father's words assaulted me. I could hear his voice saying, "If you play you're gonna pay." FUCK YOU! I thought, hating that he was right. "Fucking hypocrite," I said out loud to the trees, thinking of the magazines under his bed with naked spread-eagled girls. Is that all men ever wanted? Fuckers . . . Shit . . . What was I going to do? My rage turned to whimpers as I left the school campus, heading for the beach. Calm down, I told myself. There must be a way out of this.

I blew off school the following day and spent my time circling want ads in the local newspaper. I wasn't sure what I was going to do about the pregnancy. I was scared to death at the thought of being someone's mother at fifteen. I couldn't take care of a helpless baby. What if I did a bad job and it got hurt? How could I bring a child into my cruel world? It was a mindfuck. I really needed to talk to someone—anyone. I had hoped to find the courage to tell my mother, but her absence and my shame guarded my secret. I couldn't find the courage to tell

Lorraine either, but whatever I decided, I knew I was going to need money. And money meant I needed a job. Fast.

I did my best to ignore my predicament, but it was hard. I was already two-and-a-half months pregnant when I found out. Having always been blessed with light menstrual cycles, I'd thought nothing of it until my period stopped altogether and the home pregnancy test I took explained why.

Over the next few days, I concentrated on landing a job. I answered ad after ad, but nothing ever came of it. Apparently my age was a factor. I applied at Bob's Big Boy for a waitressing job but couldn't pull off the interview. I was smart but shy and completely unsure of myself. The manager nicely suggested I come back in a few years.

Roger then introduced me to his friend Lynn. She was a single mother in her late twenties who worked at night and needed someone to take care of her two little girls. I started baby-sitting. My mom seemed pleased I had a job, and said she looked forward to me contributing to the house. But it was hard for me to speak to her, and I could barely look her in the eye.

I had scheduled the procedure for the following week, feeling that I could always change my mind and wanting to find a way to keep the baby but scared to death of what would become of us. As the day crept closer I had serious doubts about what I was going to do. Was it wrong? Could this fetus feel pain? Thoughts like these tested my sanity: I had never hurt a fly—what was I doing? I had to find another way. I called a hotline for unwed mothers, but after an hour of religious mumbo jumbo, I hung up. They were selling guilt and I'd had enough of that.

It's hard to put into words the conflict I felt on the day of the procedure. I met Roger in the morning and as he drove me to the clinic I felt my stomach turn inside out. I was beside myself and asked him several times if he thought I was doing the right thing. His words were soft and reassuring as he reminded me that if I didn't have the abortion I would end up a penniless fifteen-year-old single mother, a thought that horrified me.

As I was prepped for the procedure, I was quiet and sweating profusely. I felt the needle enter my arm and watched the faces of masked strangers around me as the fire from the syringe ran down my arm. I started to protest, a million thoughts racing through my head, until everything went dark.

I woke up feeling dead, sobbing on a single bed in the recovery room. I wondered if Dean could feel my pain, wherever he was. Did he know how much I hurt? I thought of Ricky and how he made me lie there while he took what was only mine to give. I thought of my father who wanted so badly to punish my mother that he hadn't sent us a dime in support since we left. I thought of Hollywood Boulevard with all those stars on the sidewalk, those people so admired and loved. Why couldn't I be one of them?

I had promised to baby-sit for Lynn that evening. She'd said it was important and too late to cancel. But watching her children sleep peacefully in their beds, I lost what little composure I had left. Lynn came home and found me crying uncontrollably in her bathroom. I told her my whole story, how trapped I felt, and that I was convinced all this was happening because I was a weak kid and I didn't want to be me anymore.

She held me while I lost my mind and calmed me with reason, saying it would all pass. She offered to help solve my job problems by getting me a fake ID and giving me a reference. I just had to promise to say I'd stolen the birth certificate if I was ever caught. I remember thinking that was silly. I mean, who would care if a fifteen-year-old tended bar or waited tables or something?

I ditched classes the next day and walked into the Department of Motor Vehicles in Torrance with the borrowed birth certificate, had my photo and prints taken, and walked out a different person. I was now twenty-two-year-old Kristie Elizabeth Nussman. It was no different to me than when my sister and I switched identities in school, except this time I was leaving Nora Kuzma behind for good. She was the one who had been raped, used, and abused—and I didn't want to be her anymore. And as for the consequences of my actions, why would I ever even think of them? I was an angry fifteen-year-old acting blindly from a place of rage and desperation, so I never once contemplated the price I would ultimately pay for giving false information to the DMV.

It was payback time now and as I strode across the street from history class toward the Varsity deli I spied my target: Dean. He was laughing with a group of guys from the football team—the very same ones who'd recently started calling me "Nora Whora." I was further insulted to hear from friends that my boyfriend had been openly bragging about what a sweet piece of ass I was. I walked full speed ahead looking to blow that mother outta the water. I'd put on the shortest skirt I owned and a borrowed pair of heels from Lynn. As I clicked my way across the street, I felt the power of those shoes.

Smiling, I made a point of looking those boys right in the eye as I walked toward Dean. They all smiled back. Saying I had really good news for him, I flirtatiously asked if he had a minute. We walked down the street, and when we were out of listening distance, I turned on him. I told him that if he didn't give me money for an abortion, I was going to tell his parents about how we had sex in the bathroom and that I got pregnant.

He turned white and agreed to everything. I told him he had twenty-four hours, turned my back on him, just as he'd done to me, and walked away. It was his turn to pay up. The next day I coldly accepted his two hundred dollars. It didn't satisfy my anger toward him, but at least I knew he'd suffered in some small way.

When my ID arrived several weeks later, I lined up a few interviews. One was for a hostess job at the Red Onion and the other had something to do with modeling. I'd been told on the phone that I only needed to be eighteen and it didn't matter if I had a portfolio or not. They were in the business of breaking new talent.

Roger was my chauffeur for the day and I excitedly showed him all the ads I'd answered. He seemed impressed with my plans, so I continued to rattle on about my conversation with Mr. North, the modeling agent. Roger wanted to know what kind of modeling it was. I told him it was called "figure modeling," and that I'd have to model bathing suits and stuff like that. He looked at me strangely, then just smiled, never informing me that I had naively answered an ad for nude models. Looking back on that day, I realize he knew exactly what was going on.

We pulled into the parking lot of the restaurant where my first interview was scheduled. I checked my hair and hopped out of the car, excited by the prospect of employment. The interviewer at the Red Onion was a really young guy and I saw him checking out my cleavage. I was sure I'd get the job.

Instead, I got asked out.

That afternoon we headed to Hollywood for the modeling interview and my spirits were down. I was scared no one was going to like me. What if I wasn't pretty enough? Roger had taken me shopping for a new outfit and made a big deal of telling me how beautiful I looked. But I wasn't convinced. I was really nervous so we stopped for a cocktail. He held my hand, made me laugh, told me how special I was, that I just needed to believe in myself, and that he'd be there every step of the way. He told me it didn't matter that he and my mom had split, he was still my stepdad and he loved me.

And in that moment I loved him too.

As we walked down the corridor, a girl with the biggest hair I'd ever seen walked by, making me feel even more self-conscious about my flat, flipped Farrah Fawcett hairdo. Roger seemed to sense my insecurity and squeezed my shoulder in support as he led me toward the office. I could hear a man with a Southern accent talking on a phone. "She gets paid double for a DP and she chooses the guys." A DP? I'd learned in film study that meant a director of photography, but I wondered why she needed more guys.

Nearly a year later, on the set of a porn movie, I was horrified to find out a DP was not a director of photography in the porn world. It was slang for a double penetration scene. This particular sex act involved one woman and two men. Both men entered her at the same time, one vaginally and the other anally. Did people really do that?! Didn't it hurt? I'd never do that, I vowed.

High school girls just didn't have anal sex.

We stood in the doorway waiting for the man to finish his phone call. I was transfixed by the row of eleven-by-fourteen-inch glossy photographs lining the walls on both sides of his desk. He was small, thin, and weaselly, with a skinny mustache. His hair looked greasy and was slicked straight back. Standing up, he flashed a big smile for me, and I couldn't help but stare at the silver tooth peeking out of the corner of his mouth. I looked at his feet to find a gleaming pair of cowboy boots staring back at me. He caught me checking him out and laughed, offering us a seat. He commented on how hot it was in the Valley and how much he looked forward to moving into his new office in Beverly Hills. Excusing himself briefly, he came back with a bottle of champagne. He poured us a glass, raised his, looked right at me, and said, "Forgive my manners, miss. My name is Tim North and I'm gonna make you a star. Sir, your daughter is a looker."

I was flushed with excitement. He was going to make a call right then and there and get some pictures of me taken. He pointed to a sign on the wall that explained the fees, saying he'd always try to get me as much money as possible but all he'd ever take was a flat fee of forty dollars—period.

I went to the bathroom to catch my breath. I felt drunk and high on life. On my way back, I heard them talking about taking Polaroids and saw Mr. North hand Roger what looked like a lot of money. Roger saw me watching and said we were all set. He had the address of the photo shoot and Jim advanced us some cash for expenses. All we had to do now was take some topless photos of me in the back room. *What?!!! You mean now? Right now?* I lost my breath, panicking at the thought of being photographed nude.

Roger laughed and handed me a fashion magazine with beautiful black-and-white nude photographs in it. I felt my cheeks go hot, blushing a deep red at the sight of nudes. "It's fashion, Kristie," Tim North said. "If you're really serious about modeling you're going to have to get used to doing nudity." I looked at Roger skeptically, but he just smiled back and nodded in agreement with North.

Was I being immature about this? Is this the way the modeling world worked? Was I blowing my chance to be one of those high-society ladies I used to see lunching on the university lawn near Granny's hill? I thought of the days as a seven-year-old when I had jealously hurled crab apples toward the people laughing on the grass. How much I wanted to be one of them. I could still hear my mother whispering about "social class." I was tired of not belonging anywhere, of being a social outcast.

Maybe this could be the beginning of something new . . .

Mr. North interrupted my childhood memories, snapping at me impatiently, "Now, I'm a very busy man so if you could please go change I'd appreciate

Los Angeles, 1983.

it. Oh, and leave your heels on honey, okay? How about another glass of champagne? Want a line?"

Roger and I disappeared into the back room and I started sweating. I wasn't sure about this, but Roger calmed me down. He said he understood that it was scary, that it was natural for me to feel nervous and not to worry—he was there and nothing bad was going to happen.

North showed up in the hallway with the Polaroid camera. I was still dressed. He looked frustrated. He said he understood it was my first time, but I needed to relax. He told me Marilyn Monroe had started out as a nude model for *Playboy* and then went on to become a huge star.

I said I needed a minute.

When they left, I snorted a line of white powder North called "coke" from a mirror he'd left in the little dressing area. I'd never snorted coke before and it gave me a weird, jittery burst of energy. Suddenly I felt charged, brave from the drug and champagne.

Shyly, I stepped out of my pale pink dress.

I was naked in white panties and high heels when Roger and North walked back in. They both looked approvingly at my breasts.

Roger stood in a corner as Tim positioned me against a wall. "Arch your back and place your hand on your rear end," he said. "Close your eyes halfway and make a kiss with your mouth." He took half a dozen photos and then I got dressed. On our way out he asked for my ID, saying he needed a copy for his records.

Roger was in high spirits afterward. He was proud at how grown-up I was becoming and wanted to drive me to my first photo shoot—at some magazine called *Velvet*.

I asked if it was for a clothing store.

He said, "Sort of."

The jittery coke feeling was wearing off and I wiggled uncomfortably in my seat, replaying the afternoon's strange events. My memory felt fuzzy, though—maybe from the champagne. I remembered getting the Polaroids taken and watching North's beady eyes peering at me. All of it felt strangely . . . exciting. Maybe that's because I was being photographed topless? Or was it the way North—and especially Roger—had stared at my breasts? Was it sexual?

I flashed on my father's face again. It had been so long since I'd seen or heard from him. Did he even love me anymore? I pictured myself naked and spread-eagled in one of his girlie magazines. Would he love me then? Would everyone love me? My body seemed to be the only thing men wanted from me anyway. I fell asleep on the way home.

10

Angel Is the Centerfold

I woke up the next day panicked. I was late for school again and I'd already used up all my absences. I had been warned about truancy twice this quarter.

The night before, Roger had insisted I stay over and offered me his bed. He took the couch. When I awoke, my head was throbbing from the champagne. It was quiet. Roger must have gone off to work. Pulling on my clothes, I realized it was Saturday and let loose a huge sigh of relief.

The previous day's events played through my head.

I felt sick to my stomach thinking my mother would find out I posed naked for Polaroids, but then I found a note from Roger. He said I should go home, change into something cute, and be back by noon if I wanted him to drive me to work.

Work?

Oh yeah . . . *I was a model!* All my doubts about Mom finding the pictures of me went out the window. They were silly, I reasoned. *She doesn't even notice when I'm home.* How could she find out about this?

No one was home when I got there.

I showered, put on some tight shorts and a tank top, and was on my way. Roger was waiting when I got back with a stack of magazines he'd bought, like *Vogue, Teen, Playboy,* and some foreign nude ones. We hit the drive-thru on the way to the Valley, and I snacked on a Big Mac and chocolate shake, flipping through the magazines and rambling on about the models I saw. He told me I needed to memorize all the different poses, be cooperative with the photographer, and most of all act like a professional. *What did that mean?*

We arrived at the studio fifteen minutes early. The photographer was arranging the set and I was introduced to a man wearing more makeup than I ever had. He said his name was Coco. He'd be doing my makeup and showed me where I could change.

Coco mixed me a vodka cranberry and had one himself while Roger talked to the photographer in the other room.

"You have the most flawless skin I've ever seen," he said. "What's your secret?"

"I'm an Ivory soap girl."

He laughed and said it ran in the business, referring to Marilyn Chambers. I had no idea what he was talking about but pretended it was the funniest thing I'd ever heard. I only got the joke years later, when I crossed paths with the queen of porn herself. Apparently Miss Chambers, star of the X-rated film *Behind the Green Door*, originally gained fame as the Ivory Snow detergent girl.

When Coco finished painting me I changed into a blue pleated skirt and a tight sweater. My teased hair made me look at least five feet ten and I couldn't believe the image in the mirror staring back at me. My lips were painted huge and so glossy they looked like they were going to drip. I wasn't sure if I looked pretty or not, but the photographer seemed pleased. A pair of white bobby socks and really high heels completed the outfit. The photographer showed me where to go and I climbed up on a white bed filled with big pillows and pink bows, realizing then that this shoot couldn't possibly be for a clothing store. But Roger was there, I told myself, and he wouldn't let anything bad happen to me. And I had to start somewhere.

The photographer talked me through a dozen poses and I had three more vodkas in between film changes. My eyes were watering so much from the liquid eyeliner and the false eyelashes that we had to keep taking breaks, and I couldn't help but wonder if this would be considered unprofessional. But the vodka eventually washed away my worries—and schoolgirl innocence.

I was the center of attention for the first time in my life. I remember feeling important, even powerful. My sexuality had robbed me of so much, and now it suddenly gave me something that had eluded me in every aspect of life—control. I got off on the power my body held over that entire roomful of adults.

As I lay on the bed, the photographer showed me where he wanted my rear end. Then he asked me to really arch my back as I bent forward. Cupping my naked breasts, I slid my panties off, closed my eyes, and made the kissy face Tim North had taught me.

I spread my legs and caressed my breasts. Through a dreamy fog, I spotted Roger sitting in the corner of the studio, his hand buried beneath his coat, watching me. *What was he doing?* He caught me staring and immediately stopped. *Was he masturbating?* Disgusted by the thought of my honorary "stepfather" doing such a thing, I avoided his gaze, and when we finished the shoot minutes later, I dismissed the incident as a vodka-induced hallucination.

I dressed quickly and, with the vodka buzz finally wearing off, felt unsettled by the afternoon's events. I'd been turned on by the attention I'd received, and now it confused me. I became flooded with shame as I got dressed.

I had to get out of there.

Roger collected the two hundred and fifty dollars cash I was owed for the shoot. Apparently, the girls were paid at the end of the shoot in cold hard cash. I quickly lit the first of the series of cigarettes I would chain-smoke that night.

Quiet on the way home, I listened to Roger cheerfully jabber on about how gorgeous I looked while I was modeling. I wondered what would happen if I said something about what I thought I saw him doing. Would he get mad? Would he tell my mom I was a nude model? Would I be in trouble?

11

I, Traci Lords

I was fifteen years old when I was hired to model for *Penthouse* magazine. I was told I needed a "sexy" stage name so I chose Traci, one of the "popular" names I'd longed for growing up. During a rerun of the series *Hawaii Five-O* later that evening, I took actor Jack Lord's surname. In my mind, his Steve McGarrett was the perfect fantasy father. I added an "s" to Lord because there were three of us: Nora (my birth name), Kristie (my fake ID name), and now Traci (the girl everyone wanted).

From then on I was known in the sex industry as Traci Lords. The buzz in the business grew as North hyped me. The talk of the town was his new girl with the baby-fat bod, pouty lips, and appetite for destruction. The combination of little girl gone bad had photographers fighting to shoot me. It was a total ego trip. I was the flavor of the moment, the It girl. I felt like I'd won a spot on the cheerleading squad. Any doubts I had about posing nude were overruled by my insatiable desire for attention.

For five weeks I led a double life. I was high school sophomore Nora Kuzma by day and nude centerfold model Traci Lords by night. I avoided my girlfriends, ditched classes, and barely squeaked by in school. I started wearing the slutty outfits

I posed in to school. My microminis and come-fuck-me high heels raised an eyebrow or two, but no one said anything. I wanted to be stopped, yet I got off on the idea of getting away with it all.

I was playing a dangerous game.

One sunny afternoon, as the lunch bell rang, I rushed into the cafeteria wondering what the day's mystery meat would be. I was conscious of my snickering classmates as I collected my food. Something weird was going on. I paid for my tray and moved toward a half-empty table near the door. Minding my own business, I arranged my food and wondered if my tarty outfit was responsible for the unwanted attention.

The moment I slipped into my seat a beefy jock sauntered over. "Hey, Paula," he said with a stupid grin on his face. I took a bite out of my green Jell-O, ignoring this Neanderthal.

Smack! The magazine landed on the table.

On the front cover, there was a young girl in a pleated skirt with her hands over her breasts. The caption read "Pump Paula," referring to a pullout board game that boasted how you too could fuck the centerfold.

I choked on my food. *Oh my God, it was me!*

As I sat there frozen, my neighbors craned their necks for a better look.

It was me—spread-eagled in a really sleazy skin magazine that looked nothing like *Playboy* or *Vogue.*

I ran out of the cafeteria and off campus, never to return to school again. My heart pumped in my throat. *Oh my God, everyone at school knows I'm a nude centerfold! Someone might tell my sisters . . . my mother! I can't go home. I can't go back to school.*

What now? I hadn't even finished tenth grade. What am I going to do! What have I done? Panic-stricken, I forced myself to slow down. I walked briskly toward a pay phone, my thoughts racing. I had to speak to Roger. He'd know what to do. But he was nowhere to be found. I waited on his front porch for hours, praying he would come home soon. I grew more anxious with every passing car, afraid I would be caught and put in jail.

Where was he! I didn't know what to do. Kids at school knew I was a nude model! *What was I going to do? This was not supposed to happen.*

Anxiety overwhelmed me as I raced for a passing bus, making my way to Hollywood, where I was sure I'd be safe.

12

No One Rides for Free

Walking down Hollywood Boulevard, I could breathe again, grateful to be just another ant on a big hill where no one knew my name. I'd never spent any time on Hollywood Boulevard, but it was worth the three bus transfers and passing freak show I'd encountered to get there. I was curious about the other sights but knew exactly where I wanted to go first.

I found her star at Grauman's Chinese Theater. Sitting down next to her, I placed my hands in hers, surprised that they fit so perfectly. I wondered if everyone fit in them.

Marilyn Monroe was a curiosity to me. Since Tim North told me she'd had a similar start in Hollywood, I really wanted to know more about her. What I did know was when I looked into her eyes, I saw someone as lost as I was. Was she told she'd have to pose nude to be a star too?

Roger still wasn't answering his phone. It was getting dark.

I'd spent the day on the Walk of Fame and needed to move. I had a hundred dollars and change left over from my last photo shoot and figured I could clear my head by walking a bit. High heels in hand, I walked for blocks and blocks. A taxi driver offered me a free ride. Thinking he felt sorry for me, I climbed in. He took off, but no sooner had we left the curb when he looked at me in the rearview mirror and said, "Listen, honey, no sex, okay? Don't freak — I just want a golden shower."

The cab stopped at a light on Santa Monica Boulevard and I jumped out fast. I was shaken up, cursing myself for being so stupid. How could I get in a car with a total stranger? Freaks — everywhere I looked there were nothing but freaks! Who likes to be pissed on?

I learned an important lesson that day: no one rides for free.

On the walk down Santa Monica Boulevard, all these hot boys were looking at me. Some made crude jokes and pointed, and I had the feeling I'd better find a place to stay — fast. I saw a motel near Highland and made a beeline for it. But before I could get across the street, a nasty Latin kid stepped in my way, demanding to know what the fuck I thought I was doing there. "This isn't pussy town," he said. "Don't you know that? Take your cock-sucking ass somewhere else, and quick."

I was in Boys Town and these cuties were going to beat the crap out of me. I lost it, sobbing my apologies, explaining I just didn't have any place to go. I only wanted to find a place to sleep. I'd give him all the money I had if he would just leave me alone. I pulled out a few twenties and he grabbed me by the hair. Suddenly laughing, he wrapped his arm around me and pulled me down the sidewalk, calling to the other boys and saying, "The ho has dough! Let's party!"

We ended up under the overpass of the 101 Freeway, just blocks from the bus stop where Roger had first picked us up. We scored some pot and a bottle of whiskey and got high. There were five of them, all around my age. The youngest boy was about eleven, and everyone called him Tricky because he turned more business than anyone else.

They were male prostitutes and they scared me. I was sure they didn't want to rape me for pleasure but I wasn't certain they wouldn't do it for entertainment. They slept here all the time, the oldest one said. Every once in a while the cops would drag them off, the city would then throw their couches away, and the boys would be stuck sleeping in the dirt until they found new ones.

I didn't know where the night would take me, or if I'd even be alive in the morning. I felt so small I longed to sit beneath the clothesline in my daddy's backyard as my mother folded laundry.

Tricky asked me to sleep next to him. Afraid to say no, I curled my body against him and laid still. He was so young. As he fell asleep he told me everyone he loved had left him. It was sad, looking at his baby face covered with cigarette burns and scars from who knows what. I wanted to wash all those bad memories from him. That night, I didn't sleep at all, and when the sun rose I had no choice but to leave Tricky too.

I found a motel that charged by the hour. A lot of girls probably worked there, I thought, but I didn't care. I needed a shower and a washing machine to tidy myself up before work. I still couldn't find Roger and was due in Hollywood in a few hours for a photo session. I asked the manager how far away Vine Street was and discovered it was within walking distance. I cleaned myself up and made it there with a few minutes to spare.

The clients and photographer were all waiting for me. The shoot was for a book on couples and sex. I was there to do the photo illustrations. A stunning man in his early twenties showed up about an hour into the session. The director said we were playing a married couple and we'd be shooting some lovemaking poses together. We'd be dressed in our underthings and it would be tastefully done. The man who had written the book stood nearby and was watching the entire process intently.

I was outfitted in a beautiful white lace teddy with stockings and garters, and my "husband" had on red silk boxers. The set was a garden, which reminded me of one of the corny romance novels my mom collected. The guy was instructed to kiss my neck softly and hook his fingers under my bra strap as if he were going to remove it. He was an amazing kisser and I found myself enjoying his touch. We spent the entire afternoon being photographed in a series of simulated sex acts.

I got a real education that day. I had no idea so many positions existed! It was like Sex Ed 101. The author was a chatty man in his fifties who proudly boasted about how the book was to be used for sex education classes in colleges. He said he wanted to help young adults come to a healthy conclusion about their sexuality. I wanted to scream, *Help me! I need a healthy conclusion!* I wanted this wise fatherly man to see through the persona I'd created and save me from myself. Instead I finished the job, collected my two hundred dollars, and left.

During that photo shoot I found myself completely turned on and hoped to God no one could tell. I had no idea sex could be more than what I'd experienced until that point. There was so much I didn't know and couldn't understand, but it was strangely exciting. The other model was really nice and didn't try anything with me unless he was specifically asked. But that confused me too, until his boyfriend showed up to take him home.

Was everyone in Hollywood gay?

13

House Pets

It was August 1984. I was sixteen years old. I'd been in the business for seven months now, and one photo shoot bled into the next.

I was constantly hungover from something. Between the downers I took and the cocaine I snorted nearly every day, I was a walking zombie. When I was high, I could deal with life.

My "chauffeur" Roger could no longer meet the demands of my chaotic modeling schedule, saying he "had to work," although that had never stopped him before. I wasn't sure why he was suddenly distancing himself from me, but I was sick of him leering at my naked body anyway—even if it did mean spending half my earnings on transportation. At the time I was making two hundred dollars a shoot, and although that was more money than I'd ever had in my young life, it barely paid for the taxis I took from Roger's Redondo Beach house, where I'd been staying for the past few weeks, to the heart of the Valley.

One afternoon my agent, Tim North, summoned me to his office in Van Nuys. When I got there he presented me with a check for a whopping five thousand dollars.

Oh my God!

Stunned to have that kind of money in my sixteen-year-old hands, I tried to cover my shock quickly as North explained what it was for. I didn't want to appear immature or desperate, so I listened quietly as he told me I'd been chosen as the September centerfold for *Penthouse* magazine.

At the time, I had no idea what an "honor" being a Penthouse Pet was in the porn world. But I did notice several of North's favorite girls giving me dirty looks as they milled about his office, eavesdropping on our conversation. I had no idea why they were so jealous. It was just another skin magazine, hardly an "accomplishment." So fucking what? I thought, licking my lips at the thought of all the coke I could buy with five grand!

It must have been my lack of excitement that drove North impatiently to say, "This is like getting the Oscar in the porn world!" He turned his attention to the tarts milling about the office. "Right, girls?"

God, they *are* old, I thought, staring at their bleached-out hair and hooker makeup. They must be at least twenty-one, maybe even older. They smiled meanly at me. They obviously hated the amount of attention I received from North, and I couldn't have cared less. Having no friends in the porn world made it easier to keep my true identity a secret. I cozied up to North, smoothing over the tension between us. "I'm just tired," I cooed softly in his ear. Then I gave him a wet kiss that left him smiling and me desperate for a shot of tequila. I disappeared down the hallway wiping his saliva from my mouth, amazed at how easy it was to get what I wanted.

As I left North's office, *Penthouse* check in hand, I heard him on the phone talking up his new girl, Christy Canyon. He was bragging about how young she was and what a "sweet little pussy" this eighteen-year-old had. Disgusted, I stepped out onto Ventura Boulevard and took a cab to my dealers, desperate to turn down the volume on my life.

I scored a gram of coke, spending all but twenty bucks of my remaining cash, and headed back to Roger's house, check still in hand. What was I going to do with a check? How could I cash it? I didn't even have a bank account, as I'd always been paid in cash. I got high and contemplated this situation in the privacy of Roger's garage apartment. I was glad he wasn't home, thinking bitterly of the man I once trusted. Angry tears stung my eyes as I snorted line after line in Roger's room, the smell of his musky cologne everywhere.

I had been sleeping at Roger's for several weeks now and my mom had started asking questions. She knew I was gone, but she didn't know where I was or what I was up to. I still checked in with my girlfriends, and Maria told me she'd called and was worried. I'd sent a message back that I was okay, paranoid my mother might hunt me down at Roger's.

Or was it hopeful?

Regardless, Roger and I were on the outs and I had to find a new place to live. I'd been woken days before by him stroking me in my sleep. But this time when I awoke, I waited, needing to know if it was real. And it was.

I wanted to hit him and run and scream and cry, but I couldn't. I had nowhere else to go. I needed his shelter for the moment. And so I lay there, still, not moving at all, and plotted my revenge.

The next day I made my way to Hermosa Beach and walked down the Strand toward my old hang. I stood staring at the ocean and remembered how Lorraine and I used to surf those waves. I missed her. I wondered if my family knew. I wanted to call them up and explain, end the lies, stop the game. But my shame wouldn't let me.

I couldn't go home.

The Poop Deck was directly in front of me. Many a summer, my school friends and I had tried to sneak in for a cold one and were always promptly thrown out. But this was a different time, and I was a different girl. I marched straight through the wooden net-covered door, my tight T-shirt clinging to my breasts. Without missing a beat I beelined for the bar and looked the bartender right in the eye.

"I'll take a screwdriver, please."

The crusty old-timer who carded me made a big deal of checking out my ID and looking me over. Finally he shrugged and brought me my drink. I paid him with my last twenty, wondering how the heck I was going to cash my *Penthouse* check.

Wandering out onto the patio, I perched in a corner in the sun. It was weird being near all these partying adults. I tried not to stare but was interested in how older girls acted toward men. I was surprised that these girls were as silly as the cheerleaders and surf bums I'd gotten drunk with in the past. One rather fat girl named Heidi was clearly two sheets to the wind, swaying to Billy Idol's "Rebel Yell" and raising her top to show off her multiple rolls of blubber. But her strip routine was nonetheless met with hoots and whistles from the horny drunk crowd.

I was well on my way to being wasted when yet another drink arrived, compliments of Blue Eyes at the pool table. The waitress pointed him out and he raised his glass to me. His friends were all grinning, slapping him high-fives. He reminded me of my father, though, so I escaped to the bathroom to collect my thoughts. As I came out, he stepped into my path, smiling that smile. Unsettled, I feigned indifference.

He smiled at me and I smiled back. He kicked up a tangerine-sized beanbag into the air and, when it got to his elbow, swatted it again. "Hacky Sack" was a popular sport in this beach community, and Blue Eyes was swept up into the frantic energy of beer-induced competition. I watched the crowd of drunk men fight for possession of the tiny orange sack, hanging around simply because I had nowhere else to go.

The beer was cold, the sun was hot, and I was drunk. When he offered me a ride home, I knew what he meant, I needed a place to sleep, and so I said yes. Sex was all I had to bargain with. I didn't think I had anything else of value to offer, and wondered if other girls felt the same. *Did all teenagers do battle with their hearts and bodies like I did?*

I longed to matter to someone, to feel loved and needed. Was this man the one I'd been waiting for? *Was he my knight in shining armor?* As unlikely as that seemed, I was homeless and willing to sacrifice my body to bandage my soul.

He drove a motorcycle and I climbed on the back, both of us wasted. I let my dress blow in the wind, unconcerned by the gawking motorists.

He was a forgettable lover, and when I woke up the next morning, I crept out of his room ready to make a clean getaway. But I was busted by his roommate, Eric, who greeted me with a "Good morning" cup of coffee and then asked about me. I told him I was a model, my name was Krissie, and I was looking for a new apartment. He was a sweet one. I wished I'd ended up in his bed while we sat for a while chatting until the blue-eyed stranger appeared in a towel.

His name was Sonny and he was handsome, even though he had a jagged scar that cut down his check to the corner of his mouth. *God,* he reminded me of my father: blond hair, blue eyes, tan. I made a move toward the door, but he stopped me by offering breakfast and a hot shower.

Breakfast turned to lunch and once again I was tearing down the highway with a man who had gone from stranger to friend in just one night. We spent the day commiserating about life, but I was careful about what I revealed, admitting only that my real name was Nora. I needed someone to know the truth. It made me feel like I wasn't totally alone.

"Your secret's safe with me." He laughed, having no idea how many secrets I really had.

Soaring down Pacific Coast Highway, I squeezed Sonny tighter.

As Wanda Woodward on the set of <u>Cry-Baby</u>.

With Ricki Lake on the set.

On the _Cry-Baby_ set as Wanda, in a giant champagne glass.

The _Cry-Baby_ gang (from left to right): Robert Tyree, Kim McGuire, Darren Burrows, me, Johnny Depp, Ricki Lake, and show children.

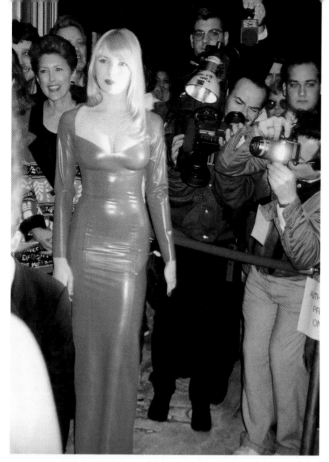

At the premiere
of John Waters's
Serial Mom
in Baltimore.

A limo ride to guest on *The Tonight Show with Jay Leno*, Los Angeles, 1999.

Brook and me.

Modeling for
Thierry Mugler
in Paris, 1989.

With costars William Shatner and Christopher Atkins during the filming of <u>Dead Man's Island</u>, a Movie of the Week.

Goofing on the set of <u>MacGyver</u>, 1990.

Striking a pose for my calendar, 1990.

On the set of "Control," the first music video for the album 1000 Fires, Los Angeles, 1996.

The covers of the album 1000 Fires and "Fallen Angel," one of its singles.

On the set of <u>First Wave</u> with director of photography Henry Chan.

On the set of <u>Virtuosity</u>.

Near a New Zealand
waterfall on location for
<u>The Tommyknockers.</u>

Hanging out, Los Angeles, 1995.

With costar Arly Jover
during the filming of
Blade, Los Angeles.

On the NBC lot as Jill
in the series *Profiler*,
Los Angeles, 1999.

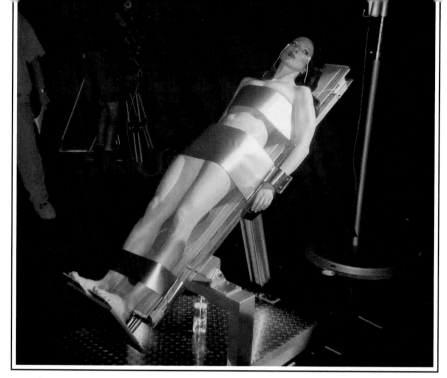

On the set of First Wave, my character, Jordan, is tampered with by the alien force known as "the Gua."

With alien fighters Rob LaBelle, Roger R. Cross, and Sebastian Spence on the set of First Wave, Vancouver, 2001.

On the set of <u>First Wave</u> with Rob LaBelle,
Vancouver, 2000.

In Tahiti, May 2001.

Jeff and me, Malibu, California, 2001.

14

Hell Is for Children

On a crisp fall day, only weeks after I'd first gone home with Sonny, I found myself washing his dirty underwear in the kitchen sink of a house we'd rented together in the modest neighborhood of Lawndale. I was now only about a dozen blocks from where my mother and sisters were living, and although I hadn't spoken to any of them in months, I felt better just knowing I was practically sleeping in their backyard.

Homesick, I longed to push the pause button on the jagged life I was living. I wanted to take it all back, to close my eyes and hear the voice of my history teacher, Mr. Atteberry, lecture the class on war. I was sure of only one thing: you can't go back; you can only go forward.

I felt like a crazy person, terrified of what I'd do next. My tears soaked my boyfriend's clean underwear.

Sonny was far from the storybook prince little girls dream about, but his presence provided me with a little comfort, making me feel I wasn't totally alone in this big, scary world. There were things about him that scared the crap out of me from the start—his unpredictable temper for one—but for some reason I was still drawn to him. I was the moth—and no question, he was the flame.

Looking back, it's clear to me I stayed in that relationship because I needed an adult in my life, someone who might save me from myself. Just about anyone would do, and Sonny picked up right where Roger had left off.

Life was about survival and drugs were my salvation. I used coke on a daily basis, as getting high was the only thing I looked forward to each morning. My world was jagged and sharp, accompanied by a constant screaming in my head that needed to be stopped.

Sonny, my ever ready drug buddy, encouraged my partying lifestyle. He was always fine the next morning, though, whereas the morning after our binges would find me feeling desperate, worthless, and utterly hollow inside. I was like a sleepwalker in traffic, unable to wake myself. Another fix would take me away from it all, so I moved through the days feeling like an outsider to my own body.

I went along with Sonny's whims without a word of protest. I stood stupidly by as this twenty-two-year-old speed freak spent my money, slapped me around, and sadly made me feel right at home. But as much as I loathed the drama, I couldn't leave him; instead, I confided in him and pampered him. I ignored the bruises and bloody noses he gave me, feeling like I deserved all the pain I got.

At age sixteen, I found myself living a version of my parents' abusive relationship. And just like my mother, I was secretly plotting an escape.

Signing over my five-thousand-dollar *Penthouse* check to a car dealership in Torrance, I bought a shiny black '67 Corvette. Since I hadn't made it through driver's ed before I'd dropped out of school, my driving skills were primitive to say the least, so I had to ride shotgun as Sonny took control and peeled off the lot.

The speed and power of that car both scared and excited me. I was wide awake, alert, had adrenaline pumping through my veins as Sonny tore through a middle-class neighborhood toward the wide open Pacific Coast Highway, where I would take a crack at mastering the gas and brake pedals of my future getaway car. We ended up celebrating my clumsy but accident-free arrival home by scoring some blow en route, and spending the rest of the night snorting coke.

That evening he told me tales of his marine corps days and confided in me that he'd been AWOL for nearly a year. I wondered if being AWOL was a crime and stored away this drug-induced confession. I was pretty sure something would happen if I were to tell on him, but what? *Could this be my out? Who would I tell? The police? No way!* I was a sixteen-year-old runaway nude model—I wasn't going anywhere near cops. I was afraid of what they'd do to me. What would they do to me anyway? *Was nudity a crime?* Stop it! I ordered myself, snorting another line and searching his blue eyes. Wow . . . he was in the same boat as I was—on the run and always looking over his shoulder.

Sonny rambled on about the jagged three-inch scar that crossed his face, saying his father had given it to him. Apparently, he'd been taken away from his parents several times as a child and was only four years old the first time one of those beatings sent him to the hospital. I listened as his body shook with emotion, feeling that I understood him now. His pain flooded my heart with sympathy, pity, and total rage. *How the fuck do these things happen to children?* I wanted to tell him that I understood what he felt, but stayed silent, stuffing the words back inside, doubtful I'd ever tell my deepest, darkest secrets to anyone. I knew then that I would never hate Sonny. But I also knew that the time bomb ticking in this man was even closer to exploding than my own, and I was terrified of being around when it did.

Besides Roger, Sonny was the only person who knew how old I really was and what I really did for work. He was an adult—six years my senior—and I believed he had to understand the world better than I did. He'd known my age for a while, and although I hadn't intended to tell him what I did, it just sort of came out one evening.

Tim North was pushing me to go further in my modeling sessions, and I was rattled by the pressure, so I scored some blow to take the edge off. Sonny came back later that night and sometime during our private coke party, I confessed to being a nude model. Waking up the next day, I had a pounding headache and totally forgot it had happened until my boyfriend reminded me he knew my secret. Instantly, I regretted telling him, scared he would use it against me—and later he did. He got off on it and started bragging about how he was dating a centerfold girl.

As the weeks passed North continued to turn up the heat, pushing me to do hard-core stills and porn movies, and warning me that if I didn't I'd be out of work. Panicked at the thought of not being able to buy food or pay rent or, more important, buy myself some peace-providing drugs, I sought Sonny's advice. But when I told him I might actually be fired, he had a fit and threw a lamp across the room. He was unemployed and intended to stay that way. He said he needed time to develop his skills and slapped me when I asked exactly what those skills were. I realized I'd better change my tone quickly. You're gonna pay, fucker, I thought as I put on my sweet sexy voice to smooth things over. *It's just a matter of time till I'm gone.*

The next morning I called North and apologized for being difficult. I asked him for work, but he told me I was all "shot up" in the centerfold world. If I didn't believe him, he said, I should look for myself. I did, and found out he was right. As I stood in front of the magazine rack in the liquor store on the corner of Inglewood Avenue, minutes from where I lived, I felt violated by the image of some freaky version of myself on the cover of several sleazy skin magazines. They didn't even make me look pretty, I thought, feeling like the ugliest girl alive. *God* . . . I was hyperventilating. *What do the pictures on the inside look like? Were they even worse than the "Pump Paula" pictures the jock at school had confronted me with?* I couldn't look. *Forget it . . . just forget it. . . . North did this on purpose. . . . He's trying to fuck with me . . . motherfucker. . . .* Buying my beer, I practically ran out of the store.

What North said had been true.

I'd posed for every magazine on the rack by now, and the business was all about new meat. I pictured myself lying in the butcher's case at the supermarket, the plastic wrap covering my body and a red "Reduced for Sale" sign on my forehead. The image seemed very real. I was going off the deep end. I had to shake it before I ate a bottle of pills. I was thinking about death a lot lately, and that day I felt like I was daring God to strike me dead.

North's words echoed through my head. Frantically, I searched the house for drugs looking for Sonny's stash. As I sniffed the white powder, my mind raced to thoughts of warm summer rain washing all the insanity out of my life, making it all better. *It's just a transitional phase*, I told myself. *Any day now someone will find out about my magazines and tell my mom. She'll go to the police and I'll be in trouble, but I'll live through it.* I had no idea my mother had already made several trips to the police department. But no one had done much about it, since I was just another runaway lost in the system. I fantasized about being able to tell all my secrets. It'd be like a dam breaking, and when it spilled, Ricky, Roger, porn . . . none of it would matter anymore. *But what then?* Would I be free?

I got high in our bathroom, paranoid that Sonny would come home from wherever he went and catch me doing his drugs. *Screw him*, I thought. *It's my money that bought them.* He'd been living off me since we met, and I was over it. Unable to stand the thought of seeing him, or being seen by him, I raced out of the driveway and onto Pacific Coast Highway in my new shiny Vette. I soared along the highway blasting Pat Benatar on the stereo. "Hell Is for Children" screamed through the air. *Isn't that the truth*, I thought, wondering if I could bring myself to drive off a cliff and be done with it.

I abandoned the thought in favor of liquid. My mouth was twitching from the coke. I needed to balance it out and ended up at my designated perch on the patio of the Poop Deck. I was just finishing off a pitcher of Budweiser, grooving to the soothing sound of the Eagles and feeling like nothing really mattered, when Sonny came waltzing in. He picked me up out of my chair and wrapped me in a hug. He kissed me softly, singing "My angel is the centerfold" loud enough for the whole bar to hear.

In his hands, he had a copy of the most recent *Penthouse* with Vanessa Williams on the cover. I only knew who she was because a few weeks earlier all of Sonny's friends wanted to check out the swimsuit competition of the Miss America pageant and her name had come up. But at the time I had no idea how her girlie photos were going to affect my life. Now, there she was, Miss America, on the cover of *Penthouse* smiling with George Burns at her side, and while this normally wouldn't have affected me at all, I was, in fact, the centerfold of that very issue.

I flipped to the center of the magazine. It really was me, and I was shocked to see how pretty they made me look.

I couldn't remember taking those photos, but I must have because there they were. Sonny was jazzed to be with a *Penthouse* centerfold model and I was stunned at the attention directed my way. The bar was hopping with both men and women, and I was suddenly the main attraction. Patrons were going to the liquor store next door and coming back with their own issue of *Penthouse* for me to sign.

Signing my very first autograph as "Traci Lords," I corrected the misspelled "y" to an "i" and felt important for the first time in my life, giggling about how they didn't even spell my made-up name right. I was cocky and arrogant. Becoming the life of the party, I danced with Sonny extra sexy, showing off, and lifting my skirt as I'd seen fat Heidi do on my first visit to this bar. I was completely aware of the jealous looks from the women and lust from the men. At the time, it didn't occur to me that perhaps I looked as silly to them as Heidi had looked to me. I only knew that I was "Miss Tracy Lords, September 1984 Pet of the Month," and it felt good to be Her.

By the time my buzz wore off the next morning, the reality of what was going on hit. I knew there was something wrong with my body being available for the world to view in a porn magazine, and although it wasn't the first time I'd seen myself in a nude layout, it hadn't actually registered until that moment.

Still, I couldn't stop myself. I was in way too deep and couldn't possibly turn back now. I had North to answer to, Sonny to feed, and my unrelenting hunger for approval to satisfy. Besides, now I was a star.

That became the bestselling issue in the history of *Penthouse*. While the TV reporters continued to gossip about the lesbian photos Miss America had done, there I was, right in front of the world, a naked fifteen-year-old girl staring up at them.

The attention that issue of *Penthouse* magazine brought me in the porn world sealed my fate. It was October 1984 when I graduated to doing porn films.

It just kind of happened.

The first time I walked onto a porn movie set I was wired. I hadn't slept a wink the night before, and as I drove myself to the location I was exhausted and overwhelmed by the anxiety of imagining what it would be like. I had one line, which I'd practiced a dozen times the night before. North had told me my line was "I know what gets me hot," but I had no idea what it referred to. All I knew was I was getting paid four hundred and fifty dollars a day with a guarantee of two days' work and no nudity.

I'd made every excuse I could think of to North, trying to convince him that I was worth more to him as a centerfold model than a porn star. But it didn't matter. My time had run out.

Needing the cash, I agreed. North told me it was a soft-core porn film for cable. I was hired to walk around looking pretty, and was asked to bring several bikinis and a selection of high heels. Stopping by the liquor store on the way there, I stashed a couple cans of premixed vodka and orange juice in my backpack for courage.

The movie was being filmed in a mansion deep in the San Fernando Valley. When I arrived on the set early, I couldn't find anyone who knew where I was supposed to go. I was told I should look for Richard, the director, who would tell me what to do. Continuing my search up the stairs, I crossed paths with several half-naked girls with very large breasts. They were laughing and seemed to be having a good time. I thought this was a good sign and continued along the hallway feeling more at ease.

I'd sat in traffic for almost two hours and I had to pee like a racehorse. Pleased to find a bathroom in the direction of the noise I was following, I walked in and was greeted with what looked like the hygiene aisle at the drugstore. There were condoms, jellies, foam, and douches of every flavor on the counter. An empty beer bottle sat in the sink and from the smell in there, someone had been smoking pot.

I relaxed even more. These people were just having a good time, partying and hanging out. As for all the products, I guessed someone had serious hygiene issues. I was a bit creeped out by that, but I put it out of my mind and laughed at my lack of experience with such things. A guttural moaning coming from somewhere down the hall startled me.

Again following the noise, I found my director behind a camera watching a woman having sex with two guys. Blushing, I gawked at them. I had never seen anyone have sex before, and it was so aggressive, so primal the way this woman moaned that it scared the crap out of me. *Oh my God, is that what they expect me to do!?* I turned and ran down the hall to the front door. I knew exactly what kind of movie this was now—and I wasn't having it.

I tore out of the parking lot and was gone before anyone knew I'd arrived. I called North from a pay phone a few blocks away screaming at him for lying to me. He told me to "grow up," pissed that I had left and saying I'd make him look bad. If I wanted to ever work again I'd better get my butt back there and apologize for being late. I hung up on him and sat in my car downing vodka and oj at eight-something in the morning. I knew I had to go back. *Where else would I go? What else could I do?*

I tried to imagine what having sex on-camera would be like, but I couldn't even fathom it. I decided I'd just go back, at least apologize for quitting, and hope that North would still keep me on as a model.

By the time I arrived back at the house, I had a good buzz on and was feeling braver. This time everyone was waiting for me. I was rushed off to makeup where the director greeted me. I started to ask questions, but he interrupted me, telling me not to worry. All I had to do was walk around the pool in my bikini during the party scene. I searched his face to see if he was tricking me, but he seemed serious.

I felt better instantly. I'd gotten worked up over nothing and damn near ruined everything!

Sitting quietly having my face painted, I was glad I'd come back. Several women and a few men were wandering around, and every once in a while someone would pop in and say hello to me. When it came time for my scene I did just what Richard had said. I strutted around the pool in my tiny bikini as the scene was filmed from a bunch of different angles.

The next day during the final take of the party scene, all the people around the pool spent the afternoon having sex. As the orgy started I was told I was finished for the day and could go home. Collecting my things, I made a pit stop at the kitchen to get a drink.

The image of all those breasts and asses, arms and legs wrapped around each other was fresh in my mind. It was a bizarre tangle of flesh, which I found erotic. The people had become a sea of groping, groaning bodies and I was amazed at the very matter-of-fact way the women acted. They stripped without any hesitance whatsoever and spread their legs without any hint of shame. *What did they know that I didn't and how did they find out?*

As I poured myself a vodka, the stud of the moment, Tom Byron, walked in and started flirting with me. He asked if I lived around there and how long I'd been modeling, and though he seemed nice enough, I told him nothing at first. But he had this sweet, dopey puppy-dog thing going on and I let my guard down. I was wasted by that point, and since then I've often wondered if he'd been sent into the kitchen to seduce me or if he just got lucky. I'm still not sure why I let him have his way with me. I don't know what I was thinking. All I can say is I never intended to be filmed having sex in that kitchen, and I only realized I was being filmed when it was nearly over and I had already given in to a feeling I had never known during sex—power. And with that power came pleasure. I was blind to everything around me and I wasn't acting for a camera. I was acting out.

That's what porn did for me. It allowed me to release all the fury I'd felt my entire life. And that's what got me off. Freedom, peace, revenge, sex, power. I'd finally found a place to put my energies—I was vengeful, even savage, in sex scenes, fully unleashing my wrath. At the ripe old age of sweet sixteen, I was nothing short of a sexual terrorist.

Porn was a power trip for me. At the time I didn't understand it, but in reality I was fighting to take back what had been robbed from me as a child. There was a war going on in my heart and I was acting it out with my limbs. I was a sex-crazed, drugged-out wild child and I wreaked havoc on everyone I came across.

I had no one to talk to and nowhere to go. My drug habit consumed my every thought, and sex became a typical ending to most mornings, afternoons, and nights thanks to Sonny's insatiable appetite. I'd grown accustomed to first pleasing him and then going about my own business, so sex became like this price I eventually had to pay for any measure of love I was going to receive, and that was just the way things were.

I didn't know that sex and love could be one and the same thing, so sex became something that I both loved and hated. On the one hand, it made me feel scared and uncertain, since all my first experiences were violent ones, and on the other, it was power, so it gave me the only kind of control I ever knew. But

I resented that price tag. It made me angry, and that's what I showed the world.

But on the inside, I was a mess.

And I was vicious. Maybe, just maybe, if I gave my body away, then I would somehow win back the control that had been stripped from me all my life. So that's what I did, and porn became yet another drug in my junkie life.

15

The Skin Trade

Several weeks later I found myself on the set of another porn movie. Time had lost its meaning. The movies all blended together. I was like a passenger in my own life.

The bathroom was littered with used douches. The scent of stale cigarette smoke hung thickly in the air. I could hear the groans of porn queen Ginger Lynn, having sex in a back room, and wished I were somewhere else.

I was in between scenes. Barefoot and barely dressed, I searched the kitchen and found a bottle of tequila. Steadying myself as I did a shot, I snorted the last of the mashed-up downers I had. I stared at the photos on the refrigerator. The smiling faces of a young boy and little girl looked back and I wondered what it would be like to grow up rich in a mansion like this. *Was it easier? Were the kids in the pictures really happy? Or did they receive nighttime visits like I had? What kind of parents let people film porn in their house anyway? Stupid? Desperate? Both?* I didn't know.

Ginger's moans grew louder. *Didn't she ever shut up?* I was pissed off and disgusted by the thought of the upcoming lesbian scene I was supposed to have with this bitch on wheels. The thought of kissing her grossed me out, *but I guess it's better than having to fuck a fleshy hairball like Ron Jeremy,* I reasoned, still feeling less than lucky.

Moments later the downers took hold. I lit a Marlboro Red and found the enormous oval-shaped pool in the mansion's backyard. It was pitch-black outside except for the candles floating in the pool's shallow end. I dropped my robe and slid naked into the warm water feeling heavy, like I had ankle weights attached to me.

Everything was blurry, hazy, moving in slow motion. I drifted toward the sound of laughing voices. As my body cut through the water, the voices grew louder and I reached for them, my hands pushing back water instead. I could see a gorgeous man standing waist-deep in front of me. He smiled, watching a goddess with long dark hair floating on her back, her small, perfect nipples pointing toward the heavens. I made my way toward her, and felt his hand glide across my back.

I wanted to be held, needed to disappear in her arms. But would she let me? She wasn't a porn star. She was better than that. None of these naked midnight swimmers did it on film. They were extras from some "real" modeling agency, not North's, and the producers were thrilled to have them there. We were filming the porn world's version of the movie *Splash.* I was supposed to be the mermaid, but in this version the mermaid liked to talk dirty. The producers of this film fancied themselves real Hollywood filmmakers because they had a budget that could actually afford extras.

My naked body met the flesh of the swimming creature, and I startled her by boldly running a finger across her belly. Our eyes met and I held my breath, waiting for her reaction. She smiled and splashed water at me. She was long, lean, and full of life. Laughing, she pulled me close and wrapped her arms around me. Her cool skin pressed against mine. I breathed her in, holding on to her, finding refuge in her arms. She kissed me softly and I kissed her back. It was different from all the other kisses I'd given and received that day on film. I bit into her lip, kissing her harder. I lost myself in the moment.

A wave of wooziness washed over me. . . . *Where was I?* I looked to the sky. The stars burned bright, telling me nothing. The woman bit me sharply on the nape of my neck and brought my attention back to her. I felt hands on my hips as someone slowly entered me from behind. I lost my breath, a sharp gasp escaping as he sank deeper into me. I was pretty sure it was the gorgeous man who had stroked my back, but the dark-haired woman's hungry mouth kept me from affirming it.

Moments later I was abruptly pulled from the water by a production assistant. He'd been searching for me for some time. Annoyed, he steered me inside toward the waiting film crew.

I was wanted on the set.

I was dried off, put back into makeup, and met with the smirking face of Ginger Lynn, the petite blond-haired blue-eyed twenty-something-year-old woman who had been the reigning diva of porn for the past year. She'd given me attitude from the moment I'd met her a few months earlier, clearly seeing me as competition. And she was right. Within months my tormented, aggressive sex acts and youthful good looks stole her flavor-of-the-moment title, and she made sure I knew she didn't appreciate it one bit. I ignored the daggers she shot at me. We were scripted prostitutes performing for the camera. No emotions were ever attached. It was soulless sex by the numbers—one blow job, two positions, final cum shot, or some slight variation of that formula. Sex on-camera fed a very specific hunger in me. It was the best drug of all.

Porn made me the kind of girl people both condemned and paid attention to, and that's what it was all about.

I was hailed as the Princess of Porn. They gave me awards at the Porn Oscars. Performers like Ron Jeremy spoke about how professional I was. Dicks for hire like Tom Byron bragged about how we were offscreen lovers. And the story of my poolside threesome spread through the porn world like wildfire, making me even more sought after in porn films. I was thought of as insatiable. But it wasn't that I couldn't get enough on-screen. It was that I got nothing. I was venting, releasing the garbage that polluted my mind in the only way I knew how.

Over the next six months I starred in twenty X-rated films. That's about twenty days' work. Most of the films were shot in just one day. Only later did I find out that it was a common practice in the porn industry for these "sex scenes" to be repackaged, reedited, and made into a dozen other "new" films. The stars were never paid for the additional film compilations that exploited their services, but the companies made a fortune.

I was said to be one of the highest-paid girls in porn at the time, earning about a thousand dollars a day. It seemed like a lot of money then, but I was hardly rich, earning about twenty thousand in total, which was just enough to pay the rent and feed my coke habit—a fact I would find impossible to explain to the Internal Revenue Service years later.

Thanks to my status as the It girl of the moment, I was offered a guest stripping gig in San Francisco. My agent, Tim North, pressed me to take it. He didn't have to work hard, as I needed a break from Sonny.

The cracks in my Traci Lords persona were beginning to show.

One month later in the spring of 1985, two months before my seventeenth birthday, I took the stripping gig in San Francisco. I arrived feeling like a cracked doll. I stayed high as much as possible and found it difficult to do the most mundane things like take a shower. I was strung out, twitchy, and irritable.

I walked on-stage at the O'Farrell Theater stoned and drunk on cheap wine. But instead of feeling powerful and in control, I felt like a beaten little girl. I was a deer caught in the headlights, frozen in place as the horny crowd cheered for me to take it off. I couldn't breathe and found myself backing off the stage. I panicked, breaking into a full-out run in my precariously high heels. All I could see around me were groping hands.

In a heap in my dressing room, I sobbed uncontrollably, trying to explain to the club manager that I was not used to crowds of fans grabbing at me. He laughed as I cowered in the corner, begging to be sent home. Instead, he sat me down in front of the makeup mirror and told me to fix my face. "You're not going anywhere until you finish up here," he said firmly.

"Look, baby"—he softened—"you're a pro, go make some money."

Twenty minutes and two shots later, I took the stage to Madonna's "Like a Virgin." A burning anger at being bullied into honoring my strip club contract replaced my stage fright, and I took my rage out on the patrons who'd scared me. It was a sellout crowd and I gave the bald businessmen what they wanted, wiggling in their laps and stripping naked as the tips came pouring in. I thrust my breasts in their faces, sold my panties to a guy in the audience, and then strutted from the stage, flipping the club manager the fuck-you finger as I slammed my dressing room door. I'd given them everything I had.

Then I fell apart.

A stripper named Raven who found me in my dressing room felt sorry for me and took me home to crash on her couch. When I woke up the next morning I was a basket case. I didn't know what I was going to do. I was strung out. Broke. Unemployed. And agentless, having fired North during a heated phone conversation about my unprofessional attitude the night before.

Gathering my things, I got into Raven's car, bound for the airport. I sighed deeply, dreading the wrath that awaited me in Los Angeles. I had called Sonny looking for a sympathetic ear but was given a tongue-lashing instead. He screamed at me over the phone, furious I had fired North, and demanded to know how I was going to support us now. I knew he was going to beat the crap out of me when I got home.

As we soared down the highway, I told Raven the whole story. It felt good to talk to someone who lived in the same world I did. She drove in silence, listening to my sad tale. When

I'd finished she told me I needed to get a grip and that North wasn't the only agent in town. "That's just what he wants you to think," she said.

She suggested I check out another agency in Hollywood that she worked with from time to time, saying it needed a girl for a video that afternoon in Los Angeles. It was an R-rated bondage video, and she'd only turned it down because the San Francisco club manager wouldn't give her the night off to fly to L.A.

I knew nothing about tying people up, but she told me not to worry. The Japanese clients were really nice and she'd worked with them many times before. That gave me a glimmer of hope. *Maybe this could be my way out of porn?* Giving me the address, she told me she'd call the agent to confirm, and I'd meet him after the job.

I thanked her profusely, unaccustomed to receiving help from anyone.

16

Strippers, Tippers, and Pony Clippers

I arrived in Burbank later that afternoon, nearly an hour late. The flight's delay had made it impossible for me to be on time for the day's shoot, and I only hoped my tardiness wouldn't make Raven look bad. I was anxious and suffering from a pounding headache as my taxi finally delivered me to the location somewhere deep in the San Fernando Valley. I scrambled to gather my things as the car pulled into a long dirt driveway. Wrestling with my luggage, I dug up the hundred-and-twenty-dollar cab fare and silently cursed Sonny for not picking me up, costing me my hard-earned tips from the night before.

The taxi left me standing in a cloud of dust as it pulled away. I had no idea where I was, but by the looks of the sparse surroundings it was the middle of nowhere. Hobbling down the dirt driveway, I struggled with my bags, feeling weak and irritated from lack of sleep. I stopped to check the address in my purse, hoping Raven hadn't sent me on a wild-goose chase. Up ahead I could see a weather-beaten red barn and some horse stables.

According to my watch I was forty-five minutes late. Crap— so much for making a good impression. This was the first job I'd booked without North and I really wanted to start off on the right foot with Raven's agent. I hoped the clients were still there and hadn't reported my tardiness by now. Man, I hate being late!

The dust from the driveway tickled my throat and I couldn't stop coughing as I approached the barn. I couldn't believe this was the place. Dropping my things, I gave the thick barn door a pounding. Helloooooooooooo! I was hot, sweaty, and wanted to get on with it. No one answered. I was screwed, in the middle of nowhere without a car or phone. I started to think Raven had tricked me when I heard some voices. Walking around to the back of the barn I saw a film crew standing in a field. I couldn't believe what I saw next.

There in the middle of the field was what looked like a large, circular clothesline attached to a six-foot metal pole stuck in the ground. Hanging down from four equally spaced positions on

San Francisco, 1984.

the line were black leather leashes, and attached to those leashes were women. Three spots were taken and only one was unoccupied. *That's my spot!* I realized with horror.

I stood gaping at these "pony women" trotting around in circles. It was a bizarre spectacle. They wore tall black leather boots, black studded leather G-strings, and black bras with the nipple area cut out. One had a horse gag in her mouth. A hooded man, well over six feet tall, stood in the center of the ring, whipping their muscular asses and ordering them to "mush, mush" as they trotted by.

I was paralyzed with a mixture of fascination and disbelief. It momentarily struck me as funny, but my amusement quickly vanished as a tall Japanese man, who I later realized was the director, noticed my presence. Rushing to my side, he started rattling on in a language I didn't understand. Then an unbelievably tiny Japanese lady, maybe four feet five inches, started circling me and tugging at my clothes as if I weren't in them. I felt like I was on another planet. I couldn't understand what these people were talking about, and although this tiny grandma of a woman wielded a rather ominous-looking riding crop, she struck me as harmless. Politely bowing, she offered me a leather straitjacket, which seemed to me appropriate, since I'd been feeling suicidal for months.

A crazy laugh escaped my mouth as I glanced toward the galloping pony people nearby and wondered exactly what they had in store for me. I'd never seen leather work like this and was mesmerized by the sight of one particular pony girl with dark-chocolate hair. She was being spanked lightly and purred in pleasure. *Was she for real? Did that feel good?* I had no time to contemplate this further, as I was quickly undressed by the grandmotherly-looking woman and outfitted in full-on leather, studs, and a cat-woman mask. It was the middle of the summer, ninety degrees outside, and I looked like an X-rated Saturday-morning cartoon.

The clients were dead serious about what they were doing, but their stoic demeanor made it impossible for me to keep a straight face. I felt as if I'd fallen into the twilight zone. Had the whole world gone crazy?

Led to the post and tied up with the other "horses," I suddenly gave in to a fit of laughter, the kind that shook my whole body. My "mature" adult persona completely fell away as I stood half laughing and half crying in my tall boots. I wondered if my giddy behavior somehow gave away the fact that I was only sixteen. But the other "models" trotted along obediently, oblivious to my hysteria.

The shoot ended a few hours later as the sun went down, and I caught a ride to Hollywood with the chocolate-haired model I came to know as Cheri. We stopped off at a local Hollywood watering hole called Barney's Beanery, and after several brewskis I dared to ask her if she liked her job. She erupted in a deep, throaty laugh and said, "We just made a grand apiece. What's not to like?" She then polished off her beer.

I could see her point. "Some people just have weird kinks," she said, her Japanese clients being some of the oddest. She told me our shoot had been tame compared with some of the stuff she'd been booked for. I was curious. *Really? Hmm . . . like what?*

Over the next half hour Cheri schooled me, telling me "splosh" videos were all the rage. "Sploshing" is getting tied up and then having food thrown at your naked body. Cheri's only rule was that she got to wear sunglasses to protect her eyes.

"Are you messing with me?" I said, squinting my eyes.

"Nope." She smiled. "Coconut cream pies smell nice and feel sexy when they slide down your belly."

Wow. . . . I pictured a cool pie sliding down my tummy. I didn't really get the sexy part, but I found it amusing, and my new friend and I sat giggling in our booth watching the traffic go by.

An hour later Cheri dropped me off at her agent's office in Hollywood.

She'd already given me the lowdown on him. He specialized in rock videos, Playboy Channel soft-core erotic movies, and pinup-type modeling. He was an R-rated version of North minus some of the sleaze. Cheri told me she made a pretty good living for a nineteen-year-old who'd never gone to college. Saving her money, she hoped to one day make it big and star in a movie with Sylvester Stallone.

"Whatever you do, Krissie," she said, "watch out for the porn guys. They'll mess you up bad."

My stomach dropped. I looked away. If she only knew . . .

"Don't worry," she said. "You're beautiful. You'll do fine."

I was taken aback—beautiful? I didn't feel beautiful. She said she'd never done anything that she couldn't live with, and I couldn't help but think I'd never done anything that I *could* live with. *Where did that leave me?*

She dropped me off minutes later, gaily waving good-bye.

As I watched her drive away I wished I'd met her years earlier. She was like an older, wiser sister and I missed mine. Lorraine had always known the way out of tricky situations. *Why couldn't I go back home? How much worse could facing my mother and sisters be than this?* I kicked a can and walked down the block to where I was safely out of view. I spat, disgusted with myself. *What's wrong with me? Why can't I just fucking stop this crazy shit?* I paced the sidewalk and tried to collect myself.

I had to do something . . . something right. If I could just fix this mess, do one good thing . . . maybe, just maybe, I could face my mother again.

Fixing my makeup, I took a deep breath and walked into the office, determined to get my life together.

I didn't want to be a porn star forever.

17

Crash and Burn

Later that evening I arrived home in Lawndale. It was nearly midnight. The meeting with the agent had gone well and I now had new representation and an audition the next day.

I crept quietly into our house, not sure if Sonny was there or not, and if he was, I wanted to let sleeping dogs *lie*. But the house was empty. Looking out the back window, I spied an empty space where my Vette usually sat. *Shit.* My car was gone.

I knew he'd taken off in my Corvette to get at me. *Great,* I thought. *Where did he go?* I'd been worried all the way home in the taxi, hoping that Sonny's foul mood would improve with word of my new agent, but now I'd just have to wait for him to come crawling in.

Standing at the front window, I watched the cars come and go, sinking my toes into the scarlet carpeting. Why couldn't I just leave Sonny? What was this power he had over me? I was disgusted with my own helplessness. Fighting the urge to smash every lamp in the room, I watched time tick by, wondering if he'd come home at all.

The bars closed in a few hours and I contemplated hunting him down, pretty sure he was at one of our regular drinking haunts in Hermosa Beach. I checked my watch and decided against it. It was almost last call. He'd be wasted by now. He was a mean drunk and I was too tired to fight.

I scrubbed my face and climbed into bed, my world quiet for once. I fell asleep. It was the first time I'd done that in a very long time. Usually I just passed out.

My peaceful slumber was interrupted by the ringing phone. It was Sonny. He was in jail. He'd been arrested for a DUI and sobbed into the phone about how sorry he was. He didn't mean to wreck it. *What?!* Would I come get him?

The policeman I spoke to said I couldn't collect my car or my boyfriend until the morning. All I could do was wait.

At 7:25 in the morning I saw my beautiful black Vette sitting in the police impound lot. She was a total wreck. Jagged cardboardlike pieces of my precious getaway car glared accusingly back at me, and I had no idea what to do next. I felt numb and utterly defeated as my eyes drifted down to the gravel that my dream car rested on.

I was such a loser. Why had I let this happen?

Leaving the impound lot alone, I made the two-mile trek home leaving the car and Sonny behind. *My car was gone—history. I was screwed. How was I going to get to my audition? I didn't have a credit card or bank account. I always got paid in cash. And I didn't have enough of that to replace the car.* The questions screamed through my head as I hailed a cab to Hollywood and sucked in a smoky drag of my Marlboro Red. I smiled to myself as I imagined Sonny sitting in jail. *Fucking asshole—let him rot.* Running my fingers through my hair, I contemplated life on my own.

I lit another cigarette and tried to squash my growing panic. I was only a kid! Who was going to take care of me now? *Maybe I should have bailed him out. It was an accident. He loved me. He told me that all the time.*

Tears threatened to blow my cool demeanor as I arrived at the casting session, but I pulled myself together as I walked into the office. An attractive Asian receptionist greeted me, inviting me to have a seat and saying Mr. Bell would be out shortly. I

counted ferns in the plush waiting room—six in all—and tried
to remember what I was auditioning for. Popping a wintergreen
mint in my mouth, I prayed I didn't stink of this morning's
blow-and-booze breakfast. I straightened my miniskirt and
crossed my legs protectively, almost groaning out loud as I
imagined someone throwing hams at my nude body.

Jesus, I wasn't in the mood for any bullshit.

Scott Bell was all smiles when he greeted me. He looked like
a Hollywood version of Sonny, with perfectly highlighted blond
hair moussed into a Ken doll coif and crystal-clear blue eyes
that screamed, "Hi, I'm a nice guy!" His name should have been
Skip, and his overeager friendliness seemed really false. He was
the type of guy who'd probably never struggled a day in his life,
and in my pissy state of mind I wanted to slap him.

I played the game instead, returning his smile, hoping to at
least get a job out of this. He had to be around thirty-five and
reeked of cigarettes. His pet project was a softcore film he was
making. He casually slid his wedding ring off as he asked for a
picture and résumé. I lied, telling him I was all out.

His eyes seemed to devour me as he probed me with questions, digging into my personal life and making a point of telling
me he was recently separated from his wife. Losing my
patience, I wondered, *What is this?* The Dating Game? He
asked if I acted under my real name, Kristie Nussman, or if I
had a stage name. I had to get out of there. Did he know something? Was he going to start trouble with my new agency? Or
was he just another guy who wanted a piece of me? Fed up
with this game of cat and mouse, I interrupted him saying I had
another audition. I no longer cared if I had the job or not.

I walked toward my new agent's office on Santa Monica
Boulevard with a bad case of the blues. Kicking stones to pass
the time, I felt like I could sleep for days.

There was a lot I wanted to forget.

I walked faster, trying to shake off the itch to score some
drugs. Dealers littered the street corners, tempting me with

their very presence. They laughed among themselves, seemingly carefree. I was no longer scared of them, though, no longer a stranger to their world.

I forced myself down the street. I wasn't going home. After leaving Sonny in jail, I wasn't about to face his punishment just yet. I'd check in with my agent, and then satisfy my need for speed later. I decided I'd lie low in Hollywood for a few days, passing several motels along the way and guessing any of them would do.

I dragged myself into my agent's office a half hour later and began to tell him what had happened at the audition. He stopped me, saying Scott Bell had already called. Bell had told him that I was really Traci Lords and that he was interested in discussing a possible business deal with me. He'd asked the agent to set up another meeting. It was scheduled for 7:30 that evening at a restaurant called Mirabelle's in Hollywood. "That's all I can do for you, Traci," the agent said. "I don't handle porn girls." Humiliated, I left his office. *I'm not a porn girl anymore!* Bell had cost me my agent.

I checked into a cheap motel up the block and had a soak in the tub. I didn't know what to do next. I was alone in Hollywood, agentless again, and had a dinner date with a guy I wanted to punch out. Did he know that he just ruined everything for me? Had he done it on purpose? What did he want from me? Was he really a legit filmmaker like my agent said? I was no longer the gullible girl from Ohio and something told me the whole thing stank. The least he can do is feed me, I decided, setting out in search of something to wear to dinner.

Later that night, I headed for the restaurant. I'd been told Mirabelle's was a fancy French place and I hoped the short black dress I'd bought was a winner. I strutted across Sunset Boulevard amid a sea of catcalls, which made me question my choice of wardrobe. The dress was on sale for $19.95. Did I look cheap? Insulted by the propositions of two different men, I quickened my pace.

Minutes later, I entered the softly lit restaurant and was

shown to Mr. Bell's table. I was flustered by the walk there and
still pissed Bell had complicated my life. But I was determined
not to let it show. As I took a seat, the waiter offered me a drink
and I looked around the room to notice what the other women
in the restaurant were having. They were all enjoying light-
colored beverages in slim glasses. I wanted to be as sophisti-
cated as they were, so I said in my most adult voice, "I'd like a
glass of Tott's, please," having no idea it was the cheapest champagne one could buy.

Scott laughed, saying what a kidder I was, and promptly
ordered me a glass of Pinot Noir. He condescendingly told me
Tott's was "low rent." Embarrassed, I was about to tell him
where to stick it when the waiter returned to card me. Scott
smiled, but I could tell by the deepening redness on his forehead
that he was mortified. I was clumsily searching my purse for the
Kristie ID when the contents fell on the table.

"Oops," I giggled, returning my switchblade to my bag.
"Girl's gotta be careful." I innocently smiled to the stuffy waiter.
Bell was speechless. I presented my ID, swallowed my drink,
and walked out the front door. Fuck it. I was done.

Bell came after me, apologizing for his bad manners. I stood
fuming in front of the restaurant and aware of the attention we
were drawing.

"Please, have some dinner with me. I'm really sorry, Kristie.
I have a business proposition that is going to make you a very
wealthy woman. Just hear me out."

One lobster and a bottle of wine later, I listened as Bell made
his pitch. He said that he had an investor who would bankroll
a film production company. It would be called TLC, the Traci
Lords Company. It would produce three X-rated films starring
me. I would be required to perform three sex scenes per film.
He would write and direct.

Embarrassed he was talking so casually about this in public,
I kept checking for eavesdroppers. How had the day gone so
wrong? Stupid Sonny wrecked my Vette, I lost my agent, and
now this guy was trying to get me back into porn. I couldn't

take any more. I told Bell I wasn't interested. Thanking him for dinner, I left abruptly.

Tears drenched my face as I walked home feeling sorry for myself. Life sucked, and I was sure I was at the end of the road. I'd only gotten a few blocks when a horn blared at me. Startled, I shot the Benz driver a nasty look only to realize it was Bell. Quickly, I wiped my eyes, not wanting him to know he'd upset me.

"What?" I snapped.

"Kristie," he said, "get in. Let me give you a ride." I hesitated for a moment and then wearily climbed in. He was a jerk, not a killer, and I was dead tired.

18

Checkout Time

It was four in the morning and I hadn't slept a wink. I was simply lying in my motel room in the heart of Hollywood, listening to the cars of the rich and famous drive by. I couldn't bear returning home to Sonny, so there I stayed, stone sober and feeling everything.

I kicked the covers off and walked to the window, watching the hookers work the street as night turned to day. Was I really any different from them? "Everyone has a price and anything can be bought." Bell's words nagged at me as I replayed the evening's events.

Only hours earlier, I'd sat comfortably in Scott's car. I'd never been in a fancy automobile before and I now understood what people meant when they asked for a "new car smell" at the car wash. I'd barely said a word on the drive to my motel. But it didn't matter; he was happy to do all the talking. Scott Bell was the kind of man who enjoyed the sound of his own voice. He was a fast talker who bragged about everything from the fabulous vacations he'd taken to the numerous cable movies he'd produced, none of which I cared much about.

Then he revealed his softer side. He was a father, and when he spoke of his three-year-old son, his whole demeanor changed. The arrogant L.A. hotshot producer was replaced by a caring family man. He was proud of his little boy and spoke sadly about his recent divorce. I was moved by the genuine love he expressed for his child and was touched by his gentleness. *Maybe I was wrong about this guy. Man, was I ever going to be able to tell the good guys from the bad?*

He asked me why I was staying at a motel and I told him that I was ending a relationship, careful not to reveal too much about myself. He was thirty-six years old and I felt very sixteen around him. "We'd make a great team, Kristie," he said, warmly reaching for my hand. "Let me help you." I got out of his car promising him I'd think about it. And I spent the whole night doing just that.

As I watched a girl climb in a car, it seemed Bell was right. Everyone does have a price and anything can be bought. I needed what he offered, but I wasn't sure I could do what he asked. Staring at the streetwalkers outside, I wondered which fate would be worse: dying on the streets or dying in front of a camera? I closed my eyes and tried to imagine having sex on film again, but the thought was too disturbing. I got dressed and headed up Sunset Strip looking for an escape. I scored some downers and bought a sixer, and then went back to my room, drinking until my eyes were heavy and my thoughts were swimming in Budweiser. I woke to the maid pounding on the door. It was checkout time.

19

Paris

I returned home to Lawndale that afternoon and found an eviction notice stuck to our front door. *Fuck!* Sonny was naked and sobbing in the living room. Unaware of my arrival, he was snorting a line of cocaine and watching Jimmy Swaggart on television. I took in this bizarre scene and quietly backed out of the room.

Heart pounding, I made my way through our trashed house to the bedroom, unable to get the image of his snotty face out of my head. He was a disgusting animal and I was repulsed. *Anyplace is better than this*, I thought. I had to get out of there.

Throwing a few things into a bag, I planned to make a quick getaway out the back door, but Sonny cornered me in the bedroom. *Fuck!* He slapped me in the mouth and ripped a dress out of my hands, then grabbed me by the hair and threw me across the room. Tasting blood in my mouth, I slowly crept along the floor to the switchblade in my purse, praying I wouldn't have to use it.

Hurling himself at me again, he collapsed at my feet in sobs, begging me to forgive him. Frightened and confused, I stroked his damp hair and told him everything was going to be all right.

He was so fucked up. I couldn't help but feel sorry for him, no matter how badly he'd abused me.

An hour later he passed out in his own vomit. I called 911 and left him for good.

Later that night I called Scott from a dingy bar in Hermosa Beach. Crying hysterically, I told him I'd do whatever he asked me to do, pleading with him to just come get me. I felt like I was making a deal with the devil that night. But at the time it seemed like the only thing I could do.

Once again my life became a constant blur of sex and drugs as Scott quickly took on the role of business partner, boyfriend, and pimp to the porn industry. Over the next twelve months he produced and directed me in two porn films. He even leased me an apartment in Redondo Beach.

In May of 1986 he took me to Paris.

I wanted to admire that beautiful city, but it was almost impossible to appreciate. We were there to film a French porn movie and I was achingly sad, more depressed than I had ever been in my life. I just couldn't fathom Scott's willingness to direct me in explicit-sex movies if he really loved me. It was obvious I was suffering. My drug intake was at an all-time high, my weight had dropped to ninety-four pounds, and my five-foot-seven-inch frame looked more frail than ever. I was rotting in my own self-imposed prison. And no one around me seemed to notice or care.

As publicity for the French film, I was scheduled to be the main attraction at a Parisian club that night. I was lowered from the ceiling in a giant gold birdcage while a sea of faces stared up at me. Wearing diamond-studded shorts and white cowboy boots, I kicked my legs to soar even higher on the swing as I descended in my fancy cell, quietly humming "Happy Birthday" to myself on the way down. Below me, I could see the club owner doing shots at the bar with Scott. I wanted another drink myself.

The fans were now face-to-face with me, but the bars on my cell kept me safely out of reach. My breasts were covered in glitter and they shimmered in the flickering lights as strangers reached for them and bulbs flashed mercilessly in my face. Voices called to me in French and the motion of the swing was starting to make me queasy when I was finally pulled upward toward the heavens.

The evening's work finished, I sat alone in the darkness of my dressing room, downing another shot of tequila in tribute to my very special, very secret day.

It was 12:01 on May 7, 1986. I was eighteen years old.

The following morning we started filming *Traci, I Love You.* Scott banged on my dressing room door and summoned me to work. I unlocked the door and downed a glass of vodka as my love led me onto the set. My eyes met his as I unbuttoned the stranger's pants, and his smiling face dug deep into my heart as he watched from behind the camera and motioned for me to continue.

Nothing made sense anymore, everything was twisted and surreal. Millions of fans would later mistake my guttural moans for pleasure.

20

King Harbor

Days after I returned from Paris, I woke up sprawled out in a pile of sweat-drenched clothing, the sun's glare punching me in the face. I had a serious case of jet lag and it took me a few minutes to figure out who I was, where I was, and what I needed to do that day to survive.

I vaguely remembered having sex with some guy but couldn't quite put it together. My answering machine had screamed at me most of the night—or was it the day? I was supposed to be somewhere, but I couldn't remember where. I felt thick. My head was pounding and I needed water but couldn't bring myself to move. So I just lay there, sprawled out on the cream-colored carpet of my 2,400-square-foot apartment overlooking King Harbor in Redondo Beach.

It was a gorgeous apartment, the kind you get when you "make it." But anyone could tell something was a bit off. The living room was completely empty except for the antique mirror my mother had given me years earlier, now lying in the middle of the room with remnants of the previous night's coke binge on it. A bottle of spilled red wine stained the otherwise immaculate carpet, and bits and pieces of discarded clothing littered the room. I'd been on a bender for two days, and now I guess I finally had come home.

It must have been the cop who'd dropped me off. I had a thing for cops. Actually, there was one in particular whom I liked. His name was Chris and he was my favorite. He'd usually catch me coming out of the Poop Deck and save me from a DUI.

I'd returned from Paris to an empty apartment and a serious case of suicidal thoughts. Maybe it was the jet lag, maybe it was that I suspected Scott was lying about being divorced from his wife, maybe it was birthday blues, or maybe it all just finally got to me. I was at the end of my rope and losing what little grip I had left.

I got high to forget, but after a while even that didn't quiet the storm in my head or stop the film loop of my life from tormenting me with its perfect memory. The sex dreams were the worst. They had become a montage of body parts and I could never seem to separate fantasy from reality. I saw dicks everywhere—dicks and fat faces and beady, Ron Jeremy eyes. It made me crazy.

I was losing my mind.

21

A Man Named Meese

Forty-eight hours later, facedown on my water bed, I watched the hands on the bedside clock move. It was 4:23 A.M. and the stench of an all-night binge hung thick in the air. Sprawling across the water bed, I searched the overflowing ashtray for one last puff of a used cigarette. My hand shook as I sorted through the butts, desperate for a toke as the remnants of the cocaine I'd snorted started to wear off.

"I fucking hate this part," I mumbled loudly in the direction of Scott's passed-out form.

He'd shown up unannounced late the night before and promptly fallen asleep. He was no doubt fighting with his "ex" again. I glared at him as I ground my teeth, turning to watch the dead fish in the aquarium next to my bed floating belly up in the murky water. I pictured myself floating alongside them, my lungs slowly filling with water. I pushed the image out of my head. My mouth was so dry I could hardly swallow and I couldn't seem to move.

Lying there miserably in the darkness, I contemplated scraping my tongue when suddenly the whole apartment shook violently. *What the hell is that?* The noise thundered closer toward me and I bolted upright thinking it was an earthquake. My bed-room door burst open and three men stormed in pointing shiny black guns at me. Not believing what I was seeing, I tried to focus my eyes. The dim light from the aquarium cast a blue glow over the surreal creatures, lighting up the yellow FBI let-ters across their backs.

FBI! I gasped, wondering if it was a hallucination. Had I died and gone to hell? I spoke to the blue men and demanded to know if this was a dream.

Scott was dragged roughly to the floor and slammed face-down into the carpet when reality finally hit me. Pushing myself into the corner of the bed, I pulled the covers protectively over my body.

"Stop it!" I screamed as the armed men surrounded me and aimed their guns in my direction. *Oh my God . . . Oh my God. . . .* I closed my eyes and waited for bullets to tear into my flesh. I felt the sweat roll down my body. "GET THE FUCK OUT OF BED NOW!" I was ordered. My legs trembled as I tried to obey. My eyes darted around the room and took in their smirk-ing faces as I was tightly handcuffed and led down the hallway out the front door. I tried to remember where I'd hidden my stash, certain that it had to be a drug bust. *What else could it be? That motherfucking dealer ratted me out! But how did he know where I lived? He'd never been to my place. . . . Ouch!* I hit my head as I was stuffed into an unmarked car, shoeless and naked beneath the knee-length Metallica T-shirt I'd worn to bed.

"WHERE THE FUCK ARE YOU TAKING ME?!" I demanded. "What am I being arrested for?" I wailed as the car took off. "You can't do this!"

I was being kidnapped and I didn't know why.

The sun started to blind me as it came up on the long drive. I had no idea where we were going and no one was talking. I hadn't been read my rights. I wasn't even sure I was being arrested and I certainly wasn't convinced they were really FBI agents. I was on the verge of hysteria, questions pounding through my mind. *Who would want me dead? Could this be my ex-agent North's doing? He was furious when I went into business with Scott. He'd sworn he'd get even. Was this payback time?*

"WHY ARE YOU PEOPLE DOING THIS! ANSWER ME!" My heart raced, but everything else remained silent. I sank helplessly in the backseat, the handcuffs digging into my flesh.

Utterly spent, I sat scared and defeated as the car wound through traffic toward the tall buildings downtown. I pictured myself escaping, running through the streets in my long nightshirt, helicopters chasing me, but I didn't move a muscle—I just sat there, thinking of my mom hanging clean clothes on the line, the wind in her hair, laughing. I was so little then, maybe four or five. . . .

The federal building in downtown Los Angeles wasn't as glamorous as I'd seen in the movies. They took me in the back way and led me toward an elevator. By now I was certain I was in serious trouble. They must have found my drugs, I thought. *Would Scott rat me out? Was he here too?* Staring down at my chipped red toenail polish in the filthy freight elevator, I wondered what would happen next.

A ding of the elevator signaled our arrival. The monstrous army of blue men walked me out and into a cramped white room with a VCR, stacks of videos, and a lady with a tiny typewriter. A fat-faced man told me to sit in a yellow plastic chair in the center of the room and I did, crossing my legs extra tight. They were all gawking at me and I glared at every one of them, memorizing their faces: one . . . two . . . three . . . seven—seven of them in one room with me.

The fat-faced man stepped forward and introduced himself as Detective Rooker. Then he said the words I'd been longing to hear for the past three years: "We know who you are, Nora. We're here to help you; but first, you're going to have to help us." And then the bottom fell out of my world.

My stomach dropped and I wanted to scream, both in outraged grief and in relief I cannot explain. Someone had finally stopped me. It was over. But it wasn't the rescue I'd dreamed of. I was in a room full of leering men who seemed to be getting off on my hysteria. If they were trying to help me, why were they doing this? I looked Rooker dead in the eyes, trying to see if he was a good guy or a bad guy, but before I could even make up my mind he sealed his own fate by popping a triple-X video of me having sex into the VCR. Someone in the back of the room whistled and Rooker scolded them. I exploded, remembering how my mother had gently scolded Roger years ago for looking at my "poached eggs."

"Fuck you people!" I spat. "You're not here to help me! You just want your piece." I was livid—all the pain and rage I'd felt for years shot out of my mouth in the shape of four-letter words. The lady with the tin typewriter pecked nervously in the background. I felt like a caged animal ready to attack, but as we watched film after film of me having sex with strangers, my fury gave way to numbness.

"What took you so long?" I asked the fat-faced man.

He told me I was part of a sting operation that had something to do with a man named Meese and that they'd been gathering information on me for a while.

The Traci Lords case was three years old.

I couldn't believe what I was hearing. *"YOU PEOPLE KNEW THE WHOLE TIME?"* I went berserk.

"Hey," Rooker said, trying to calm me down, "what are you crying for? Tomorrow we're all going to be famous. Isn't that what you want?"

I just looked at him, not understanding. "Famous for what?"

22

Running on Empty

As unexpectedly as I'd been ripped from my bed in the wee hours that morning, I was returned home later that afternoon. The police dropped me off unceremoniously on the sidewalk in front of my apartment and sped away.

I forced myself forward toward the apartment, ignoring the curious stares of my neighbors. The front door was hanging on its hinges, and as I walked through it, I cautiously listened for voices.

Rounding the corner into the living room, I was confronted by Scott Bell. He demanded to "hear it all come out of my mouth." I broke down and collapsed in a sobbing heap in the corner of my living room, the fight totally beaten out of me.

I had no idea how to begin to explain myself, but I had nothing left to hide. "Look," I started, "I never meant for any of this to happen." Scott rolled his eyes and that set me off. "I WAS TIRED OF BEING RAPED IN MY FUCKING SLEEP, OKAY! CAN YOU UNDERSTAND THAT?" I screamed. I went nuts, punching walls, sobbing. I curled up in a sad little ball and looked him right in the eye. "I was out of porn when I met you," I whimpered, watching him turn white. He softened, moved closer. He was scared. "We have a lot of people to answer to," he said, but I wasn't really listening. I was too tired. I just needed the world to stop for a minute . . . to rest.

Elegant, shiny black shoes walked right up to my head, and I stared eyes-to-laces as I awoke from my momentary slumber. As I started to get up, a shoe stepped on my hair and held me to the ground. It belonged to one of two porn producers I'd seen in Scott's office days before, and one of them got right in Scott's face, telling him he better make sure his little girl kept her mouth shut.

"Please let me go," I pleaded from the ground. "I don't know anything." What did everyone think I was going to say?

"Listen, Kristie," the one accosting Scott said, "you better just keep as quiet as a fucking church mouse or that pretty little face of yours won't be pretty for long." With that he kicked me in the mouth and left me bleeding all over the beige carpet.

Later on I learned that the porn industry thought I had turned myself in. They believed I could identify certain individuals by their real names (apparently I wasn't the only one with an alias), but in truth I had told the FBI nothing. I knew nothing.

I didn't know who had produced which film. I had to rely on the porn box covers for answers. I didn't understand why, but the cops were really annoyed that I didn't have personal relationships with these people and didn't even know who they were. Why was I even being asked these questions? None of it made sense at the time.

Once I was alone, I packed my remaining personal possessions into big brown boxes. The feds had confiscated every photograph I had of my family, and I felt even more alone without my mother's picture to talk to. I had to speak to her. But how? Was she still close by? Did she hate me? It didn't matter. I was no longer safe living in her backyard. King Harbor had become the dead zone. I'd have to leave first and find her later.

I found a new apartment the next day. It was in a large complex by the sea in Marina Del Rey, the kind of sprawling building I could get lost in—and that's exactly what I wanted to do.

I was hiding out and licking my wounds. Fighting to survive. I had no credit, a couple thousand dollars in cash, and no ID, since the feds had confiscated the Kristie one. Nora was gone in my heart and I couldn't be Kristie anymore, so only Traci remained. But was that who I was? *Was I Traci Lords? But I just made her up. How could she be real?*

Scott was civil toward me as the days passed. He cosigned for the apartment in the Marina. I was surprised that he stuck around after all that had gone down. For a while I entertained the idea that he really must love me, but I soon realized his motives were more complex than that. There was the very important matter of the only legal X-rated film I ever made, the one in Paris. In the middle of all this chaos it hadn't occurred to me that the countless news reports about me and the sex scandal would give it added value. The fact that I owned it (it was a Traci Lords Company production) only helped to solidify my reputation as a brilliant Machiavellian businesswoman.

The following weeks were torturous.

I woke up and took long walks along the ocean, the wind stripping some of the haze of my life away. But every day was a new challenge. It was hard to stay sober at a time when everything hurt so much. The massive amount of media attention I got needled me on a daily basis and I was so vulnerable to the cruel titles with which seemingly intelligent reporters crowned me. I was called a porn queen, a naughty Lolita, the princess of pornography. Hypocrisy runs deep in our society, so it's no surprise that the same news channels that reported on the teenage runaway victim Traci Lords now followed that story with nearly nude images from my porn films. The media frenzy drove the price of the now illegal tapes up, and while those in the porn industry complained bitterly that I had cost them a fortune, in reality they became richer than ever. Thanks to the news coverage they were given a free advertising campaign and I was further exploited, left to gather the broken pieces of my life. It was hard not to be bitter.

I'd made about thirty-five thousand dollars during my three

years in the porn business, and all that money was now gone—
spent on rent and drugs. And despite what the media reported,
I had never looked for porn stardom. My life had simply led me
there, and my emotional hunger had made me a prime target for
that kind of exploitation.

I went into therapy the summer of 1986 and began the long,
painful process of unraveling the web of my life. There I
learned, much to my surprise, that it isn't uncommon for children of sexual abuse to act out in many of the ways that I had.
I was told I wasn't a sex-crazed freak but an abused child, and
that was very hard for me to accept. I didn't want that title.
Those words were painful to hear and they stabbed at me. I
knew my therapist was onto something, but it would take me
years before I could allow myself to be that vulnerable in therapy, where I could actually let those words in and see the truth
for what it was.

I had to strip away all the masks I'd been wearing for years
to protect myself, and it was heartbreaking to confront my
demons. I was angry about Ricky, my father, the abortion, dirty
Roger, my mother's blindness, and the ugliness and poverty I
grew up in. But most of all I was angry with myself. I felt that
I should have found another way. I should have been stronger.
At eighteen, I blamed myself for everything, and I felt the
weight of the world on my shoulders. I condemned myself, and
it took me years in therapy before I finally began to see that I
wasn't the only one who was guilty of abusing me.

On one sunny afternoon toward the end of the summer of 1986,
Scott visited my Marina Del Rey apartment. Months had
passed since the FBI bust, and the paperwork for the distribu-
tion deal for the final porn movie I owned was ready to be
signed. I had serious issues about signing over the rights, but
my world had closed in on me and once again it was about survival. I was being bombarded by subpoenas from the federal
government, which wanted to use me as the poster child for the

Reagan administration's task force on child pornography. Apparently, in the countless cases of child pornography across the United States most of the young victims were unknown and I was the only one who was readily identifiable. And although I didn't want another soul on this planet to go through what I had, I was a shattered mess myself. I was so fragile at that time I just couldn't imagine surviving the ordeal of looking at images of myself and other children engaging in sexual acts. It was just too much. I was broken, raw, bleeding from my own battles with drug withdrawal and the undeniable shame I was wallowing in. And I was unnerved by the unpredictability of the subpoenas. It seemed every kiddie porn case in America had suddenly requested me as a witness. No matter what the intentions of the prosecutors were, I felt like I was being thrown to the wolves.

I was a drug addict, only months clean, and battling to remain drug free at a time when the last thing I wanted to do was stay conscious. And the subpoenas just kept coming. I knew the prosecutors of these child pornography cases had a job to protect other children from being abused. I was all for that. But I had someone to protect too: me. Struggling to regain my own sanity, I was hit from every angle. With the federal government, the still-circulating death threats from the porn industry, the IRS, and the local media who hid out in my bushes and stalked me daily, I was going down fast. I don't know exactly where I found the strength to stay off drugs, but somehow I did. Looking back, I think there was something about the feds' constant presence at my doorstep that served as a powerful drug deterrent.

As miserable as I felt in those days I knew something was changing in me. I've heard people call it a survival instinct and I think that's exactly what it was. I had two very clear choices: get on with living or die. I chose to live. I don't know exactly how or when, but sometime over those next few weeks I started fighting back—not lashing out but fighting for my life. I was so far down I could only go up, so I started climbing out of the hell I'd been sentenced to years before at the hands of perverts and pedophiles. Yes, my life was a mess. But I was still standing. I was not another statistic. I was the one who got away and I was going to fucking make it all count. So I did what I thought best. I sold that fucking movie for a period of ten years and with it bought myself some shelter from the storm. It was an agonizing decision, and one that made me a harder person, but it had to be done. I hated the fact that *I* had made it possible for someone to go into a video store and rent it. But selling that film gave me some control over my life. I made two other life-changing decisions that afternoon: I doubled my therapy sessions, and I hired a high-powered lawyer named Leslie Abramson.

23

My Hero

Leslie Abramson was the first protector in my life. Ironically, I found her through a lawyer Scott knew named John Weston, who represented porn clients and was one of the first people to publicly state that I was washed up and would "never make anything" out of myself. I thought he must really hate me to say such cruel things, especially since I'd never met him, but his words only fueled my determination to prove him wrong. Weirdly, he turned around weeks later and recommended the lawyer who gave me my life back, and although I've never understood his motive, I've always been grateful that he led me to Leslie.

The FBI was relentless in its disruption of my life. After giving the initial statement at the federal building downtown and never being booked or read my rights, I had good reason to question authority. I couldn't walk outside my apartment without being stopped and served subpoena after subpoena to appear for prosecutions around the country, and I saw these prosecutors all over the news talking about the Traci Lords case. There was no longer any doubt in my mind about why they wanted me to appear. It wasn't only because I was the most readily identifiable child in porn but also because wherever I went, the media followed.

A dozen cases popped up out of nowhere, mainly involving distributors selling my underage movies after it was publicly announced they were illegal. Certain individuals were actually advertising them as kiddie porn and selling them at hugely inflated amounts to federal agents involved in sting operations all over the country. Then these same distributors gave interviews claiming they were victims of the lies of the teenager who said she was of legal age, swearing they were family men who would never use minors in their movies. This went on for months. I wasn't interested in protecting the people who had exploited me. But I wasn't going to be victimized by a politically motivated administration either. I felt raped by all of them as well as a hostage to everything that was going on, and that's when I met Leslie.

When I walked into her office on Wilshire Boulevard, I was a nervous wreck and out of cigarettes. She was sitting behind a huge desk overflowing with stacks of folders. All I could see was a mound of curly white-blond hair sticking out over the papers and books. Smoke drifted over the desk and circled me, and her big blue eyes suddenly peered over the mountain of work and sized me up.

"Come on in here, close the door," her raspy voice demanded. "You," she said to Scott, "wait outside." I felt like I was in the principal's office. Shaking, I did what she told me and sat down in a big brown chair. "Can I have a cigarette?" I asked her in a small, tentative voice. "Yeah," she said, leaning forward with the pack. "You can even have one if you ask in a big girl's voice."

I swallowed hard, fighting the tears that had been building all day. I sure didn't feel like a big girl.

Then she looked at me, really looked at me, and what was left of my tough-girl façade crumbled. The cat was out of the bag. Tears welled up in my eyes as she handed me the whole pack of smokes. This woman was a fireball. She was a hard-ass and I don't believe she feared anything. But she also had a heart, and it was her kindness that ultimately undid me. For the first time since I'd been abducted by the feds, I felt like someone really got the magnitude of what I'd been through. No matter how much life experience I had, she realized I was still an eighteen-year-old girl, and she was the only person who seemed to truly get how fragile I was.

Years later, she told me that when I had walked into her office she immediately understood how it had all happened. She said the first thing she thought was "My God, what a beautiful young girl—those assholes."

Leslie got on the phone right away, barking at the various prosecutors to call off the hounds. They didn't need me to testify in their cases, she said. It was a dog-and-pony show. She demanded that they use my mother instead of me if they truly needed my identification in those movies, and when the prosecutors weren't satisfied and said they needed me, Leslie shot back that they needed a cold shower. Launching into them, she said she couldn't believe it took so many agents to bring in one little girl. She slammed them for not allowing me to get dressed before taking me downtown, and then warned them she was an excellent public speaker and not at all media shy.

I sat there taking it all in. It hadn't occurred to me until that very moment how inappropriately those agents had handled everything. This woman I didn't even know was defending me, protecting me, and I was so used to getting the short end of the stick that I didn't know how to respond. But I can say it touched me to my core. I was indebted to Leslie Abramson for what she did, and I always will be. It was because of her that I had a chance.

The months went by and I crawled into a protective shell, isolating myself from the judgments of the outside world. I spent most of my time in therapy, trying to figure out what had happened to me. More than once, I felt like I was losing the battle to recover from my past, and years later I realized my feelings were totally justified. What had happened to me is not something a person can recover from. You can only make peace with your past and move on. And man, that takes a lot of time.

I must have cried a thousand tears, wishing I could take it all back. It tortured me morning, noon, and night—craving and resisting the solace one lousy gram of coke would surely bring me. Life was hard, but time went on. I started running on the beach and painting vivid pictures in my living room when I couldn't sleep. Unknowingly, I was learning how to cope in life without the crutches of sex and drugs to hold me up.

The trials and subpoenas continued. Every day was another battle and it became clear to me that I couldn't survive much longer without a bigger army.

It was time to call my mother.

The first thing I said to my mother was "I'm so sorry." I told her I wanted the madness to stop and I wanted my life back. It was an intense reunion. I wasn't ready to discuss Roger or porn or any of it, and she didn't push me to. But for everything I didn't say, I know she saw it plainly on my face. I told her about the trials and subpoenas and how crazy it all was. And she told me I was going to be okay. But I wasn't so sure. I knew I couldn't be okay with prosecutors torturing me on a daily basis, and my mother volunteered to testify in my place.

"You would do that for me?"

"Absolutely," she said. "I'm here for you." My mother's willingness to testify in my place gave me room to heal and proved to me that I really did matter to her. After all the battles we'd fought against each other, we were finally on the same side.

24

Dynamite

Six months later, my time in therapy began to pay off. I was on the road to recovery. At least I now was beginning to understand why I'd behaved as I had. I was making progress. Each day brought a new set of challenges as the indictments and trials raged on, and I dealt with them moment by moment. The intrusion they caused in my life was like salt in an open wound. I felt the sting, paying dearly for the choices I'd made. But I'd had enough.

As the days passed, I was taking my life back, unwilling to continue to live in limbo. I had things to do. I wasn't sure what I wanted to be when I grew up, but decided to try acting—for real. After all, hadn't I been acting my whole life? I made my move. I auditioned and was thrilled to be accepted into the Lee Strasberg Theater Institute. Orientation was set for the next day. I was like a kid on Christmas Eve—so excited I couldn't sleep.

I woke up the next morning and scrambled out of bed, eager to begin the day. I was excited but nervous and had no idea what to expect. Would the acting class have many students? Would they know who I was? Was it a dream to think anyone would take me seriously? Was I about to make a complete fool of myself? *Come on, girl, you can do this.* I dressed quickly, heading out the front door before I lost my nerve.

Cranking the radio, I peeled out of the driveway feeling like my luck was about to change. It was good to be alive. Two stop signs later, I spotted an undercover cruiser in my rearview mirror and was instantly brought back to reality. This was harassment. I'd already been served three times that month. They knew who my lawyer was. When were they going to leave me alone? I had to be in Hollywood in half an hour and I had no time or patience left for these games.

I sped onto the 405 freeway feeling like an outlaw, feds in pursuit. I'd just pretend I hadn't seen them. I thought I'd ditched them when I was stopped at the Santa Monica Boulevard off-ramp. The indignant agent slapped the subpoena on my windshield and said, "Consider yourself served, you little brat."

Adrenaline pumping, I arrived at school with no time to spare. I signed in and finally found teacher Hedy Sontag's classroom on the second floor. As I approached I could hear voices. Class had begun without me. I entered the room aware of a dozen eyes following me to the only empty chair. Being out in public was intimidating. Were the students staring because I was late or had they seen me on the news? Paranoid, I studied the crevices in the floor, wishing I could slip between them.

Hedy sat in the corner watching us. Rising from her chair, she said, "Good morning, ladies and gentlemen. You are here to learn to access the 'well' that life has provided you in your work as actors." I was intrigued: the "well"? At the time, I didn't know that method acting was based on emotional recall. The "well" Hedy spoke of was one's own personal experiences. I had stumbled upon another form of therapy. The three months I spent at the Strasberg Institute gave me insight into myself as an actor and as a person. My confidence was growing.

One afternoon, I was asked to read a monologue from a play, set in the 1950s, about a girl who refuses to join her schoolmates in a bomb shelter. The girl runs across the playground convinced that the world is about to end. Pleading to the sky, she asks God why she can't live longer. She confides in him that she wants to make love at least once before she dies. She continues on, talking about how she needs to know what it's like to have her legs parted and a man enter her. I finished the reading to stunned silence and then applause. Afterward, I was congratulated by my classmates who, one after another, commented on how brave my performance was. My teacher had pushed me toward the subject I most feared: sex.

25

A Few Wise Guys

Three months later, on the last day of school, Hedy told us we had to do three things to succeed as actors: find an agent who believed in us, give incredible auditions, and never give up. The following morning I placed an ad in the *Hollywood Reporter* seeking representation. Scott had agreed to field any calls that came in but only under the condition that he use an alias to protect his reputation. I couldn't believe what I was hearing. He was the one who directed me in those movies and now he was embarrassed to be associated with me?! Although I was hurt, I could understand his desire to leave our sleazy past behind.

The ad I placed attracted the eye of William Morris agent Fred Westheimer. He said, "If she looks anything like her picture, I want to meet her." I drove to Beverly Hills the next day.

My high heels clicked along the marble corridor as I was escorted to Mr. Westheimer's office. He was a well-dressed man with a dry sense of humor. Several people popped by to see if we needed anything and I was impressed at how important he was. I waited for him to ask about my porn days, but he didn't— and I didn't volunteer a word. Instead we chatted about the Strasberg school. I told him how serious I was about my acting career. He promised he'd give serious thought to representing me.

I called Fred the next afternoon. He said he had good news and bad news. The bad news was that the agency refused to represent me. He didn't say exactly why, but he didn't have to. I already knew. The stigma attached to being in porn movies was a big problem. I had no idea how insurmountable it was really going to be.

TRACI LORDS

My first headshot.

My spirits began to sink.

"Traci . . . hello . . . are you still there?"

"Yeah," I muttered, depressed and ready to hang up.

He gave me a pep talk for a few minutes and said he'd be willing to send me out on a few auditions. But it would have to be between us, on the hush-hush. I'd heard that one before, and immediately wondered what the catch was.

Westheimer was a man of his word. He sent me on an audition the next day. Arriving at a silver-and-black highrise, on Hollywood Boulevard, I waited anxiously to meet the folks at Stephen Cannell Productions. I was auditioning for the role of a call girl on the TV show *Wiseguy*. It was a role I knew something about. I booked the job! I was overcome with gratitude, promising God I'd never do anything bad again in my life. I was being given a second chance and I wasn't going to blow it this time. I left for Canada the following week.

26

Lucky Star

I was poured into a stunning black lace couture dress and my hair was teased up high. Walking down the hallway in my heavy mink coat, I felt like a million bucks as I rang the doorbell, cooing "I'm Monique, Herb" to the man who answered. He reached for me and the director's booming voice broke the moment. "Cut. Print. Moving on. Great, Traci!" bellowed the director, taking me by the hand. "Next scene we're in the bedroom. It's postcoital. Camera pans your back as you get out of bed, we follow you down the hallway, and then we all go home. Got it? Good. Get changed."

It was the final day of shooting on *Wiseguy*. Everything was moving at lightning speed. There was no time for butterflies as I hung on the director's every word. I was a sponge, amazed at how much there was still to learn about acting. I was so green! In the past few days I'd learned the basics. I now knew that the colored piece of tape on the floor was called "a mark," which was the target I had to land on before delivering my lines. It was trickier than I'd first thought because I had to do it without looking down! Later in my career, I became a master mark hitter, but in those days I was lucky to land a foot away. Fortunately, the cameraman took pity on me by placing a "sandbag" on the floor that was impossible to miss.

All in all, the five days I spent on location went off without a hitch. I had no problem memorizing dialogue and nailed my lines in a few takes. I was proud of myself, certain I hadn't embarrassed Westheimer. As I said my good-byes to the cast and crew I was pleased to receive a dinner invitation from the show's heartthrob, Ken Wahl. The attraction between us was intense and I happily accepted.

Ken was tall, dark, and brooding with a mischievous smile. He took me to dinner that night at a down-home Italian joint near my hotel. It had a low-key vibe and sensational food. He was a star with simple tastes, which impressed me. He was kind to people and bantered easily with the staff as he leaned back in his chair. The white T-shirt, faded jeans, and ancient motorcycle jacket he wore completed the package. He was one sexy man. I'd only had two boyfriends in my nineteen years and this man was very different from them. His contagious laughter put me at ease and the conversation flowed. As the evening passed, I found myself not wanting it to end.

Headshot, 1994.

27

Top Billing

I sat staring out the window, cloud gazing on the way back to Los Angeles, the night's events fresh in my mind. I wondered if this was the part where I was supposed to feel guilty. I had slept with my leading man. But I was grown-up and hadn't acted irresponsibly, I reassured myself. I was a healthy nineteen-year-old woman and it was about damn time! Ken was the first civilian I'd made love to post-porn. And it was a bit of a head trip. I wondered if his attraction was fueled by that taboo part of my history. Was I the girl every guy wanted to screw but would never take home to his mother? And did that matter? Yes, I realized, it did. As the descent into Los Angeles began, I knew my views on sex had changed. While I had no regrets about the one-nighter with Ken, I realized then that I wanted something more than sex. I wanted a loving relationship.

When I stepped off the plane, Scott greeted me with flowers. He'd missed me, he said, and I felt a twinge of guilt. Was it possible to cheat on a relationship that was all but over? I was confused as I hugged Scott back. I wasn't in love with this man, but I kept him around anyway. Why? Was he my daddy figure? Was it the history we shared? I wasn't sure. But I knew I had a lot to talk about in my next therapy session.

On the ride home, Scott must have felt the distance. Annoyed, he snapped, "I asked you a question." "Sorry, I'm feeling spaced-out from the trip," I fibbed. "What was your question?" He repeated himself, the irritation obvious in his voice. He wanted to know all about the filming. *He's jealous*, I realized—jealous I'm doing what he's always wanted to do. With one episode of a television show under my belt, I was already more legit than he was. Was my thirty-six-year-old lover showing his true colors? Or was I just finally seeing them?

I met Jim Wynorski the following Monday at Roger Corman's office in Brentwood, California. Corman was producing a remake of the Beverly Garland classic *Not of This Earth* and Wynorski was set to direct it. They were searching for a leading lady to play the part of Nadine Storey, the film's sarcastic, quick-witted sexy nurse, and I was up for the part.

When I arrived I was given three scenes to read and, much to my surprise and delight, I realized I had a near photographic memory. Memorizing the lines was easy, calming my nerves was another matter. I was intimidated by the boisterous Wynorski, a horror film legend at Corman's.

I hoped "audition" was not just an excuse to meet me.

Over the past few months, I'd found that horny men from all walks of life wanted to meet the notorious teenager in the news, so I had become suspicious of everyone. Just the thought of Wynorski having ulterior motives annoyed me enough to want to win. I didn't know it at the time but my paranoia was actually an asset. Seeing myself as the underdog, I overcompensated. I was twice as prepared as everyone else and I believe that hunger—that brutal determination and take-no-prisoners attitude—is what helped me succeed. I was absolutely relentless in my pursuit of a legit acting career.

I won the role of Nadine Storey and was set to begin work the following week on Roger Corman's soundstage in Venice.

Since I had no agent at the time, Scott negotiated a fee of

double minimum for me, about three grand a week, and two topless scenes in the movie. While I was uncomfortable with the nudity, I thought they'd laugh if I protested. (I was two for two now: two auditions, two jobs!) But life was far from smooth. I was dealing with the pressures of a new acting career, the continuing harassment of the federal government, and the emotional roller coaster of therapy. I felt like everyone was watching to see if I would fail, and at times I believed I might. The more "real" my new life became, the more doubts I had about being in the public eye again. *What if I messed up? What if I started using drugs again?*

Sometimes, I just wanted to hide under a rock.

But I didn't. I was so desperate to make a new life for myself and change the world's perception of me that I kept moving forward. I morbidly kept thinking, *What if the porn world makes good on its threats to kill me . . . and I die today?* I was repulsed by my contribution to the world so far. *What would my tombstone say? Here lies a cocksucker? Good God!* I felt solely responsible for my own mess and was determined to change my destiny, to redeem myself, to redeem my family. It was an impossibly heavy burden and I wondered if I'd ever get out from under it.

I reported to the set of *Not of This Earth* completely prepared. I wanted to be liked, and greeted everyone with a pleasant smile, hoping to win some kindness points from the cast and crew. I nailed my lines, got along with my costars, and finished up feeling confident that I'd made a good impression. But as I changed out of my nurse's outfit I wondered if the "pink elephant" still overshadowed my efforts. I honestly don't know what I would have done if someone had mentioned porn, but it wouldn't have gone well—just the word made me feel like ripping someone's head off.

Midway through the ten-day shoot, I realized method acting was useless in some scenes. I mean, seriously, how could Hedy expect me to use my emotional "well" to pretend my Ray Ban–wearing costar, Arthur Roberts, was a man from outer space as he chased me through Griffith Park?

I decided to throw my acting "technique" out and hoped I wasn't making an awful mistake. I hadn't studied comedy but I'd studied the role of Nadine and appreciated the character's quick humor. As I played the scenes I was surprised and gratified when the crew laughed at all the right places. *Huh?* I thought. *I'm funny? Who knew?*

Wynorski was a real screamer on the set. A passionate director, he was clearly frustrated with the short shooting schedule of the movie but his tantrums were never directed at me. I avoided all conflict by mastering the art of disappearing at the right times. And despite his sometimes gruff ways, I liked him. How could I not? He was the man responsible for hiring me.

I was biased.

We worked like dogs throughout the picture, filming twelve to fourteen hours a day and completing the whole project in just ten days, which I was told was unheard of in legitimate films. Then the Roger Corman machine went to work quickly editing and completing the film. They wanted to get it out as soon as possible to benefit from the ongoing publicity around the Traci Lords scandal.

Not of This Earth opened in a theater in Westwood only four months later, and people said Corman and Wynorski had done the impossible, putting an ex–porn star in theaters across mainstream America. The *Hollywood Reporter*'s review read, "The answer is yes. She can act." I was ecstatic and thought I was finally on my way to leaving the past behind for good.

Fueled with a newfound confidence, I agreed to promote the film. Corman and Company jumped at the opportunity, setting up several interviews in the days to come and taking full advantage of the press's desire to speak to me. Having no experience with the press or doing interviews, I trusted all the wrong people, agreeing to speak to *Hard Copy* and *A Current Affair* about my past as long as they focused on my present life and the new movie. I spoke candidly about my struggles with drugs, pornography, and the pain of recovery—really deep issues that I had never shared before. And I got knocked flat on my butt.

Film Review

'Not of This Earth'

By DUANE BYRGE

The answer is yes — she can act. Traci Lords is better than most TV soap stars and as good as the majority of primetime fashion queens. Faint praise to be sure, but what she shows is more than adequate for what this Roger Corman opus demands.

Sci-fi buffs and Traci-in-the-buff buffs should turn out in semi-respectable numbers to not only add a few coins to boxoffice tills but provide a bonanza of left-behind raincoats for theater managers.

In keeping with Roger Corman's deserved reputation for inspired production values, all the money is clearly up on the screen. In this case, easily several thousand dollars. Quite sagely, little valuable production money has been frittered away on costumes for Ms. Lords.

The plot, in keeping with sci-fi story standards, is appropriately uncluttered. Similar to its big-budget brethren, "Earth" is composed chiefly of goo, blood and flashing lights. Members of the Academy of Science Fiction, Horror and Fantasy, with their unique levels of appreciation and special insights, may note that "Not of This Earth" encompasses classic story forms with modern permutations — the bloodsucking alien wears sun glasses.

In this cheeky production, Lords plays a nurse. Undeniably, she's invested a lot of everyday nurse-stuff into her performance. Bending, reaching, stretching — Lords stuffs a lot of acting into her form-fitting, snow-white nurse's uniform.

The Steubenville, Ohio, native is not the only cast member who has seemingly heard of the Lee Strasberg school, however. A bevy of supporting actresses, likewise endowed with Lords' particular assets, bring their considerable thespic thrusts to the forefront as well.

For those of us who took notes, "Not of This Earth" revolves around the alien's (Arthur Roberts) attempts to find a suitable supply of blood for his dying planet. Evidently, the blood of large-mammaried females is especially valued. Like most garden-variety aliens, he's sensitive about his physical predilection and goes about his business

---

NOT OF THIS EARTH
Concorde Pictures
A Roger Corman Film

Producers .... Jim Wynorski, Murray Miller
Director .... Jim Wynorski
Screenwriters R. J. Robertson, Jim Wynorski based on the original script by Charles B. Griffin, Mark Hanna
Director of photography .... Zoran Hockstatter
Editor ....Kevin Tent
Art director .... Hayden Yates
Costume designer............................ Libby Jacobs
Color/Stereo

Cast: Traci Lords, Arthur Roberts, Ace Mask, Lenny Juliano, Roger Lodge, Cynthia Thompson, Becky LeBeau, Rebecca Perle
Running time — 80 minutes
MPAA Rating: R

---

in the quiet privacy of his fashionable L.A. basement. Indeed, he's a high-tea kind of chap, quaffing his blood with fastidious regularity every mid-afternoon.

In keeping with the special nature of this movie, the dialogue is often hilarious, including some which comes directly from the screen. To be sure, this unique movie inspires audience participation, and "Not of This Earth" spills forth with double-entendre witticisms.

Someday the French will devote several forests worth of print on this particular oeuvre. It's likely they will distill the varied thematic-philosophical-cosmological essences that co-writer, director and co-producer Jim Wynorski has sprayed around in this low-budget whiff. And it's likely they'll unravel the etiological significance of the vacuum cleaner salesman — the one victim in the film who does not fit the physical or sartorial requirements of the alien. Undeniably, there's a lot to chew on here.

Although "Not of This Earth" does not augur a new aesthetic age for Roger Corman, this essential entertainment combines the artistic rectitude of neo-minimalism with the populist integrity of modern baseball stadium design: Visually, the film is bolstered by effects and flourishes usually only realized by ballpark scoreboards; orally, the film's spare, yet bouncy, musical score resonates with the single-finger purity and stirring breadth one typically only associates with stadium organ music.

The Hollywood Reporter review of Not of This Earth.

Both programs broadcast footage from the illegal porn films, showing clip after clip of explicit photos with the smallest blockers allowed on prime-time television to cover my private parts. They referred to me as "the porn princess" and claimed I'd starred in more than a hundred porn movies, as if twenty weren't enough. They even interviewed people from the porn world who either didn't know me or barely knew me, and they all swore I was some kind of child genius who'd deliberately plotted to destroy them.

How could I have been so stupid? God, it hurt. And the worst part was my mother knew about the new movie and the TV interviews, and I was sure she'd seen it all. Once again I'd screwed up, shaming myself and my family in the process.

I was a wreck, and it nearly drove me back to drugs and out of the film business for good.

28

Not of This Earth

Not of This Earth opened and closed within days. The film's failure coupled with the brutal press experience of the previous week pushed me further into a dark hole. I had gotten drunk way too many times that week, and I knew my drug abstinence was seriously at risk. I hadn't yet given in to the overwhelming urge to score, but I was itching. The little part of me that had dared to dream I could be something other than a porn girl was crushed. I had no hit movie, no mainstream success, and nothing to look forward to.

Depressed and feeling sorry for myself, I stayed in bed for days. I thought about how hard it had been watching myself as Nadine Storey at the cast and crew screening I'd gone to weeks before with Scott. I was so critical about my work I wanted to redo the entire movie, sure I'd be even better if I got another chance. Maybe the *Hollywood Reporter* was wrong about me and I really sucked. Had my lousy acting ruined the film's success? Or did it have nothing to do with me and it was just a B movie destined for a video release from the start? I didn't know. But I knew I didn't like the girl staring back at me on *Hard Copy*, and I didn't understand why anyone else would either.

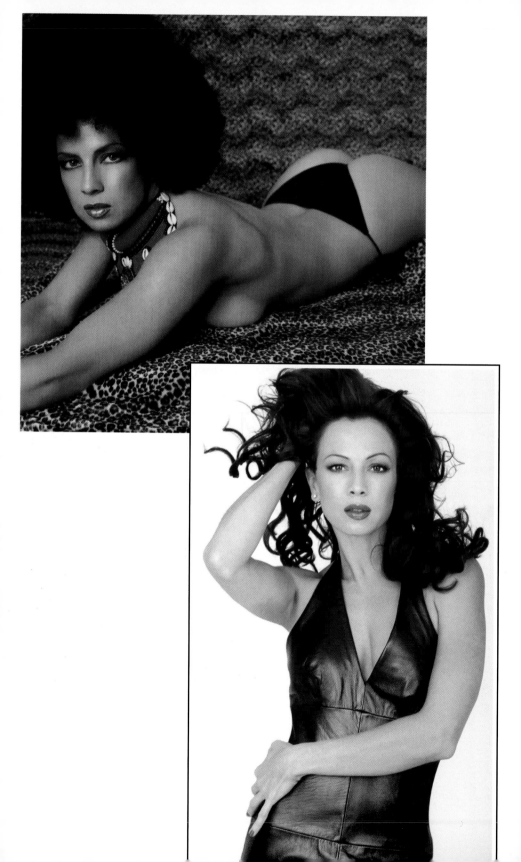

A barely sober eighteen-year-old, Los Angeles, 1986.

As the months went by I returned to my old regimen of running on the beach and weekly chats with my therapist. Slowly, I started to shake off the depression and constant urge for a drug-induced peace. I was living to fight another day, and once again, the time had come to do just that.

Though *Not of This Earth* had failed at the box office, it made a killing in video. Based on that success, Corman offered me another film on the condition that I appear nude again. But this time, although I wanted the work, I wasn't willing to sell my body to get it. I remembered how embarrassed I'd been sitting in the screening room between Scott and Wynorski when my nude scenes first came on. I'd cringed, fully aware of how gratuitous those scenes were, and promised myself I wouldn't allow that to happen again.

Keeping that promise, I turned down Corman's offer. This time I was going to try things differently. I didn't want B movie–queen stardom. I wanted something more. I wanted to be a serious actress.

Hoping I wasn't cutting off my nose to spite my face, I looked to Scott for reassurance, but he only made me feel more uncertain than ever. Amused by my concerns, he crassly reminded me that "everyone had already seen my tits anyway." I chose to disregard his advice to "go for it," opting instead to hold my ground and wait.

During the weeks that followed, print interviews for *Not of This Earth* in publications like *Rolling Stone* and the *Los Angeles Times* trickled out. It was the same rehashed sex-scandal story again and again. I knew I should ignore it, but it was hard not to be affected by the cruelty. I was tired of being called a "porn queen." If I'd known then how much longer that title would haunt me, I probably would have just given up. Instead, I marched along blindly—although cautiously—into new territory.

As the media continued to milk the kiddie porn indictments around the country, I tried to find new opportunities for work and healing. I explored the possibility of working with an organization called Children of the Night, which provided a safe haven for runaways and abused children. The founder of the shelter was a woman named Dr. Lois Lee and we made plans to do a series of public-service announcements together.

I was proud to be Children of the Night's spokesperson and hoped my experience would somehow give me the credentials to reach other lost kids. What I didn't realize was that the kids would be helping me as well. Through them I saw firsthand that I wasn't the only child who felt disposable, used, and guilty of things she had no control over. It made me even more angry at the world.

But this time, it was an active anger, one that fueled my desire to take a stand. One day, I promised myself, I would reach even more of these kids.

For the next few months I existed in a transitional prison. Tabloid photographers were still staking out my apartment, so I closed every blind, locked every window, and was glad I lived on the second floor.

Peering through cracks in the blind one day, I searched the trees closest to my balcony for men with cameras. I had a full day's schedule and couldn't wait any longer, so I made a mad dash to my Camaro in the garage. Reaching the car door, I was almost home free when they appeared out of nowhere.

"Come on, guys," I pleaded, "give me a break." I struggled with my keys, modeling portfolio, and the morning's coffee, my patience wearing thin.

"The movie closed ages ago!" I yelled. "I'm old news."

Ignoring my misery, they snapped away. There must have been four or five of them pushing at one another to get to me. In addition to the tabloid guys there were the autograph hunters. Those vultures were the worst. Pissed that I refused to sign nude photos, they thrust explicit penetration shots in my face in retaliation. "How about this one," one said, presenting a photo of my young face with a penis stuck in my mouth. The guy just laughed.

I wanted to rip his eyes out.

I roared away in my car, cursing at people as I made my way through traffic. *Was this shit ever going to end?* I had a meeting with a modeling agent in Beverly Hills and was so shaken by the raunchy crowd that I just prayed he was going to be kind.

The owner of the modeling agency was Dennis Vaughn, and the head booker was a guy named Craig. Although my five-foot-seven-inch frame is considered short in the modeling world, Dennis signed me anyway, conceding to Craig's argument that I could still do beauty and swimsuit catalogues. I signed an exclusive agreement with the Vaughn Agency that day, giving them all rights to my modeling services for a period of one year. As we were wrapping up, Dennis suggested I use my real name, Nora, to avoid any problems.

Tired of being persecuted for the name Traci Lords, I agreed. I decided I deserved a break.

That afternoon I was sent on a casting call for Frederick's of Hollywood, and I signed in as Nora. When Delores, the casting director, called my name, I just sat there not realizing at first that she was talking to me. The clients were three older women dressed very conservatively in navy blue suits and low-heeled shoes. Whispering to the casting lady, they looked me up and down. I rolled my eyes and expected the worst, my foul mood beginning to take over. I only had two photos in my portfolio, and the waiting room was packed with models, knockouts of every shape and size. I didn't think I had a chance in hell. *I wish they'd hurry up and throw me out so I could go find a new place to live.*

Approaching me sheepishly, Delores asked if I would mind trying on a bra-and-panty set for the clients. I had no body shots in my portfolio and the clients needed to be sure I had a good figure. I couldn't believe it. I had managed to meet the only people in the world who hadn't seen me naked! Greatly amused, I modeled my undies for them.

They were pleased I had natural breasts, apparently an increasingly rare commodity in Hollywood. I got that job, as well as several other bookings as a bra model for them, and over the next few months I was photographed from the nape of my neck to the middle of my stomach, a headless torso for hire. I felt like a complete jackass, but the job was harmless and the much needed income and very much appreciated anonymity were welcome. But it almost came to an end when I made an even bigger splash as Vaughn's new girl by modeling two swimsuit covers for *Muscle & Fitness*.

Twenty-year-old "Nora" for Vaughn.

The first cover hit the stands with me as Nora Kuzma and my anonymity was secure. But a few days later the *Los Angeles Times* ran an article about how the face and body of the model looked strangely similar to Traci Lords. The owner of the magazine was a clean-cut ex-bodybuilder named Joe Weider, and he issued a statement saying that he didn't know anything about his model being a former porn star. I was hired strictly for my physique. He even ran a second cover later on in spite of the fuss—*or was it because of it?* I was next hired to model for L'eggs pantyhose, which was a huge commercial job; however, the client canceled my booking at the last minute. They refused to say why, but off the record I was told they found me "morally unsuitable."

They felt I'd misrepresented myself by using my birth name.

My modeling agent told me not to take it personally. But how could I not? It *was* personal. I knew I'd made a mistake as a young girl, but did that mean I'd have to continue to pay for it forever? Hadn't I suffered enough? I wasn't doing porn anymore. I wasn't doing drugs. I was really trying to change my life! Couldn't anyone see how hard I was working? Didn't that count?

I felt like I just couldn't win. What do you do when your past is your present? How do you leave it behind?

I chose to stop running from it. Instead, I owned it, legally changing my name to Traci Elizabeth Lords.

That's who I was, and that's who I was going to be.

29

Pencil-Thin Mustaches

Months later, on a warm November morning in 1988, I moved into a spacious suburban home in Woodland Hills with Scott. The prying eyes of the media had finally driven me from my Marina Del Rey oasis, and while I missed the clarity I got from long runs on the beach, it was a fair trade for the sanity I found in my new neighborhood.

Being tucked away in the gated, pretty Valley home with a swimming pool and rooms full of rented furniture was a blissful departure from the daily harassments I'd grown accustomed to dealing with. I woke to birds singing and children playing catch in the street. I finally began to relax. Everything seemed to slow down in that southern California version of Mayberry and I felt enormously relieved to be there. I'd made it out of the fast lane and now I could slow down and safely reevaluate my options.

Though Scott and I were getting along, I was concerned about living with him. He was the person I trusted more than anyone else, but I had made the move more out of financial necessity than any growing love I had for this man. It wasn't that I didn't care for him, because I did. But his elitist attitude and condescending air continually left me feeling inadequate and stifled. He hated when I "acted my age" and scolded me for my immaturity. I was a twenty-year-old woman and I'd been given a new lease on life. How could I not be giddy?

My last two years in therapy were helping me cope with a lot of these feelings. My emotional need for Scott was diminishing and I think that scared him. The anger that had served me so well in life was growing into a pure hunger *for* life — a new and positive one. But it was a life that most likely wouldn't include him, and maybe on some level he knew that.

Setting my goals high, I enrolled in another acting class with a teacher named Vincent Chase and started looking around for a theatrical agent. I studied comedy and shared coffee with my classmates, opening myself up to judgment but also friendship. It was a major emotional gamble — and it paid off. The other actors were supportive and most had their own stories to tell. I wasn't the only one who had struggled with drugs and I found that prostitution came in many forms. I was still sensitive about my past, so I never spoke about it with anyone (especially after the *Hard Copy* nightmare), but it wasn't a fresh wound any longer.

I wasn't bleeding as much.

In the following weeks, I booked modeling jobs for swimsuit ads and continued to model for Frederick's of Hollywood, earning enough money to pay my portion of the rent and finance my schooling. During this period, my relationship with my family was also starting to grow, although slowly. So much had happened in all of our lives that being together was difficult. I wasn't the only Kuzma sister who had issues with our parents. My three beautiful, strong, but emotionally battered sisters had suffered as well. They might not have ended up on the streets, but they wrestled with their own demons while growing up and acted out in their own ways. Somehow, though, we all seemed to be landing on our feet.

Scott spent most weekends with his son at his ex's place somewhere on the other side of the Valley. Over time, these overnight and weekend visits became more and more frequent. I was pretty sure he was sleeping with his ex, but since I had little interest in sleeping with him myself, it didn't really matter. I was more concerned about his trustworthiness. He was starting to look like a real fair-weather friend. He'd shown his true colors during the aftermath of the porn scandal. He didn't have my back. It seemed like he was just out for himself.

The question wasn't if I would leave him—it was when. But how would I untangle myself from a man I'd been with since I was seventeen years old? We had a lot of history together—mainly traumatic, but still history. What is it about stepping away from something familiar that's so difficult? I'd done it in every other way, with porn, drugs, and physically abusive men.

Why couldn't I do it with him?

As November flew by I welcomed December and the festive mood the Christmas season put me in. I spent the next few weeks running around on go-sees for my modeling agency and sending out eight-by-tens trying to get a theatrical agent. At the Samuel French Bookstore on Sunset Boulevard, I bought a book that listed all the agents in Los Angeles, and decided the best way to get one was to do a mass mailing.

I only made it through "h" before I ran out of pictures, résumés, and stamps, so I sent out fifty-five requests for representation.

I got four responses the following week.

After meeting with Don Gerler, I decided he was the best choice. He was a pleasant man in his late fifties who had a simple office in a strip mall off Ventura Boulevard. He had a kind face and fatherly way about him, and I liked him right away. He seemed to understand my passionate plea for clothed roles, so I left his office excited by all the prospects the new year might bring.

Yayyyy! I finally had an agent!

When I was a little girl I baked tiny cakes in my Easy-Bake Oven. I considered myself a fine baker indeed and once thought I would grow into a jolly old plump woman with rosy cheeks who lived on a big grassy hill and baked breads and cakes for the little Russian village I came from.

It's a weird thing, self-image, but at my new home in Woodland Hills I found myself constantly venturing into the kitchen to play chef. Although I hadn't cooked much in my life, learning wasn't difficult. My father once told me that the best thing about cooking was that you get to eat your mistakes, and he was right.

As I stood in my kitchen remembering his words, I was filled with a longing for him to be near me. How could he have let so many years slip by? Where was he now and what did he think of me? Was he ashamed? Would he be surprised to know I'd dug through his *Playboy*s as a kid? Did he realize how much he scared us when he drank and slapped our mom? Was he sorry it all turned out to be such a mess? Did he have the same desire to fix everything that I had?

Did he know how much I needed him?

The kitchen became my outlet for self-expression. When I was angry, the sauces were bold and spicy; when I was sad, I whipped up garlic mashed potatoes and homemade chicken pies.

I cooked because I loved it.

Christmas came and I invited my mother over to help me roast a turkey. Just as I had once found common ground with my father in the kitchen, I found it again with her. My mother and I were growing closer.

January greeted me with a few auditions that led to a few forgettable, but clothed, roles in lame B action movies. I was presented with the opportunity to make some money doing an exercise video with Scott. I'd only been to the gym a dozen times in my life, and although I was in good shape from running, I didn't know anything about "jazzthetics." No one seemed to care. Scott, apparently no longer afraid to be associated with me, put the video together quickly.

Tanya Everett, one of the teachers from Strasberg, was hired to choreograph the video. She was so good at what she did that I actually looked like a professional dancer. Scott directed the video, choosing a two-piece yellow leotard for me to wear. I thought I looked ridiculous, but Scott said it was perfect. I learned all the required dance moves but paid no attention to the shots Scott set up during filming. Oblivious to camera angles and lighting, I was mortified to see the final product. It was an embarrassingly cheap video with crude angles and a cheesy soundtrack. The exercises themselves were shot in a vulgar manner that exploited the otherwise innocent bending and stretching I did, and as I watched the camera pan invasively up and down my body, I wanted to strangle my boyfriend. "How could you do this?" I demanded.

He seemed to have no clue why I was upset.

Looking back now, I think, Man, was I stupid or what? The guy was only out for himself! What did I expect? Good taste? But at the time, I naively believed Scott wanted to better himself and make films he could actually show to normal people. Gullible? Absolutely! He had been plugging away in the back office of our house, trying to raise money for the same softcore movie that he'd been "casting" since the first day we met. I couldn't ignore the obvious.

I spent the following week looking for a new apartment, going on auditions, and avoiding my boyfriend. I couldn't believe how much money it cost to move! How would I make it on my own? I could get a roommate. No, I was still too vulnerable. A new boyfriend? I'd been down that road and I didn't want to step into something worse, so I saved my money and bided my time.

The opportunity I'd been waiting for finally arrived in the spring of 1989. My agent, Don Gerler, called to say a director named John Waters wanted me to audition for a role in his new movie *Cry-Baby*. I'd never seen a John Waters film before but I was excited just the same. *A famous director wanted to meet me!* After months of doors slamming in my face and the workout-video fiasco, I was eager to meet a real filmmaker. I tried to picture him in my mind, remembering a television interview I'd seen him do a few years earlier.

I think he has a very skinny mustache, I thought to myself as I drove over to my agent's office to collect the script.

30

Cool Waters

It was a gorgeous spring day in Los Angeles.

Eager to meet John Waters, I got up early and ate some Cheerios. I hadn't slept well. I'd rehearsed the two scenes I was supposed to perform a zillion times while walking around our backyard, determined to give a great audition.

Scott thought I was nuts. I'd asked him what he knew about John Waters and he just laughed, telling me a horrible story involving an actor eating dog poop in one of his movies. *Jesus,* I thought, *he's kinkier than the Japanese sploshers!* Thankfully, I found his new script *Cry-Baby* to be turd free. It was a PG comedy romp set in the 1950s. The central character was a bad-boy Elvis Presley type named Cry-Baby, and Johnny Depp was to play the role. I'd seen Johnny on TV before when he'd starred in a series called *21 Jump Street.* He was a real babe.

John wanted me to read for the role of Wanda Woodward. She was a member of Cry-Baby's gang, a tough-talking teenager who wasn't really bad; everyone just thought she was. I hadn't done much comedy in my career, and while I loved the idea of it, I was scared that I wasn't funny.

I waited for my turn to audition in an empty waiting room at Imagine Films, repeatedly mumbling the scene's dialogue to myself. I was so nervous that I couldn't keep my Cheerios down, and thankfully made it to the ladies' room just in time to toss my breakfast. Oh no! Horrified I might smell, I ate a pack of mints and splashed cold water on my face. I studied my appearance closely. I looked younger than my twenty years, which was a darn good thing considering I was supposed to play seventeen for this role. Pleased with the Levi's and white T-shirt I'd chosen to wear, I headed back to the waiting room and was stopped in my tracks by a voice that inquired, "Miss Lords?"

I turned to be greeted by the pencil-thin mustache of John Waters. I had to force myself not to stare at it, wanting to watch his lips make the little black line jump.

He smiled warmly, a twinkle in his eyes.

Leading me into an office, he introduced me to the producer, Rachel Talalay, who said my audition would be taped by an assistant sitting in the corner. John told me I should play the part "real." He didn't want camp. So I did the scene, often distracted by John mouthing along the words as I said them, and finished with a snarl, saying, "I wouldn't be caught dead in a full skirt!" John laughed. Then I thanked them all for their time, and was out the door and on my way home.

I had no idea if I'd done a good job or if Mr. Waters was just being nice.

I wanted to know if I had the part. Why did they always make actors wait? It was torture! I needed the role of Wanda Woodward for many reasons. I thought being hired by Imagine Entertainment/Universal Pictures could be the endorsement I needed to put my past behind me. If a big studio hired me, maybe other studios would take that risk as well. Also, the prospect of working with a famous director on location in Baltimore for three months was the answer to my personal problems. Baltimore was a long way from Los Angeles and I definitely needed the space from Scott.

I fantasized about working on a big Hollywood movie. *Would the actors have stars on their dressing room doors? Would the crew*

*look at me funny, trying to remember where they'd seen me before? Was
I still just "that porn girl"?*

I tried to push these thoughts out of my head and concen-
trate on the actual work. *Was I really ready to do a musical comedy?
What if I was still too green? What if my singing voice was embarrassing?* I'd never sung professionally before and there was a big
difference between singing into a hairbrush and performing in
a movie. *Man, if I get this role, could I pull it off?*

I waited for the call all afternoon, the agony of not knowing
eating away at me. Scott was on the phone in the back office,
talking on his private line about the success of my recent
appearance on the first MTV Music Awards show. That had
been a wild experience.

My entertainment lawyer, Alan Dowling, had passed along
an appearance request from another client of his who was man-
aging a band called Guns n' Roses. The band was set to perform
at the awards and they were also up for Best Artist of the Year,
but lead singer Axl Rose didn't want to accept an award and
then have to play right after that. His manager, Alan Nevin, said
it was too distracting, so I was asked to accept the award if they
won.

Scott took the call and urged me to accept this nonpaying
appearance. I was leery of the media, having only recently been
left in peace, and wasn't sure if I was ready to face the wolves
again. But Scott convinced me that it would be good for me to
be seen with successful people. All I had to do was walk across
the stage and smile. What could go wrong?

The event took place the following afternoon. The band sent
a huge white limo to pick me up. I arrived at the auditorium and
was immediately whisked backstage. The guitarist of the band,
Slash, introduced himself. He wore a top hat and under that had
a mountain of curly hair even bigger than Leslie Abramson's.

My white leather dress felt out of place in the dark sea of
rock and rollers. I waited in the wings backstage. Peeking
through the curtain, I was shocked at how many people filled
the auditorium. The place was packed and totally unruly! Slash

appeared at my side moments later, smiling shyly at me and saying he'd decided to walk with me "if" they won. I got the impression they already knew they had won, but kept the thought to myself, just glad I didn't have to walk out there alone.

Guns n' Roses won, and Slash grabbed my hand as we walked across the stage to the podium. *Snap!* The photograph of us holding hands was all over the place the following week. I could tell Scott was jealous. But he said nothing. It had been his idea. *People* magazine ran the photo with the caption "Guns and Poses" that implied Slash and I were an item. I was amused. Although Slash wasn't my new boyfriend, I did secretly like him. He was a rock star and I was intrigued. It was exciting playing a part in the early days of Guns n' Roses, even if I was only there as a press stunt. It was the kind of energy that sucked me in, and I couldn't resist saying yes when Slash asked me out and scribbled his address on the back of an empty cigarette pack.

The following afternoon at five, I arrived at Slash's rundown apartment above Sunset Boulevard. *Evidently rock stars don't get paid much,* I thought as I stepped over the smoldering cigarette butts embedded in the carpet outside his door. Knocking softly, I wondered what I was doing there. *Could this go anywhere or did he just want sex?* It had been a year since my fling in Canada and I wasn't interested in a one-night stand. This bizarre guitar slinger was kind of sexy. Perhaps this could be something more?

He answered the door looking like he'd just woken up and smelling faintly of last night's booze. He had company, another one of the guys from the band. He apologized for running late and invited me to have a seat while he and his friend went into the back room to finish up their business. I was settling into the sofa, feeling uncomfortable at being alone in Slash's living room, when something cool slid across my back. I turned around and there, slithering across the back of the couch, was the biggest snake I'd ever seen in my life.

Freaking out, I jumped up and ran out of the apartment as fast as I could.

I hate snakes!!!!!!!!!!!!!!!!

By the time I got home my fascination with Slash was a thing of the past. My brief glimpse into his world was enough to make me realize he wasn't for me. It was a little too fast, what with the snake, cigarettes, and rock and roll. I wanted a simpler life. He left a message on my answering machine saying he was sorry he had kept me waiting, thinking that was why I had left, and asked me to come back over. I didn't return the call, and I never told him about my encounter with his slithery friend. Instead, I chose to simply remain a fan of one of the greatest guitar players of our time.

That evening my agent finally called.

I got the role in *Cry-Baby*.

I shrieked! Putting down the phone, I cried like a baby. What a day! It was one of those moments every actor dreams about and I was jubilant. It made up for the countless doors I'd had slammed in my face. It was a dream come true and I was on top of the world.

31

Faster, Pussycat! Kill! Kill!

A week later. I checked into a quaint little Baltimore hotel called the Tremont. It was a few blocks away from the *Cry-Baby* production offices in the new Tremont annex. Many a film crew had passed through the doors of the Tremont, if not to rent a room, then to hang out in the Celebrity Lounge, a small bar lined with the head shots of actors who, like us, had lived at the Tremont while making their movies in town. As seasoned as the staff was, we still managed to raise an eyebrow or two with our unruly behavior.

The cast of John Waters's *Cry-Baby* was a handful. At twenty-two, our faithful leader, Johnny Depp, was the oldest member of the cast. Darren Burrows, Ricki Lake, and I were all twenty, or closing in on it, and Amy Locane, who played Cry-Baby's girl, Allison, was the baby at seventeen. Our hotel mom and dad were Susan "Sue Sue" Tyrrell and one of the gods of punk, Iggy Pop, whom I always referred to as Mr. Pop.

Johnny lived in the penthouse suite of the ten-story hotel and the rest of us lived on different floors below him. I was the resident of suite 801, with Sue Sue above me, Ricki Lake below, and poor Amy banished, for her own safety, to the new Tremont building down the street under the watchful eye of her mother.

On my first day I barely had time to unpack before I was summoned to the wardrobe chamber of designer Van Smith. As I walked to his office, I took in the local scene. Characters from all walks of life waited for buses, spit on the sidewalks, or strolled out of the local beauty parlor with fresh beehive hairdos. Some of these ladies reeked of Aqua Net and probably still wore chiffon scarves over their hair to bed. I was charmed by the thick Baltimore accent of the voices chattering up and down the street, and especially the local peculiarities. Everyone was called "hon," and rat sandwiches (American cheese with gobs of mayonnaise on sourdough bread) were the town staple.

Paranoid I'd be late, I left my hotel way too early and ended up in the lobby of the big Tremont about twenty minutes before my fitting. The scent of hamburgers cooking pulled me toward the deli in the corner of the lobby, but I ordered the local favorite instead to get a taste of Baltimore life. Rat sandwich in hand, I sought out the elevator and climbed aboard, chomping away at the tasty new delicacy as I pressed the button for the twenty-first floor.

Several businessmen entered and left on the way up, until I was left alone with a long-haired man in his twenties. He was sweating profusely and engrossed in his shoes. I followed his gaze and saw he was wearing Dr. Martens. *I hadn't seen combat boots since junior high school. Maybe they were in again?* By the looks of them they had traveled a few paths.

On the twenty-first floor, the shoe man zoomed out in front of me, practically knocking me over. What an oddball, I thought as I watched his chocolate-brown ponytail swing away.

Van Smith greeted me in the wardrobe department. He was a no-nonsense, been-around-the-block-and-built-a-shopping-mall type of guy who chain-smoked as he told me to undress. "Don't worry, honey," he said in his raspy voice, "I like dick." I giggled as my foul-mouthed fairy godmother put me into a knee-length white-gray tight skirt and an off-the-shoulder black top. The incredibly uncomfortable pointy bra gave me cone-shaped breasts, a thick red belt cinched my waist, and my feet were clad in short white bobby socks and black mary janes. It was weird putting on those shoes! I remembered the last time I'd worn ones like them, as a little girl on a bus from Ohio to L.A.

Ensemble in place, I was presented to Mr. Waters. They started chatting about my hair, and just then a plump pretty girl walked in. Van pointed to her pin-curled bangs and suggested this hideous style for me. I silently voted against it. John told me the girl played Pepper, Cry-Baby's pregnant sister, and when I was introduced to her, the girl smiled sweetly and said, "Hi! I'm Ricki Lake."

The shoe guy from the elevator squatted in the corner watching the action. He had a furrowed brow and seemed very serious. John asked him something about Pepper's switchblade and he bellowed to an assistant named Lester, who brought in several blades for Ricki to try out. John called him Brook. He was the show's property master. I remember thinking he looked more like an Angus or Storm, something a bit more butch than Brook.

I was caught daydreaming by Waters, who wanted to know what I thought of pin curls. I told him they weren't my favorite. Van snarled, saying, "It's either that or baby bangs, hon." I didn't know what baby bangs were but chose them anyway and headed off to the hair department, thinking they couldn't possibly be as ugly as poor Ricki's pin curls.

I got my bangs cut super short—about an inch and a half below my hairline. Feeling silly, I twisted the back of my hair into a ponytail and tried not to look disappointed, but John loved the Wanda do so I was free to go. I went back to my room at the Tremont Hotel and collapsed into bed. Exhausted from the day's travails, I fell sound asleep.

I woke up to the blaring of my alarm clock. I had dance rehearsal up the street. A map had been slid under my door. I pulled on my jeans, grabbed a cup of coffee, and walked to the rehearsal studio a few blocks away.

My fellow cast members greeted me as I walked through the door, but seeing them all in one room unnerved me. I wondered what they thought of my past. Had Waters told them I'd done porn? Did they think I was a trashy girl? Did they remember my face from the five o'clock news? Was I being paranoid? I swallowed hard, wanting to fit in. Johnny Depp saw me first. He walked right up to me and smiled.

"Hey, I'm Johnny. You must be Traci."

"Yeah," I said shyly, "nice to meet you."

He was so cute, it hurt to look at him. A sweet smile played across his lips and I felt my face flush, embarrassed by my attraction to him. Feeling like the geek of the century, I positioned myself on the other side of the room, hoping he hadn't noticed how nervous he made me, and scared of falling under his spell.

We spent the entire morning practicing the jitterbug. The mood was jovial as the cast got to know one another. We had fun laughing at our poor dance moves, and the choreographer, Lori Eastlake, had the patience of a saint.

By that afternoon I'd grown more comfortable with the gang. I got to know Johnny, Ricki, Amy, Darren Burrows, and finally Kim McGuire, who played Hatchet-Face. She was the palest woman I'd ever seen, and her tiny five-foot frame and ice-blue eyes were a huge contrast to her booming Broadway voice. She reminded me of a Great Dane trapped in a poodle's body. Like her character in the movie, she was the loudest of the bunch.

Darren was a handsome but gangly guy who towered over us at about six three. His lighthearted personality made him impossible not to like. On the dance floor, he was like a puppy that hadn't grown into its paws yet, and trampled through his routine as gracefully as an ox. Ricki Lake swooned like a schoolgirl, sneaking peeks at him every so often. She was by far the best dancer of the bunch. Her effortless moves won both the praise of our instructor and Darren's attention. Amy Locane had already been in several big movies and was a seasoned actress. Clearly intimidated by her more grown-up cast mates, she seemed to be searching for the same thing I was—approval.

Johnny was the quiet one—or was that me? We both took up space in opposite corners of the room, with him close to the window. He listened carefully to the teacher's instructions and was very focused in learning his moves, grabbing smoke breaks between dances and flicking his ashes out the window. He had a gentleness about him, and when he spun Amy Locane around and around, they looked great together.

I liked these people.

John Waters turned up at the dance hall just as we were finishing for the day. He'd come by to check out our progress, remarking that it was a good thing we'd started rehearsal early as he watched us with a raised eyebrow. I guess we weren't quite there yet. Or maybe he was just razzing us. He had a sharp tongue and an odd sense of humor that made it hard for me to tell when he was serious.

As homework, he brought me several videos from the 1950s to watch. One was called *Faster, Pussycat! Kill! Kill!* I giggled at the title. Not understanding why he wanted me to view the tapes, I told him I didn't have a VCR in my room. Johnny spoke up, casually saying I could use his room. I thanked him, blushing at the thought of being in his room. Waters smirked as he took in the exchange, telling me the tapes would help me understand the time period. He wanted Wanda to be a sexy, tough Russ Meyer bad girl. I was nervous I wouldn't please him.

I hopped a shuttle with the rest of the cast back to the hotel. Johnny stopped me in the lobby and handed me the extra room key he'd gotten from the front desk, innocently saying he'd be gone all afternoon working through the script with John and that I was welcome to watch my videos in his room. I took the key, thanked him, and raced away, only breathing again when the elevator doors closed.

Taking a shower, I contemplated Johnny's offer. Why did the thought of being in his room make me so nervous? What was I afraid of? I was just being weird. It was no big deal and *I wasn't going to let myself make it one. He's just being nice.* He had a girlfriend anyway—some actress named Jennifer Grey. *I wondered if she was pretty.*

Oh, crap! I thought I should call Scott, but what was I going to say?

I'd been gone for two days! I couldn't just keep ignoring him because all my stuff was at our house. I just needed to keep the peace until the film was over so I could collect my paycheck and move on. *Just call him,* I told myself. *I'll tell him Waters is keeping me running, which was not a lie! Okay—here I go.* I dialed his number. Scott answered, his tone unmistakably cool. He was very curt, and halfheartedly asked how it was going. I told him that I really liked everyone and I was going to a cast gathering later that night. He said he missed me. Then he hung up.

I hadn't even thought of him since I arrived.

I knocked on Johnny's door to make sure he wasn't there, then walked into the living room. He had an incredible view from his penthouse perch. The windows were open and the white curtains floated in the breeze. The room smelled faintly of cigarettes. The VCR was not in sight. I found it in a cabinet close to his king-sized bed. Popping in the video, I settled back on the bed, wondering if I should be sitting on a chair instead . . .

The movie was nearly over when I heard the front door open. My heart raced as if I'd been caught doing something wrong. Johnny walked into the bedroom, put his script down, and climbed into bed next to me. He smiled and asked how the movie was. I pretended to be fully engrossed in it, but in truth I was nervous as heck with him so close. We watched for a few moments in silence. Uncomfortable being there with him, I asked about the read-through with John. He said it had gone really well, and then commented on how cute my new bangs were. Reaching over, he pulled the hair band out of my ponytail and smiled, saying it looked better down. His fingers in my hair freaked me out. His face was way too close to mine. I tried to ignore the closeness of his lips and act cool, yet I felt anything but. The film mercifully ended minutes later, and I thanked him for letting me use his VCR and tried not to run from the room.

ARGGGGGGGGGGGGGGGGGGGGGGGGGGGGGGGGG! Why was I so nervous with men? I slammed the door to my room on the way in, embarrassed at how totally flustered I'd been. Had he noticed? I wasn't sure.

John Waters had referred to my character Wanda as "a sexual terrorist" just days after I'd arrived in Baltimore. Was he confusing the defiant teenager who had once used sex as a weapon with the twenty-year-old who was trying to figure out who she really was? Had he made a mistake in casting me? Was I doomed to fail? How was I going to pull off a role driven by sexual power when I was so unnerved by it? How could an ex–porn star explain to anyone that I had these kinds of head trips? Who would believe me? Clearly I had urges, and God knows I'd had sexual experiences, but it was all so tangled up inside. I didn't know how the whole dating and sex thing worked in the real world. The majority of my sexual experiences had taken place stoned in front of a camera. *Would a normal guy like . . . say . . . Johnny expect me to be amazing in bed? What if I wasn't? How could I possibly date anyone, let alone sleep with him, with all this pressure? True, sex hadn't been a problem with Ken, but I knew I was leaving Canada the next day. Was that the buffer I needed? Was that the real problem? I wanted to be respected. Arggggg! What did any of it mean?*

I was ready for a real boyfriend but scared of making a bad choice. *Was I a good girl or a bad girl? Was it possible to be both?* That's where the fear came in. I was afraid of what might happen if I just let loose. What if a sexual terrorist lurked within me? Would she behave reasonably or wreak havoc? Where would sexual freedom take me?

And what would people think?

I unpacked the rest of my luggage and got ready to go to the Celebrity Lounge, choosing snug jeans, cowboy boots, and a pair of big hoop earrings. I walked in late to a packed house, the underage cast drinking anything they could get their hands on. The mood was loose. Darren and Johnny were sitting at the bar and everyone was letting their hair down.

Waters and a few crew members showed up with the casting

director, Pat Moran, whom I'd met at my audition. She was a
red-haired fireball. She was about five feet tall, her sky blue
eyes vibrant beneath thick red-framed glasses, and her voice
boomed through the bar. She sat like a queen with John, drinking martinis and talking loudly. I relaxed amid the chatter of my
cast mates and downed a beer at the bar with the boys. My new
earrings pinched at my lobes and annoyed me, so I took them
off and laid them on the bar. Johnny and Darren helped themselves, wearing one earring apiece and looking like pirates. We
laughed and listened to the latest Sinéad O'Connor. My beer
buzz signaled an end to the evening and I excused myself, leaving my pirate costars with the earrings.

Getting to my room, I crashed out in a deep sleep.

I woke the next morning with a crashing headache. I swallowed some aspirin and quickly headed over to dance rehearsal,
cursing my hangover. It had been a long time since my partying
days and I was shocked at what a lightweight I'd become. *Man,
if a few beers had me hurting like this, what would anything stronger do?
Kill me? I'm too old for this,* I decided, huffing and puffing as I
climbed the stairs to dance class, cringing at the blaring 1950s
music that thundered through the room.

The cast arrived slowly. From the looks of things, the boys
had pulled an all-nighter. They looked green as they entered the
room, and I couldn't help but smile at Johnny's obvious pain,
glad to be in on the joke. John entered moments later and lec-
tured us on being "responsible teenagers" as he turned up the
music. "Heavy hangs the head that last night wore the crown."
I believe he enjoyed punishing us for staying out late. He said
we were on his dime now, and then made us work even harder.
We moaned, staggering our way through class and sweating out
the night's mischief.

32

Just a Kiss Away

A week had passed since our descent on Baltimore and the cast, myself included, had made the rounds. We'd managed to stagger through dance rehearsals and tame the oh-so-proper Tremont housekeepers who no longer woke us at the crack of dawn to make our beds. And most important, we'd gained twenty-four-hour access to the hotel's restaurant/bar! Of course no one knew we were lurking in the stairwells in the wee hours of the morning. We'd sneak into the chef's kitchen to fix midnight snacks and then settle deep in the rear of the restaurant and light candles to conceal our trespassing. We were like a bunch of kids playing, hoping not to get caught but secretly excited by the possibility. We all became fast friends.

Although John encouraged cast bonding, he grew suspicious of our late-night prowling and sent around a memo warning that the hotel disapproved of underage drinking and mischief after dark. It tickled me to think of John Waters as our "keeper." He was as open-minded as they come, so while I felt the boozing of the cast was rather tame, I understood his fears. He clearly had his priorities in place, and I tried to be a young den mother, quietly encouraging my coworkers to behave.

In the front seat of the cast van, Ricki Lake sang a pitch-perfect rendition of Madonna's "Cherish"; Johnny and Darren were dead asleep in the backseat; and Amy, Kim, and I gossiped happily as we made our way to the stages where we would start filming the following week.

John greeted us at an enormous building in the warehouse district of Baltimore, where the air reeked of butchered animals. He was wide awake at seven in the morning. Dressed in his standard uniform of casual suit and white shirt, he looked like he was ready for his close-up. He led us through the various sets, showing Ricki where the orphanage scenes would be shot, and Johnny went off to check out Cry-Baby's house, particularly interested in the pool table.

John showed me the massive champagne glass I was to sit in for an upcoming scene and invited me to climb on up. Just as I'd made my way up the ladder, one foot in, about to have a seat, the property master, Brook, appeared out of nowhere, anxious because an actor had intruded on his territory in his absence. He looked nervous, pacing around beneath us. John told him to relax.

As we made our way back to the van, I noticed my picture hanging on the wall in a cubicle marked "Art Department." It was the photo from *Rolling Stone*. I was lying on my side, tousled hair in my face, Mona Lisa smile on my lips. *Odd . . . no one else's photo was on the wall. . . .* Catching up with my exiting costars, I felt like I was being watched. I looked around and locked eyes with Brook, who was staring at me from behind his desk. The horn of the departing van broke the trance and I took off out the door yelling for Cletis the driver to wait up.

Later that night, Darren Burrows's wife showed up unexpectedly. We were all hanging out in the Celebrity Lounge, watching cars zoom backward up the one-way street looking for a parking place. Teamsters sat soaking up beers, and a poker game raged in the back. The livid Mrs. Burrows rushed in brandishing the pirate earring that she'd discovered on Darren's bedside table. When he innocently told her it was mine and that Johnny had one too, she stormed out, convinced he was having an affair with me, the prime suspect.

Apparently, he hadn't been calling home much. I guess that was going around.

I thought the whole thing was ridiculous and would have said so if I'd been given a chance. I clearly had no interest in Darren, and "home wrecker" was not a role I wanted to play. I wondered if all this drama was really over an earring—or if it was because it was *my* earring.

As the night went on, Mrs. Burrows's intrusion into our movie world was all but forgotten. Ricki and Darren hung out chatting at the bar and I had a dance with my pal Johnny in the center of the dimly lit room, moving to the slinky music of the Cure's "Lullaby." My eyes met Brook's. He sat in the corner of the bar, feet kicked up on a chair, and stared dead at me. I stared back. The moment broke as the song ended and I took my place at the bar with some of the others.

Who are you? I wondered as I looked over my shoulder at him. He studied the large raindrops that splashed in the street. I stood there watching him watch the rain and I was drawn in. He was an odd mix of things, rock-and-roll tough yet calm and somehow soulful.

I finished my beer and walked outside into the pouring rain, feeling giddy as the droplets drenched my face and the water washed my mental cobwebs away. My skin was cool, my head clear, and without even looking I knew Brook was watching me. I walked up the hill away from my costars, away from the hotel, away from my fear of the unknown. *Would he follow me?* My heart raced as I heard footsteps behind me, and I walked faster toward the city's monument. I was shaking in my drenched T-shirt, my long hair plastered to my head, adrenaline pumping through my body. *What if it wasn't him following me?* Panicking, I spun around suddenly and came face-to-face with Brook. We just stood there for a second, inches apart and staring into each other's eyes. Then without a word he kissed me so deeply I forgot who I was and what I was afraid of. It was like magic—fireworks—the kind of kiss that made every hair on my body stand up.

Instantly, I fell completely and hopelessly in love with him.

33.

The Lipstick Trick

Alone in bed later that night. I felt like I'd been hit by something. I wasn't sure what had happened. I didn't believe in love at first sight. I wasn't even sure I believed in love at all. *Was the rush I felt when Brook kissed me pure chemistry? Was it lust at first sight? How could I be in love with someone I hadn't even had a full conversation with? What if he was just out to score? What if he was a porn fan?! What if he doesn't really like me at all! How could he? He doesn't even know me! Man, why do I think so much? Get it together, I told myself. I'm here to film my breakthrough movie! Don't get distracted. Just be cool, do your job, and proceed with caution.*

I spent the night tossing and turning, getting no peace from my thoughts and wondering if rumors of the kiss in the rain would spread. Was I about to become the set "ho"? I thought of Darren's wife's accusing eye after she found my earring in his room. *Good grief, I didn't do anything. I was innocent! Oh please — can I just get away with one little kiss?*

Brook called the next day to invite me out. As nervous as I was about the consequences of mixing business with pleasure, I couldn't say no. I wanted to be near him and said yes, cursing my weakness as I hung up the phone. *No, no, no, no, no, no, no! That's not what we agreed on, self!* I was pissed that my laserlike

work vision was being clouded by thoughts of boys. But deny-
ing there was something between us only distracted me further.

Taking control over the date the only way I knew how, I
reserved a car and driver for the evening. It was a gorgeous,
stormy night in Baltimore. Brook lived just ten blocks from the
hotel and he was punctual, sliding across the backseat toward
me right on time.

We headed downtown to an ancient movie theater called the
Charles in the heart of Baltimore. I don't remember what was
playing. I wasn't paying attention, distracted by my date. He
gave me a little history of the place, telling me his mother, Pat,
used to run the joint and he worked there selling popcorn as a
teenager. Hoping he wouldn't expect me to talk about where I
worked as a teenager, I shifted coolly in my seat. Mercifully, the
opening film credits ended the conversation before I had to go
there. When we left two hours later, we were in good spirits.
Laughing easily, we climbed back into our chauffeured car and
I felt myself relax. I liked being with this man.

I was glad I'd said yes.

Brook suggested we stop for a drink at one of his favorite
watering holes, the Club Charles up the street, and I was happy
to comply, not ready for the evening to end. And since the hotel
was within walking distance of the club, we sent our driver
home, thereby eliminating the only witness to our budding
romance.

Brook and I agreed to keep our date a secret, since neither
one of us wanted to be the topic of set gossip. But just as we
were finishing up our drinks and flirting coyly with each other,
a booming voice behind us announced, "I approve." The pencil-
thin mustache of Mr. Waters wrapped over his martini glass.
He looked tickled pink. *Oh man!* We were busted. My heart
dropped. Would he think I was completely unprofessional by
dating a crew member? Brook and I both automatically acted
like we didn't know what he was talking about. "Oh please," his
raised eyebrow proclaimed.

We all started talking at the same time.

"What does *she* think about this?" John said.

"Who's she?" I asked, turning to Brook. "Please don't tell me you're married."

"Oh, he doesn't have a wife, just a mother—and oh, what a mother." John laughed.

I was completely lost.

"What are you talking about?" I asked a bit defensively, thinking John meant that Brook's mother would have issues with him dating an ex–porn star. "Who's your mother?"

John nearly choked on his drink.

"I see," he said, disappearing into the club.

I turned on Brook. "What's the deal?"

"Traci, my mother is Pat Moran. She cast you in this movie—you know, the kooky redhead? Talks real loud?"

Holy crap! I'm messing with the casting director's son! What if it all

Brook and me in Baltimore during the filming of *Cry-Baby*.

goes sour and she hates me for breaking his heart? Then what? People talk in this business. Man, these are just the kind of complications I don't need!

Reading the look on my face, Brook just laughed. "She's my mother. She won't like that I'm dating a cast member, but she adores you and she wants me to be happy. It's a good thing," he said, kissing my fears away.

An hour later we'd picked up a bottle of wine and plotted our entrance into the Tremont. We decided to arrive separately. I went first, frantically straightening up my hotel suite before he got there. He knocked on my door minutes later, narrowly escaping the clutches of a drunk and horny actress. He said she'd groped him as he made his way to the elevator, and slurred into his ear he didn't know what he was missing. According to her, she had the "pussy of a twelve-year-old."

"Grossssssssssssssssss!" I squealed. "What did you do?"

"Nothing," he said. "How does a person respond to such an invitation?" Beats me, I thought, pouring wine as we cozied up on the couch.

Listening to the Cult, the Cure, and Sinéad O'Connor, we talked the night away. He told me about his life in Baltimore and spoke fondly of his family. He said they were like a version of the Addams Family, quirky but solidly together. His godfather was the late great actor Divine, with whom he'd traveled around the world, doing lighting for his/her concert tour. He'd even appeared in one of his "uncle" John-as-in-Waters's films as a nude child who played doctor with a little girl. Most of his adolescent years were spent walking around John's sets, dispensing props to all the actors.

Brook had seen a lot of death in his twenty years on the planet. His father died when he was a toddler, and his mother remarried an amazing man named Chuck. He was the only father Brook had ever known and he loved him. But his own father's untimely demise tugged at him. He said his dad died of an overdose. Of what, I don't know. He'd also lost many close friends to AIDS. Some of these people had been friends of his family since he was a child, and his eyes burned with rage and sadness as he spoke of music composers, stylists, and designers who "had IT." Thankfully, though, his mother had ingrained the importance of safe sex in him at puberty.

We were both disease free. But neither of us was an angel. Brook didn't ask about my porn days, but I suddenly felt compelled to explain them. I told him I'd been heavily into drugs and I didn't remember a lot of the specifics of those hazy days. We spoke candidly about sex and porn, and I was surprised at how willing I was to share my very private thoughts with him. He asked me if I liked kinky sex, and I laughed, saying I wasn't even sure what that meant. I was a virgin to anal sex, thankfully missing that phase in porn movies. "And I don't particularly like to be tied up," I said, "although a cool pie does feel rather nice sliding down one's body," I teased, breaking into hysterical laughter as I remembered the stories of sploshers.

"The only thing I ever really learned from porn was how to give a blow job without messing up my lipstick," I said, then excused myself and headed for the bathroom, fully aware of the amused look on his face. Unreal—I'd actually made a joke about the most painful part of my life.

The evening ended with us in bed. All thoughts of ulterior motives and what-ifs were gone. He knew who I was, what I'd done, and I wouldn't have been surprised if he'd even seen my old movies. But none of that mattered. I was crazy about him and fully aware of what I was doing. We played, laughed, and made love all night long. It was exactly how I'd imagined it would be . . . just right.

34

Cry Babies

Filming on <u>Cry-Baby</u> started in late April. We were like a traveling circus, wandering all over Baltimore on location. We shot in amusement parks, an old prison, and people's backyards. My mother on film was none other than Patricia Hearst, and we had an unspoken agreement: I didn't ask her about robbing banks and she didn't ask me about porn movies. We got along just fine. . . .

The dance lessons paid off. All of us bopped along well to the music and the atmosphere was like summer camp for juvenile delinquents. John was our faithful leader and set father. Pat Moran, Brook's mom, was definitely our set mother. We worked hideously long hours and pulled a lot of night shoots, going to work at seven in the evening and finishing at nine the next morning. Everyone was punch-drunk. As for me, well . . . I was dizzy in love. Brook and I were a hot item. We didn't even bother to hide it anymore, spending all our free time together. Pat was not surprised to hear of our relationship and her warm acceptance of me dissolved any fears I'd had.

The cast jitterbugged and snarled our way through the first month of filming and I had the time of my life, discovering the joy of working with an outrageous personality like Waters and the satisfaction of ending each day in the arms of a man I really loved. I was walking on air, a part of something bigger than myself and grateful for the extraordinary opportunity I'd been given. John's praise gave me confidence. He was a visionary, and I was thrilled to be part of that vision.

About halfway through filming Scott started sending me flowers and calling the hotel at all hours of the day and night looking for me. Why he suddenly seemed so desperate for my attention, I don't know. I'd been gone for almost two months, and although I hadn't told Scott about my relationship with Brook, I did say I needed some space and that when I got back, it would be time for me to move out. I didn't want to hurt him or lie to him, but I couldn't bring myself to end it over the phone. It just seemed so mean. I don't know when he put it together or if he really did, but days later it all came to a head.

Brook and I returned to the hotel at about eight in the morning on a Saturday after spending all night on the set. We were wiped out from the week's filming and lounged in bed, munching on bacon and eggs and glad for a day off. Road workers were outside the hotel making lots of noise with jackhammers and we wanted to strangle them, but who wants to go to jail? So we ended up throwing water balloons at them instead. Laughing away our frustrations and satisfied with our retaliation, we finally fell asleep.

The phone started ringing a few hours later. I unplugged it and had just fallen back asleep when I heard someone banging on the door. Pissed off at housekeeping for ignoring the "Do Not Disturb" sign, I set off down the hallway to give them a piece of my mind. But I stopped dead in my tracks when I heard an angry and familiar voice ranting outside. It was Scott.

Creeping closer to the door, I peered out through the peephole and saw him pacing back and forth. I freaked out, rushing back into the bedroom and waking Brook.

"Oh shit. . . . My boyfriend or ex-boyfriend . . . whatever — he's here! Outside the door!"

Brook was out of bed, pulling on his jeans in seconds.

"What should we do?"

"You . . . you . . . got to hide somewhere," I muttered. "We don't want a scene."

"No way!" he said. "I'm no pussy."

I panicked, trying to reason with him.

"Listen, all my stuff is in our house in California. If it goes down like this it's going to be a nightmare tying up loose ends with him. Please don't make it harder." Brook finished dressing, walked into the kitchen, and poured himself a glass of water.

"Okay, Traci," he said. "Let him in. I won't do anything unless he does. I'm just going to stand here in the kitchen. Get rid of him, though—for good."

Oh man, oh man, oh man. Okay, I thought, *maybe I just won't answer the door.*

The pounding got louder. I could hear my neighbors complaining. I stood in front of the peephole watching Scott grow redder by the minute. He was screaming at the housekeeper to let him in. *Okay, enough:* I opened the door and asked him to be quiet. He stepped right past me and headed for the bedroom. I started praying Brook would take his cue and split so I could deal with this on my own. I followed Scott as he checked the closet. Hey! He pushed me out of the way and headed toward the kitchen. My heart pounded. I held my breath and braced for a brawl. Scott backed out of the kitchen when he saw Brook leaning against the back wall with his ankles crossed and arms folded, staring daggers at him.

Silence. Scott turned on me: "You're fucking this kid? I can't believe you're fucking this kid! You better go, buddy."

I saw a smirk on Brook's face at the word "buddy." Brook and I locked eyes. I nodded. He hesitated and then walked out the front door.

I spent the day trying gently to explain things to Scott. But he was so hysterical it made no difference what I said. I apologized for the way it had all gone down, and told him I'd had no intention of falling in love with someone else. But that only made it worse. He was beside himself. I felt bad. He seemed so distraught. But I really didn't get it. We hadn't been happy in a long time. I'd been looking to end the relationship for nearly a year now. Could this have been a one-sided desire? And speaking of desire—wasn't it clear we had almost none for each other? Did he think I had no sexual appetite? Besides, this was the man who directed me in porn films! Why was he so upset I was sleeping with someone? Hadn't he always encouraged that? Or was that just "my job" to him?

I got frustrated as he hurled insults at me, knowing full well that he was hurt but finding the whole situation ridiculous. Oh, get a grip, I wanted to scream, it's not the end of the world. I was suddenly pissed he'd barged in uninvited, threatening the peaceful existence I'd created among the other misfits. *What's his problem? Is he afraid of losing his meal ticket? Is that it?* Just as I was about to say exactly that, he said, "Traci, my divorce is final."

"What?! You mean you were married the whole time we were together? No wonder your 'ex' loathes me!!" I was furious as he pitifully took a velvet box out of his pocket. It was a diamond ring. He'd come to Baltimore to propose to me.

"I'm so sorry," I said to Scott as he sobbed at my feet.

I was so sorry . . . I'd waited so long. . . .

35

The Wrap Sheet

Scott went back to Los Angeles later that afternoon, engagement ring in hand. He said he could forgive me everything if I married him when I got back. I somehow managed to stifle my anger at this absurd "solution." He left for the airport, satisfied that I had "come to my senses." I felt like a fool. *I was a home wrecker and I didn't even know it. Why hadn't his wife said something? I sure as heck would have. She let this jerk play us both!* I wondered what lies he had told her. But did it really matter now?

Man, my head was spinning.

God, I have to see that idiot again—all my things are still in Woodland Hills. How am I going to contain the situation for another month until I can get home and get out of there? Oh, screw it . . . screw him—let him throw my belongings in the street. I'm not wasting another breath on him. It's stuff, it's just stuff. I need to talk to Brook.

As I climbed into the cast shuttle bus the next day, I could tell by the looks of my fellow cast members that word of my love triangle had spread fast. Johnny offered me a smile, shrugging his shoulders and saying, "Ah fuck it—you'll be fine." He too had broken up with his girlfriend recently, and he knew the score.

Ricki patted my back, saying Brook was all pumped up

about another cock being near his henhouse. *What? Did he think for one second I wanted to be with anyone else? Didn't he know how I felt about him? Maybe it's time I said the four-letter "l" word?*

The ride to location seemed way too long. I was anxious to find my boyfriend and bring him up to speed. I was the gossip of the day and I really loathed it. I was embarrassed that everyone knew my business, and the only thing that made it bearable was that I was among real friends. I was safe.

A few hours later, I was wearing a flaming-red dress, and my thoughts couldn't have been farther away from Scott Bell. I was lost in the moment at hand. Garbed in our 1950s finest, I struggled not to fall off my ultrahigh heels as the entire cast performed as the Cry-Baby Band in front of dozens of extras. I sang backup and played the triangle. Johnny and Amy lip-synched to "King Cry-Baby" and danced hand in hand across the stage. It was the finale of the movie. The cool cats—that would be us—versus the rich geeks.

The battle of the bands raged on, finishing to thunderous applause. We brought down the house. Then we all had to shed one single teardrop of joy. Cut. Print. Moving on.

Waters paced excitedly on the sidelines. Extras milled about and the producer, Rachel Talalay, called lunch break. I kicked off my shoes and headed for my dressing room, where I could see Brook already waiting for me. He smiled and planted a kiss on my face. It was now or never. "You know, I love you, man."

"Yeah," he said, smiling, "I love you too."

Toward the end of June, as we wrapped up production, Pat Moran knocked on my dressing room door and asked to speak to me. I invited her in thinking she was there to chat. We'd become very close friends during the filming and spent lots of downtime gossiping and sipping coffee, enjoying the fact that our friendship made Brook a little nervous. I guess he was afraid I'd learn all his childhood secrets.

Taking a break
on the set.

As
Wanda Woodward
on the set of
<u>Cry-Baby</u>.

On the set with
Iggy Pop.

With Johnny Depp
on the set of
<u>Cry-Baby</u>.

But that afternoon her expression made me nervous. She came right to the point. The FBI was on the set. They'd been looking for me for about twenty minutes. John, Rachel, and the first assistant director all knew.

I felt sick, picturing myself being led away in handcuffs. *What now?!*

Pat read my mind and in her smoky voice said, "Don't worry. These assholes are not going to do anything but serve you. I'll bring them in here. No one else needs to know."

I started crying, horrified that the casting director/producer/boyfriend's mom knew what a loser I was. *Oh fuck.* I lost my composure. Furious on my behalf, she steamed onto the set, determined to solve the problem quickly.

I was served in the privacy of my trailer, but everyone knew something was up. I was completely rattled when I was called to shoot my next scene. They'd tracked me down on location to serve me a subpoena. *What if word got out that Traci Lords gets served at work? Would producers be afraid of the lurking feds? Why couldn't I go on with my life? It had been three fucking years! Enough!* My cover blown, my insecurities took over. *How am I going to walk in front of a camera now? Once a porn star always a porn star. What am I doing here? I'm not good enough. I don't deserve it.* That quickly I knew I didn't belong next to these "real actors." I was an outsider, an imposter, a loser. I fought the tears welling in my eyes as I told myself it didn't matter. *Fuck what these people think.* But it did matter . . . I loved them.

My tough exterior crumbled in front of everyone. I tried to suck the feelings down but they consumed me. *I'm not strong. I feel like no one's ever going to let me forget my mistakes.* The tears poured down my face and I found Pat immediately at my side. I stood there dressed in my 1950s garb crying on her shoulder. My boyfriend appeared and wrapped his arms around us. I was sandwiched between them, sobbing. *Oh man, what a spectacle.*

John broke the intensity of the moment, walking up to our huddle and saying, "Traci, I bet everyone here has had a run-in with the law. You're not the only one." He raised an eyebrow and looked from Sue Sue to Patricia Hearst, who smiled back innocently. I could see his point, but it's always different when it's you.

Returning to the set after having my makeup repaired, I found the entire cast and crew sitting around telling stories of their "previous incarcerations." John was right. It seemed that nearly everyone on the film had been arrested for something, ranging from drunk driving to public exposure to grand theft auto. It was much different from the recurring drama I experienced, but the fact that all these people cared so much about me that they shared their own bouts with the law just to make me feel better . . . well, it did. Clearly, no one in the land of *Cry-Baby* looked down on me.

I turned the subpoena over to my lawyer Leslie. It was the same thing as always. Some distributor had sold my underage porn films to a federal agent and once again my mother agreed to testify in my place.

Filming on *Cry-Baby* wrapped the following week. I couldn't believe it was over. The cast and crew wrap party was going to be held in the Celebrity Lounge at the Tremont. Since I was flying home to Los Angeles the next day, Brook and I decided to tell his parents we were going to continue our relationship, which meant he'd move to California in two weeks' time. He'd wanted to check out L.A. before, feeling he'd prosper from greater film opportunities there. But his love for his family had always kept him in Baltimore. He was close to them, especially his grandma Grace. He'd lived there his whole life and it wasn't an easy decision for him to make. I just hoped we were doing the right thing.

It was a loaded situation. Emotions were charged, everyone was exhausted, and there was a somberness in the air. I knew the blessing of Brook's family was important for our future and I hoped the timing didn't work against us.

We went to the wrap party that night together. Everyone was already there. We broke the news to Brook's mom and dad, and I could see Pat breathe deeply. Then she just hugged us. His father signed my script: "To Traci, the girl who stole my son away," and we all started crying.

Many tears and several martinis later, the cast and crew of John Waters's *Cry-Baby* said good-bye.

36

Home Sweet Home

Twenty-four hours later I stood in front of the home Scott and I rented in Woodland Hills, surrounded by luggage. As the taxi roared away, I took a deep breath, preparing myself for the worst. I was tired from the early-morning flight and dreaded facing my scorned ex. I hadn't spoken to him since his unexpected visit to Baltimore but things were clearly over between us. Earlier that week I'd left word on his machine that I'd be arriving this afternoon to collect my things. I'd gotten no response and I had no idea what I was walking into.

I left my pile of luggage by the garage and struggled with the front gate. He must have been waiting for me because the moment I got in, he stormed through the front door, calling me every name in the book. I kept my voice calm, not wanting to fuel the fire. I told him I was sorry to upset him and that all I wanted to do was collect my things and go, but he tried to snatch the keys from my hand and said I wasn't stepping foot in his house. His fury scared me. I turned around and walked quickly to the street.

He laughed, slamming the door behind me.

I stood there on the curb for a minute, shaking and trying to decide what to do next. I knew he was angry, and maybe even genuinely hurt by my relationship with Brook, but we were grown-ups. This wasn't the way adults were supposed to act. At twenty-one years of age, it was finally clear to me that certain types of behavior just weren't acceptable. I fumed as I thought of all the money I'd spent on rent for this house while I'd been away on location. Not to mention the countless dollars I'd given him for child support for his son. *Forget it, pal,* I thought. *We're even. I'm out of here.*

But first I needed my car.

The next few minutes moved at warp speed as I ran for the garage and punched in the code. My red convertible was right where I'd left it, and I jumped into the driver's seat. Throwing the car into reverse, I sped backward out of the garage as Scott came running after me like a crazed lunatic. My heart felt like it was going to burst from my chest as I squealed around the corner, home free.

I had no choice but to go to the cops. I showed up a couple of hours later with two cops. Scott answered the door all smiles and "yes sir's," pretending nothing had happened. I wanted to slap that smirk right off his overly tanned face, but I bit back my impulse, ignoring him as I scrambled to gather my things. I stuffed a duffel bag full of clothes and grabbed my guitar and a stack of lyrics I'd written. Even in my haste I could tell many of my things were missing. I couldn't locate the Bible my grandmother had given me, and Scott denied ever seeing it. At an autograph signing months later, it was returned to me by a fan who said he had purchased it.

As I was dragging my things out the front door, I heard a mewing sound coming from the kitchen and stopped to crane my neck for a better view. There in the center of the floor was a tiny white Persian kitten. Scott swatted at it for peeing on the floor and referred to the adorable ball of fur as "Rat," announcing that he'd named it after me. I headed through the door. I'd had enough.

"Hey!" he snapped. "Don't forget your cat!"

He threw the little creature at me.

"It's your problem now." He turned. "Happy fucking birthday, bitch."

37

Dancing in the Dark

I spent the next few days living out of a suitcase and talking long-distance to my Baltimore Boy. The Hollywood Roosevelt Hotel became my hideout as I searched for new digs for Brook and me to move into together. I wasn't sure where I wanted to live, but I was positive I wanted to be as far from Woodland Hills and Scott as I could get. Thankfully, I had some money to work with. I'd earned a decent salary for *Cry-Baby,* and although Scott had helped himself to some of it, I managed to hold on to what was left.

I pounded the pavement apartment hunting in the Hollywood and North Hollywood area, finally settling on a rather boring, sterile-looking town house that overlooked the 101 freeway. It was new, clean, safe, and the price was right. Screw the freeway — I was out of time. Brook was supposed to arrive in two days. I hoped he wouldn't hate it. *Oh, what the heck — the freeway can be our ocean.*

God, I missed him.

I signed the lease and then stopped off at my agent's office to show my face. I wanted to make sure he knew I was back in town and ready to work. Sitting in his office, we chatted about where I wanted to go in the next phase of my career, and I

stressed how much I wanted to do television and avoid exploitation films. He nodded in agreement but offered no further comment, changing the subject instead. He asked about the Waters
film, wanting to know all about the shoot. I gave him the rundown but kept the feds and my affair with Brook to myself, saying only that I'd decided to split with Scott.

I left Gerler's office unsure of how seriously he took my
desire to star in more serious projects. Over the next few days,
he reminded me several times that I could be working right now
if I would just appreciate the offers before me. It was hard to
stick to my guns at a time when I had little going for me. I
doubted myself constantly. *Maybe Gerler was right. Maybe* Cry-
Baby *was the biggest film I'd ever do. Maybe I should be grateful to star
in B movies, count my blessings, and call it a day.* But I couldn't. I
wanted something more. I just had to go for it.

It was an uphill battle. I encountered many obstacles during
that period of time, self-righteous casting directors, conservative
production companies, and people who flat-out refused to grant
me an audition. It was maddening to be judged by people who
had no idea who I really was or what I stood for. I wasn't sure I
had the guts to stay in the game.

The constant rejection and general meanness took its toll. I
nearly gave up a dozen times and I honestly don't know what
kept me going. I wondered if I'd ever be allowed to star as a
series regular on television or find myself in an A movie. I had
my doubts. But I needed to know I'd given it my all, and even
if I ultimately failed, I would not quit. I was willing to struggle
for the career and the life I wanted.

Brook hated Los Angeles the moment his combat boots hit
the ground. "Everyone is so pretty here," he grumbled, chain-
smoking Merit cigarettes, "even the straight guys shave their
legs." He was an East Coast boy and sunny L.A. made him feel
like a "fat, sloppy dirtball." But as much as he hated it, he said
he loved me. And he stayed. We were like peas and carrots,
always together.

Brook and I settled into our new life together, spending our

days hunting for work and our nights cooking meals and sharing the secrets of our lives. He landed a job working for New Line Cinema doing props on a movie called *Book of Love*. It was his first job as a Hollywood prop master, and as cool as Brook always acted, I could see the excitement bursting in his walk and in his voice when he called his mother to give her the news. I was very proud of him. He'd gotten exactly what he wanted.

Within days I could say the same as I booked a job as a ditsy dental hygienist on the television sitcom *Married With Children*. Brook and I bought a bottle of champagne and danced in the darkness of our living room to celebrate. The headlights of the big rigs that streamed by on the freeway below provided us with urban candlelight. Life was good.

The following Monday I began work on *Married With Children*. I'd never done a sitcom before and I discovered how different work schedules were for half-hour sitcoms, hour dramas, and feature films. The show ran like a well-oiled machine. The cast seemed to effortlessly nail their lines and hit their marks. I was in awe and wanted to learn their technique.

Monday through Wednesday were prep days. We did table-reads, wardrobe fittings, and dealt with dialogue changes. We reported to the Hollywood stage about 8 A.M. and finished by lunchtime. On Thursday we rehearsed in front of the cameras, and Friday was the shoot.

We performed before a live audience twice on Friday, once in the afternoon, then again at about six in the evening. The rush of performing live was a real high. I loved it. The cast members of *Married With Children* were all seasoned pros and I learned a lot about comedy just sitting in the read-throughs, watching them work. They had a rhythm when they acted. A lightbulb went off in my head: comedy was all about rhythm! It may seem obvious, but that realization changed the way I attacked my role.

Christina Applegate in particular fascinated me. I could relate to her. We were about the same age but she was light-years ahead of me professionally. She was about eighteen at the time and had a quiet confidence about her. When the camera hit her, she was a ball of energy. Whip smart, dead sexy, with incredible timing. I liked her. Over the next few years I guest-starred on *Married With Children* several times, and Christina and I became good friends. I struggled with booking acting jobs; she struggled with having a life outside her acting job.

38

Press Junk

Cry-Baby premiered in Baltimore. Brook and I were flown in, compliments of Imagine Films, to participate in the press junket. I felt like royalty as we arrived in a stretch limo at the best hotel in town. The red carpet literally rolled out to welcome us. The lobby was grand. Our room was filled with flowers and gift baskets. A chandelier hung above the Jacuzzi. The marble hallway offered a private, fully stocked bar, and Brook and I laughed at the outrageous display of wealth, shocked to be treated like movie stars.

We called Brook's mom and told her she had to see this, and the whole gang turned up an hour later, with John Waters in tow. We hung out in our room, swapping stories. The junket was weighing heavily on John's mind. He warned me I'd better be prepared to answer questions about my past. *Oh no! Again?! Why? Hadn't I done enough interviews over the past four years? I'd spoken to* Hard Copy, A Current Affair, Entertainment Tonight, *dozens of local news stations, magazines, newspapers. What was left to say? How many times do I have to relive this?*

I'd naively thought I'd already answered "those" questions.

John sighed deeply. "Honey," he said, "you'll be answering those questions as long as you live."

That statement knocked the wind out of my sails. Reality suddenly awakened me from the fantasy movie star world I'd walked into, but as I looked around the room, seeing Brook's family there, I felt comforted. No matter what anyone said, pornography was my past. Not my present. Not my future. It was my past, and I could deal with that.

I wouldn't crumble.

I woke up at seven the next morning and declined Imagine's offer of a makeup artist. I can paint my face better than anyone, I thought. Besides, I wanted a moment of quiet before the press onslaught. As Brook slept soundly down the hall I headed for the "greenroom," the hospitality suite for the talent. By the time I got there it was packed with the *Cry-Baby* gang, roaring with the excited chatter of old friends reconnecting. We headed down the hallway ready to meet the press. There were eight rooms filled with press people from all over the country. I had never seen anything like it. The cast was split up and sent in different directions to give interviews. It was a feeding frenzy.

I was nervous as I entered the first room. The public relations person from Imagine assured me that I could refuse to answer any question I didn't like. I just looked at her. The thought had never occurred to me! I'd always felt the need to explain myself, somehow wanting to make people understand that I wasn't really all bad.

I fed myself to the wolves, answering every question but not always seriously. I found myself snapping back when insulted, cringing at certain outrageous comments about my porn past, and still naively believing that my new work would speak for itself. I was embarrassed to be asked questions like What's the difference between porn movies and mainstream movies? Did you enjoy making porn movies? How many films did you really make? I'd been answering those questions for years, but I'd never had to do it in front of fellow actors. It was humiliating to be put on the spot like that. I hated that it still got to me, but I couldn't resist defending my life. I was a sucker.

The cast of <u>Cry-Baby</u> with John Waters.

As the day wore on, I became more and more irritated that no one cared about my work in *Cry-Baby*. Try as I might to throw in comments about working with John and the others, the press only wanted to hear about my porn days. It was clear that I was being exploited for an easy headline. Yet I felt that if I stopped the interviews, Imagine Films would think less of me, and I wanted to prove I could hold my own. I wished I could turn back time. I would have given anything to erase the XXX from my forehead.

On the crisp spring evening of March 15, 1990, a long line of cars crept one by one toward the Senator Theater for the world premiere of *Cry-Baby*. Brook and I shared a glass of champagne while peering at the crowd of fans and reporters from the safety of our limousine. As the car crept slowly forward, we downed our drinks, hands sweaty with anticipation. Brook was no stranger to the press, having grown up with the Waters clan in Baltimore and sharing many a photo op with his godfather, Divine.

My deep purple dress clung to my body as I exited the limo, flashbulbs blinding me. Brook and I walked the red carpet hand in hand. I met Pat's eyes as she watched her son and me greet the media. She gave me the thumbs-up and I smiled back, feeling like I belonged on the red carpet and knowing that I had backup nearby. I laughed at the frozen smile of my petrified boyfriend, squeezing his hand to bring him out of his trance.

The film was met with screams of approval from the crowd, but I don't remember seeing the movie at the premiere. My body was in the theater; I was not. The adrenaline pumped through my veins as I sat gawking at my name on the huge movie screen. I squirmed in my seat, uncomfortable to see my giant face looking down at me. I was antsy. Waters must have felt the same way because I saw him sneak out for a cigarette a couple of times.

I spent the rest of the evening accepting congratulations from strangers at the after-party. We mingled with journalists and fans. The cast signed autographs most of the evening, and the next day the *Baltimore Sun*'s headline read "Not a Tear at 'Cry-

Baby,'" featuring a color photo of John, Johnny, Patricia Hearst, and me.

Brook and I headed over to John's house, which was located in a beautiful area of Baltimore. He owned a gorgeous three-story mansion not far from the university. John laughed that with all the press that had come out over the weekend, he'd been woken up twice by cars full of college kids screaming "Traci Lords!" in front of his house.

"I guess they think I have you locked up in the attic," he said.

He was in a fabulous mood, happy with the response to the film and telling us to keep our fingers crossed. He was anxious to hear the weekend's box office receipts.

We made our rounds, visiting friends of Brook's and hanging out with his grandma Grace. She was still all aflutter about the fabulous green lamé gown she'd worn to the *Cry-Baby* premiere. I loved her. She was still every bit a diva.

We spent our last night in town with Brook's family enjoying an incredible meal prepared by his father, Chucky. After dinner we all piled onto their massive sleigh bed to watch CNN. We were like little kids lying at the foot of the bed. Brook, his sister, and I gossiped about Johnny Depp's new girlfriend, Winona Ryder, who had been unnerved by our gang at the premiere, not sure what to make of us. I was glad I wasn't the new girl anymore. I was happier than I'd ever been in my life and completely at ease in this family of oddballs.

39

Film Misses and the Mrs.

<u>Cry-Baby</u> was only a moderate box office success. It made its money back, but by industry standards it was a bomb, which was a huge disappointment for all of us. But it was hardly a loss for me. I was one step closer to mainstream credibility.

My picture appeared in newspapers and magazines all over the world, and while the press hadn't hurt my career, it certainly hurt my ego. I discovered that few people actually read the articles accompanying the photos and was horrified to realize many people still thought—and would continue to think—of me as a porn girl. Is that why I was asked the same old questions over and over again? Weren't they bored with the subject yet? Was it impossible to change public opinion?

Where do I go from here?

The studios weren't courting me, and while small independent houses had made a few offers, most of them were for poorly written exploitation films. So I continued building my résumé by choosing the best of what I was offered.

I accepted a role for an action movie called *A Time to Die*, opting to shoot people rather than perform the required nudity of a Roger Corman film. It turns out I was the perfect action hero.

I had an edge, loved the stunt work, and much to my surprise, I could handle a gun.

Slowly, I was climbing the ladder and staying true to my two rules: Make every film better than the last, and keep my clothes on.

One afternoon I came home late from filming. The walls of our house were vibrating with the wailing guitar of our neighbor, Rikki Rocket of the band Poison. He was rehearsing songs for a new album, and "Unskinny Bop" blared over and over as I headed for the shower. Stepping out of the bathroom, I noticed a trail of rose petals leading from the door down the stairs. I wrapped myself in a towel and followed the trail, wondering what was going on.

As I walked into the living room downstairs, I heard Chet Baker playing softly in the background. Brook stood staring out the window at the cars rushing by on the freeway. He was wearing a black suit, and he was shaking.

"Is something wrong?"

He asked me to come to him. Walking toward him, I noticed the wineglasses and the candles burning on our coffee table. He dropped to one knee.

"Will you marry me?" he asked.

"Yes!" I said, and excused myself to the bathroom to throw up.

40

Father Waters

Brook and I were married in Baltimore, Maryland, in the fall of 1991, in a church only a few blocks away from his parents' house. But before that could happen, the first order of business was for me to get baptized. During the required marriage counseling before the wedding, I realized the minister assumed we were both baptized, and the truth nagged at me. I certainly didn't need any strikes against me going into a marriage. Who wants to piss off God? So I brought the problem to John's attention.

Boasting he was an ordained minister, John offered his services and support. At first I thought he was kidding, but when we met the following afternoon at his Baltimore home, he'd changed into a fancy dark jacket and wore a very serious expression. He asked me to be seated. Brook stood nearby rearranging some dark purple-black tulips as John recited his résumé as a minister. He had indeed performed several weddings.

"Hmm . . ." I said out loud, "is this going to hurt?" I'd never been to a baptism before and was nervous.

"Perhaps," he shot back, his eyebrow rising. "The removal of original sin is a difficult process. As a matter of fact, I might have to charge you double for my services!"

I burst out laughing, his teasing manner lightening a surprisingly intense moment. I'd had little experience with organized religion in my twenty-three years on the planet and I didn't know how I felt about this ritual. But I was comforted by the warmth in the room. And with John and Brook by my side I was sure of one thing: I believed in love, and God was said to be just that.

Father Waters removed my sins, and about half an hour later, Brook and I went to city hall, sin free, to collect our marriage license. We were married the following day.

The reception took place at a gorgeous private club overlooking the harbor. It was all a big surprise for me. I really just showed up for the wedding. I didn't know what kind of flowers or food we were going to have. I had been in Los Angeles running around on auditions while Pat organized the day perfectly.

Cheek-to-cheek with John Waters at my wedding reception.

My dress was designed by *Cry-Baby* costume designer Van Smith, and made by Grandma Grace's personal seamstress, Paulette. The food was catered by an old friend of the family and the casting was perfect. It seemed everyone in town had a part in Pat's production of our special day. Life was funny; the woman who'd cast me in *Cry-Baby* had unknowingly given me a permanent role in her family. It was a wonderful, weepy day. We were surrounded by a hundred and fifty guests and both our families. My mother and sisters had even flown in from Los Angeles. Brook and I danced the night away, finally retiring to the bridal suite of a lovely hotel across town. It was an unforgettable evening.

   In the morning I caught a plane for Vancouver, British Columbia, by myself, as I'd been cast in an episode of *MacGyver*. No one was surprised that Brook and I went right back to work, though. We were a show business family.

41

Patio in Tow

Brook and I moved into a cozy house in North Hollywood. We called it the Hansel and Gretel house because it had a stone walkway that led up to a sunny porch overlooking a big garden. Wearing our beekeeper hats, large ridiculous bonnets we'd purchased in Chinatown, we dug around in our blooming garden. We planted sunflowers, tulips, and parsley, exercising our green thumbs. Our cat—previously known as "Rat"—had been renamed Mr. Steve McGarrett, in homage to my favorite actor as a child, Jack Lord of *Hawaii Five-O*. We had a wrought-iron gate about six feet high in front of the house, and although our yard wasn't completely private, with the exception of the occasional nosy neighbor, no one bothered us.

At twenty-three years old, I was happily married. I spent a lot of time hanging out with girlfriends like Christina Applegate, fixing dinners, playing pool, and drinking wine on the front porch. I was also making a decent living as a print model. My pinup posters hung in rock band bathrooms all over the city, and Christina liked to remind me of the days when she briefly hung out with the Red Hot Chili Peppers' Anthony Kiedis. Apparently my swimsuit poster hung above the toilet in the band's bathroom and she was scarred for life—unable to get the image of me staring down at her, as she peed, out of her head.

I've been in worse places, I'd told her.

My acting career was moving along slowly. I did a lot of episodic work, guest-starring on *MacGyver, Sweating Bullets,* and twice more on *Married with Children* in different roles. Christina and I got to know each other during those long Friday-night shoots and I came to feel that she had it all. But it's true—the grass is always greener. We spent many an evening sitting on my front porch with Steve McGarrett talking about boys and business. She longed for a solid relationship, fully in awe of my marriage. I longed for a solid career, fully in awe of her success. She was only nineteen years old. She had a fortress in the Hollywood Hills, drove a brand-new car, and had men falling at her feet. She had everything but no one to share it with. I adored her, never understanding how Mr. Right hadn't swooped her up yet.

Mr. Steve on the porch of our Hansel and Gretel home in Studio City.

Our little house was the hangout. Our friends had the fancy homes, but Brook and I had the joy and everyone wanted a piece of it.

My mother-in-law, Pat, became an even more important part of my life. We were really close. I traveled a lot in those days modeling all over Europe and it was decided by the family that I needed a chaperone. "Patio" in tow, I traveled to Paris for the Thierry Mugler fashion show. I hadn't been to France since the final porn movie I'd shot in 1986, and was a little nervous about returning to the scene of the crime. But it was nothing like I remembered. It was a completely different experience now that I was living in another world, no longer a teenager or abusing drugs.

I arrived in Paris hours behind schedule. Pat had flown in beforehand and I was sure she was looking for me by now. The flight was late and I had no time to relax or even check into the hotel before I went to work. All I could manage was a birdbath in the backstage bathroom sink before I was rushed into makeup, greeted by an excited Patio. The makeup area was a big open space with a dozen mirrors. Makeup artists scrambled to ready the faces of Cindy Crawford, Naomi Campbell, Rachel Williams, and Debi Mazar. The place was wall-to-wall six-foot-tall beauties in various stages of undress. Racks of clothes lined the walls with models' name tags attached. I could hear the crowd chanting out front. The champagne flowed, the music pounded, and finally the show began.

Models scrambled to take their places and I had no time to be intimidated or impressed by the spectacle. My makeup was slapped on in a gorgeous-mess kind of way, my hair teased into a more extreme Brigitte Bardot style, and I stripped naked next to Cindy Crawford, who wiggled into a space outfit of some sort. I hung on to Pat's shoulder as a dresser dusted baby powder on my lower half so I could slide into a pair of candy-apple red latex pants. The rhinestone bra I wore pinched my nipples, turning them into razor-sharp weapons. It was good to be armed in a sea of unruliness, and Pat and I tried, unsuccessfully, not to laugh.

I felt like an Amazon in my platform heels, my five-foot-seven-inch frame raised to six feet. It was a long way down! I moved cautiously toward the bathroom, my full bladder demanding attention. I carefully rushed along, only moments away from being called onto the stage, when a woman's foot tripped me. I fell down the small flight of steps, barely stopping myself as I grabbed for the railing. I looked over my shoulder at the platinum blonde perpetrator. A famous blond singer stared back. I wasn't sure if she'd tripped me on purpose or not, but she sure didn't apologize as her entourage laughed at my flailing limbs.

"Cow!" I said, hissing, as I entered the bathroom.

I walked the runway three times that evening for Thierry Mugler, and each costume was more bizarre than the last. I was the latex rodeo queen, the sci-fi space goddess, and finally a glittery angel. Pat watched from backstage, helping me change costumes. We were jet-lagged, exhausted, and utterly giddy at our current surroundings.

A handsome but rather dumb-looking man in his twenties walked by our changing area several times staring at me. I met his eyes, but his sour expression told me he wasn't a friend. Pat already had the scoop, having made friends with all the stylists backstage. She said he was a gay porn star named Jeff Stryker. Never having heard of him, I shrugged my shoulders. Okay — what did he want? She told me he was mouthing off backstage about how I "wasn't all that" and if I could get as far as I had in Hollywood with such limited talent, he was sure to be a huge star.

"Really," I said, scanning the room looking for the twit. If it was that easy to do what I'd done, more people would have done it. I was fuming, but the expression on Pat's face when she announced, "Oh, Traci, he's just a big jealous baby," was so priceless, I could only laugh. I realized how silly it was to take these jealous, petty comments seriously. *You're right, Patio,* I thought, smiling at her. Someone was actually jealous of my success. I guess that meant I was making progress!

The fashion show finished to a standing ovation and the press ate it up. For once they seemed to really like me — but of course I couldn't understand a word of French.

Pat and I arrived at our Parisian hotel long after midnight. We were exhausted and starving but room service was closed, so we lay on our twin beds in the dark playing the food game. I would say mashed potatoes. . . . Ummmmmmm, she would say turkey sausages. . . . Yummmmmm, creamy chocolate cake. . . .

Ahhhh, vanilla ice cream. . . . Ohhh. And it went on and on until one of us fell asleep.

The next day was rainy and gray. We pressed our faces up against the taxi's window as we snaked through the city en route to another photo shoot. The streets were filled with colorful umbrellas and the people were handsomely dressed in cashmere coats and leather gloves. It seemed so civilized there.

I was set to shoot some photos for Mugler and was the only model working that afternoon. They positioned me in an old elevator with a small French poodle and I stared at my Polaroid image thinking I looked exactly like Cruella De Vil. Finishing work early, we said our good-byes, then Pat and I headed off into the city once more.

"This is the 'veppon,'" Pat said in a funny voice, pointing at the big black umbrella she was using as a walking stick.

"Ahhhhh," I said, "you mean 'weapon.'"

"No—it is the 'veppon'!"

"Very well, then," I played along, drawing my top lip back and lowering my voice. "Where shall we go with our 'veppon'?"

"Why . . . to eat of course. Traci Elizabeth!!!!!!!!!!!"

Giggling like schoolgirls, we entered the first café we saw and pointed to items on the menu with a simple "oui" as neither one of us spoke any French. Then we took in the sights, walking through the streets of Paris hand in hand and drinking coffee.

I felt I'd reclaimed the city that day, and left behind a new history.

42

Have Your Cake 'N' Eat It 2

Pat and I left Paris days later and pounds heavier, she for Baltimore and me for Los Angeles. I was already missing her as my plane took off into the clear blue sky, returning me to my husband and an audition for a miniseries called *The Tommy-knockers*.

After the audition a few days later, I peeled into the driveway of our house bursting with excitement. I screamed for Brook, but he was nowhere to be found. I was dying to tell someone! I called Pat in Baltimore.

"I got the part!" I screamed into the phone. "I'm playing Nancy Voss in Stephen King's new miniseries!"

"Yeah!" she cheered. "When do you start?"

"Next week!" I told her it would mean going on location to New Zealand for about three months, and that I'd heard it was beautiful there. But I was nervous about Brook's reaction to my leaving again. He never complained, but I could tell he was growing tired of my whirlwind travels. I hoped he wouldn't be angry. I had to do it! I was a fan of horror and Stephen King was my favorite! I was dying to play Nancy. I must! I must! And even more significantly, this would be my first big network job.

I was all wound up as I waited for my husband to come home.

Brook was working on *House Party 2* and the hours were insane. He was wrecked. I'd spent the previous evening baking him cakes for a party scene they'd added at the last minute.

He walked in the front door covered in icing. I ran to him like an excited puppy wanting to share my news, but he wore a sour expression. He was covered in chocolate cake. Apparently he'd fallen asleep at the wheel, crashed his car into a tree, and the cakes went flying. He wasn't hurt. The car had little damage but was a sticky mess. And he was in a foul mood as he scrubbed frosting from his clothing.

My good news was met with obligatory congratulations. It wasn't that he wasn't happy for me. He just missed having his wife around. It was hard trying to earn a living and nurture a marriage at the same time. In so many ways we were like every other couple in their twenties who are trying to find balance in their lives.

With Brook's blessing, I took the job in New Zealand and left for Auckland the following week. I cried my eyes out all the way there. It was hard being away from him.

What if things changed? What if the distance took its toll?

Was my job really worth the risk?

43

Shed My Skin

The cast trailers sat in a clearing of a heavily wooded area of Auckland, New Zealand. *The Tommyknockers* had been shooting nights for the past few weeks. There's something creepy about midnight filming in the jungle, with a full moon on a horror film set. My overactive imagination ran wild and I entertained thoughts of lurking beasts as I downed my second cup of coffee. As I made my way toward the set, my white stiletto heels sank into the moist earth. Thick worms wiggled by as I walked on tiptoe up the narrow path trying not to squash them. The full moon lit my way. Creatures rustled in the brush nearby.

I climbed into the vintage Mustang convertible and offered my coffee to my weary costar, Cliff De Young. He looked like he needed toothpicks to prop up his eyelids. Fighting off the evening's yawns, we ran lines for the scene. We were postal employees whose romp in the woods led to an alien possession. In the scene my character, Nancy Voss, becomes "one of them," joining the growing army of possessed citizens in a sleepy little town somewhere in Maine. Marg Helgenberger was our leader. Joanna Cassidy played the sheriff who tried to save the town, and Jimmy Smits filled the hero spot.

It was a large ensemble cast and I was the baby of the bunch. I had enormous respect for my costars but little in common with them. Marg had her children in tow. Joanna traveled around Australia on her days off. Allyce Beasley was a thirty-something yoga fanatic. Handsome, hunky Smits had his hands full with a gorgeous fiancée. And I was homesick, missing my husband.

I hung out with the show's drivers and production assistants. They were all in their twenties and most of them had been born and raised in Auckland. They turned me on to the best clubs and took me to hidden nightspots that played awesome tribal music on the weekends. It wasn't hard to love New Zealand. The gorgeous moss-covered mountains took my breath away.

One Sunday afternoon, we headed out in search of waterfalls. Otis, my driver, led a small group of us down a steep path that he claimed eventually emptied into the bottom of a waterfall. I'd left the hotel wearing a black dress and strappy sandals, completely wrong for the muddy hill we were approaching. I grabbed my new friend Shelby's hand, giggling as we slipped down the hill, balancing ourselves against each other and nearby trees. Our legs were covered with streaks of mud and the path grew slicker. I fell, sliding on my butt with Shelby right behind me the rest of the way down. We picked up speed as we squealed down the smooth cool muddy path. It was our jungle Slip 'N Slide and it took me back to Great-granny Harris's hill from my childhood. My sisters and I used to lay down the plastic runner and connect the hose at the top to add water to our slippery runway on her hill. We then took turns running and jumping, sliding all the way down.

I'd forgotten that moment until then. I felt a layer release, freeing me from the pain and shame I'd held on to for so long. I had no idea why it happened then. Why in New Zealand??

When the path ended I was shot out into an ice-cold pond. With a rebel yell, I burst through the water, completely exhilarated and screaming at the top of my lungs, utterly giddy.

I was silenced by the beauty of the waterfall in front of us. I felt a part of the water and the wind and the sky. It was a moment of rare magic and I was overwhelmed with a deep respect for life.

Floating in that water, I felt as if I'd been reborn.

44

The Orange-Haired Fairy

Work in New Zealand was an adventure. I particularly relished my scenes with Jimmy Smits. He was a giant of a human, standing about six feet three or so, and I was the Mighty Mouse who brought him down.

I spent my free time in the hotel room staring out the window at the ocean below. Listening to a new artist named Tori Amos, I became inspired by the candid stories she told in her lyrics. She sang about being raped, and I found myself writing about the same thing, filling notebooks with random thoughts from years before. I titled that section of words "Father's Field," although it had nothing to do with my father's field. My father's backyard brought such vivid images to my mind that that's where my story character was placed.

Tori Amos turned out to be magic in concert. She played to a packed house in Auckland Hall the following month. I dragged my driver, Otis, with me. Tori wore blue jeans and red ruby slippers. I sat transfixed in our front-row seats watching her writhe around on the piano bench as she played. Her curly orange hair hung in her eyes as she wailed "Silent All These Years." Then she stood up with the microphone and walked

I REMEMBER that day. I was EXCITED. No school. I'D BEEN RAKING my FATHER's field. WEARing this stupid little DRESS. Rockin' out. RAKing it up. Sort of SWEATing. FEELing GOOD. I was lying in the grass. Making big angels. I was FEELing kind of itchy, From the grass, laying in the sun kinda liking the way it Felt. I guess I must'VE fallen asleep. I still Don't know what WOKE ME up. All i can remember SEEing were these huge eyes. Staring over ME. Right on top of ME. This OLDER boy, out of my league cuz i was no cheerleader no lipstick queen i could feel his eye lashes on my face And they were tickling ME. Maybe that's what woke me up. I was shocked. But the sun was so warm And he was so hot. I didn't know what it was but it felt Kinda good. Just the way his fingers ran thru my hair. Raking it up. I'D never REALLY had anyone touch me like that before aside from my mother. I knew there was something wrong but ... i Don't know i kinda liked it. it was sorta like. Wow. like amazing. He could hAVE been lying there on top of ME for an hour. I Don't know how long he was there. He just kept repeating Your so beautiful your so beautiful. Just this sweet voice tickling me. He was really really close And his lips were touching me. It was like A kiss but it wasn't a kiss. And then i got kinda nervous. i i got really embarrassed I felt myself getting really hot. Sort of blushing Heat Hot. And i tried to get up. And he started to laugh. And then he's sort of pulling

The notebook page on which I wrote "Father's Field."

across the dimly lit stage as she spoke the words to the rape song "Me and a Gun."

Man, she was brave. I was amazed that anyone else shared the same horrible thoughts I had entertained as a teenager, the very thoughts that had driven me to drugs, drowning me in a sea of meaningless sexual activity.

She said out loud what I'd always fought to hide. Why did I do that?

I was quiet on the ride home. Bowing out of the evening's clubbing schedule, I called Brook from a soapy bubble bath. I missed him. I felt vulnerable and had done a lot of thinking in my time away from home. I was changing. It was unsettling. I thought I'd already put the pieces of my life together. I thought I'd already dealt with everything in therapy. So why was I spending so much time thinking about these things all over again? Why did they even matter anymore?

I wanted to go home.

45

Shades of Blue and Green

I came back from New Zealand three months later with a few good stories, a few more friends, and the shadow of things past hanging over me. I was thrilled to see Brook. We spent the afternoon on our sunny front porch painting each other's toenails shades of blue. "It's clear you missed my grooming services," I teased, marveling at how long his nails had grown. They practically curled over the tops of his toes, strangely resembling Mr. Steve's claws, a comparison that earned me a playful swat from my indignant husband.

Coming home was always weird for me and this was no exception. It seemed my body arrived before my spirit did. I think I felt our separation more than Brook had. I sat there in the sun taking him in, chatting about the cast, filming in the jungle, my Slip 'N Slide ride into the waterfall, how bummed I was that I never got to meet Stephen King in person—you know, light stuff. But what I really wanted to talk about was Tori Amos and how her song had affected me. I'd never spoken about the rape to anyone, not even Brook. I searched for a way to tell him, but it all seemed wrong. As much as I wanted to share my feelings, something stopped me. I wasn't sure I would ever tell another soul my secret.

Why had I been silent all these years? Was it because I didn't want Brook to see me as a victim? Was it because saying the words made me feel so helpless? Or was it because I didn't want my husband to have that image of me? Why after all these years did I still carry such shame? *How does anyone get over these things? Maybe I needed a new round of therapy? Arggggggggg!* The thought of spending more time in the shrink zone practically made me groan out loud. I'd already done a good three years, on and off. Wasn't that enough time to unload a girl's baggage?

I listened to Brook talk shop, grateful for the distraction. He sucked on a cigarette, filling me in on the new movies going into production around town. I'd have to ask my new management team if there was anything in them for me, I thought. Brook always had his ear to the ground, looking to get the jump on his competition. He was stressed about booking another prop gig, but I took it with a grain of salt, knowing full well that Brook was always worried about his next gig. He didn't need to be, though. His reputation always put him in front of the line.

Our painting chores complete, we walked our pretty feet off into the kitchen, strapped on our aprons, and fried up some bacon. We built bacon and bagel sandwiches and brewed up a pot of coffee, falling back in sync with each other.

The next day I entered the elevator at 8730 Sunset Boulevard, pressing the button that would take me to a meeting with my new managers, Juliet Green and Alan Siegel. I didn't know them very well, having signed with them only a couple of months earlier. But I was already impressed with their connections, having booked the *Tommyknockers* film through them. I was sure they'd want to hear all about my filming adventures and readied a few quick sound bites from my trip to New Zealand for their amusement.

Juliet Green, a petite woman with curly brown hair, was like a steamroller. A straight shooter with impeccable taste, she had strong opinions about my career and what it would take to get me from point A to point B. My agent, Don Gerler, was not in these plans, and I knew that if I wanted to continue on with Ms. Green it would mean listening to her advice.

Gerler's days were numbered. Juliet wanted to see me represented by a more prestigious agency, and although Gerler had always been respectable in my eyes, I was still being offered bad-B-movie auditions while the Movies of the Week and serious independent films came and went without ever landing in my hands. Treading in unknown waters is always risky, but there was no doubt it was time to take the leap. I had never had a woman put such faith in my career, and I wondered if there were more Juliet Greens in the world. *Could this be my time? Was it possible for me to step into the next phase of my life? Was I beginning to look different to the world?*

I was a grown-up, happily married, with some good work to my credit and a reputation for being professional and kind. But how do I get people to focus on that? Juliet said there would be doors that I would never be allowed to walk through, but there would be those we could break down. It had been five years since my departure from porn and I was only beginning to get recognition as a legitimate actress. There was still much to learn, much to do, and much to forget.

The task seemed daunting. But with her at my side, I took the leap and fired Gerler, diving into uncharted waters feeling confident she'd be there to toss me a life preserver if I needed one.

46

Star Sauté

It was a scorching ninety-one degrees in Sherman Oaks, California, as my husband and a small army of movers finished unloading the final boxes into our newly rented house in the heart of the Valley. Both of our careers were in transition. We had outgrown our adorable Hansel and Gretel home but were still uncertain about where we wanted to nest permanently, so we opted to save our money and rent a three-bedroom Valley home with a pool and huge garage for Brook to store his props in. His massive collection included everything from ladies' purses to rubber guns, and our new garage was already overflowing with boxes on wheels containing his prized prop kit. It was then I discovered that a property master was just another name for junk man. Through the kitchen window I watched him methodically organize hundreds of sunglasses by brand. The sweat rolled down his face as he lovingly cleaned each pair and then placed them in their proper case.

What an odd creature, I thought, smiling to myself.

He hustled about in his Hawaiian shorts and combat boots as I watched the neighbors watching him. So much for blending in. Brook didn't care, though. He dubbed it his "festive moving outfit." What could I say? He was a constant source of amusement. *He's still cute,* I thought, taking in his oh-so-pale Baltimore bird legs and noticing the extra married poundage he'd put on, which had earned him a rather undesirable Sam Kinison comparison by the press at a recent party we'd attended. Funny how un-Hollywood the two of us really were. We rarely went out, cooking feasts in our kitchen instead, and never hit the club scene, preferring an occasional bottle of champagne in the privacy of our own home. We were recluses and I believe that served me well. There was no evidence of my wild-child party-girl days.

As I unpacked my pots and pans I watched Brook take a seat out front by the white picket fence and grab a smoke. *What are you thinking about right now?* I wondered as I studied the expression on his face, but couldn't gauge his thoughts.

Change was thick in the air — I could feel it in my bones.

I'd been spending way too much time away from home and I wondered if it was shooting holes in our marriage. There was so much I wanted to do, and ironically, the safety I felt being married was exactly what allowed me to swim in uncharted waters with sharks. *Was I naive to believe our marriage was that solid? Why was it accepted for a man to put his career first but when a woman did she was criticized?* My husband was always there to hold me when I fell on my ass, whether that meant I lost a role, got trashed in the press, or just felt beaten up and wanted to give it all up, disappear from the public eye, and get a normal job. While he supported me completely in those moments, he still couldn't hide his jealousy over the time I spent pursuing other things.

My ambition was the greatest problem in our marriage, and as I grew and added music to my career wish list, things became even more difficult. Brook always fancied himself the singer of the family, having grown up playing in bands, and he wasn't thrilled when I started studying music and hired a vocal coach named Robert Edwards to help me expand my vocal range. He wasn't exactly against it but he wasn't for it either. And it just added to the building tension between us.

I'd spent the past month working on a film in Italy called *Mafia Docks*, only to return home and win a role in the enormously popular show *Tales from the Crypt*. Thanks to my gamble on Juliet Green and a new agent named Stephen LaManna, the quality of projects I was now doing was light-years beyond the Gerler days. But I still struggled to book jobs I could be proud of while earning a reasonable income.

I got word later that afternoon that I had been offered a role in the TV version of *Smokey and the Bandit*. It was a very G-rated project and exactly the type of good-girl role I had yet to play. The only catch was it filmed on location in North Carolina. *Would three more weeks away matter?* I hated the idea. Brook and I were both edgy from the move, but it was about more than that. I was worried about how my husband was spending his lonely evenings. I'd begun hearing disturbing gossip over the last month as Brook completed work on the film *Buffy the Vampire Slayer*. Rumor had it that while I was on location in Italy he was getting cozy with an actress in the movie. I'd found no concrete evidence to support these claims, but the shadow of doubt had been cast. The source of this gossip was undeniably reliable, but I needed the cold hard facts before I would ever confront my husband with such an accusation.

The filming of *Buffy* ended without further gossip, but I wondered if my leaving town again would open the door for such temptations. We had been married for three years now. Was he bored? Our sex life was great—we had no problem in that department. So why then would he go elsewhere? *Was it the distance? Or was it something else? Conquest? A new piece? Man, what a thing to think about before leaving town. Was he capable of bringing another woman into our bed? Would he risk my leaving him?*

As I fried chicken for dinner, I thought of the actress in question. I imagined covering her with eggs and flour, and plopping her into my pan—voilà, star sauté.

I loved my husband and I wasn't going to let my imagination get the best of me. But I wasn't a fool either. This time, I asked him to come visit me on location. And I'd make sure he had a smile on his face when he went back home.

47

Sweet Dreams and Flying Machines

I opened the front door of our Sherman Oaks home and a monster jumped out at me, its snarling fangs tearing into my leg. A fit of hysterical laughter followed my shrill screams of terror. I knew immediately who the culprit was: Brook, now the puppet master, emerged, a perma-grin on his face.

"Very funny." I slammed the door in protest, realizing he must have gotten the job working on the monster movie. I looked from my husband to the gremlinlike creature he held protectively in his arms, worried I might retaliate and rip its face off. I growled back at it, making them both jump. Continuing grumpily down the hallway, I looked forward to a hot shower.

I'd just finished work on *Tales from the Crypt* that evening and was stiff as a board. I stood in the shower wondering how I was going to drag my weary bones to the airport later that night. Drying off and popping two aspirin, I could still feel the hands of the episode's lead actor, David Paymer, around my neck pretending to strangle me.

I had hoped to spend some time with Brook before I left for North Carolina to film *Bandit*, but time had run out. I kissed him good-bye and reminded him of his promise to visit me on location. He said he'd try, sending me off with an unsettling feeling in my guts. *Try hard, baby . . . real hard. . . .*

As the mechanical bird carried me off to another hotel room, to another group of people to win over, and to another credit on my résumé, I was grateful to have the job but uncertain of the price my absence would cost me at home. *Was I too obsessed with my career? Was I a bad wife? Was I driving my husband away?*

On the surface I didn't think there was anything wrong with our marriage, and I couldn't put my finger on it, but I knew there was trouble in paradise.

48

Sweet Meat

Chanel!" exclaimed the six-foot platinum blonde drag queen blocking my path as I walked through the nightclub.

"Be gone!" demanded my cross-dressing cohort, Vincent Domini Fauci, snapping his fingers in front of the intruder, reminding me of the grandmother Endora from *Bewitched*.

"See that, honey? I told you, you look fierce," Vince said, dragging me deeper into the pounding walls of the flesh-throbbing gay club. He was proud of the smoky eyes he'd painted on me. I was his makeup showpiece as we made our way toward the bar, where buff boys in short shorts danced on platforms.

Androgynous fashion plates chatted animatedly as they kicked back cocktails. I surveyed the dim room. RuPaul's "Supermodel" boomed and strobe lights danced off the club's walls, disguising the beard stubble of the woman next to me. But the meaty paw holding her martini told another story. Being a gay man in North Carolina was a dangerous thing. The gorgeous cow-grazing fields gave way to streets filled with beer-drinking good old boys who didn't take kindly to "sweet meat." This club was an oasis for the young gay population of the North Carolina hills. It was their safe zone. I was pretty sure I was the only female by birth there.

I tugged at my skintight fishnet dress as we positioned our-selves to get the bartender's attention. Catching my reflection in the mirror behind the bar, I laughed. I was a gay man's creation. I looked like an old Blondie record cover with my thick black

As a showgirl at a modeling shoot, mid-1990s.

eyeliner turning my lids slightly catty and my eye-lashes miles long. I smiled at my glitter-covered pal. He had been nonstop entertainment since I arrived a month ago.

Vince was my makeup artist on the show *Bandit,* where we'd become close after a minor mishap. The first day of shooting I walked into his trailer and took a seat in his chair. He carefully applied my foundation, his hands shaking so bad I thought he was going to poke me in the eye. Finally I asked him if he was all right, and he started to say something. But I wasn't listening. My eyes were drawn instead to his obvious erection. Adjusting his crotch, he burst into tears and walked out of the trailer. I just sat there processing this odd occurrence.

I found Vince on the steps of the makeup trailer. He wouldn't look at me. "Hey, man, what's up?" I said teasingly.

"I'm so sorry," he gushed. "I just think you're such a god-dess. Apparently my body agrees. But I swear to God I'm gay! Please don't have me fired!"

After that, I became the goddess of Vince's world. I hadn't been familiar with diva worship but caught on fast. He painted my face every weekend before we hit the town, and we shopped for ridiculous outfits in the conservative shopping mall in the city. Vince and I favored latex, finding our best treasures in the sex shop down the street. I'd never had the nerve to walk into a sex shop before, fearing I would see myself staring back at me from a porn video. But my world was different now. That fear no longer held the same weight. I was with Vince and I'd discovered an acceptance in his world—the gay community—that I'd never known before. In this company, I wasn't the only one who'd been persecuted because of sex, and I was certain no matter what I bought in a sex store, I still wouldn't be judged.

I saw the same old faces on the porn covers displayed in the "New Releases" section, happy not to be one of them. Trying not to stare, I headed off toward the dressing rooms, the image of Ginger Lynn's latest porno cover fresh in my mind. It was unbelievable that she was still doing porn all these years later. *My God—how had she survived it? I'm so glad that isn't me,* I thought as we abandoned our shopping spree for Mexican food.

Over carnitas my thoughts returned to Brook, and I poured my heart out to Vince, worried that my marriage was really in danger. Vince did his duty as a good friend, listening to me ramble on through dinner about my marital blues. Brook and I had been battling over the phone since I arrived. We couldn't agree on the smallest things. Bottom line: the distance had done its damage.

He canceled his visit to see me and I felt snubbed.

"I thought I was the most important thing to you," I spat over the phone.

He said he couldn't leave town. He was waiting to hear about another job.

"It's just a weekend! Come on! I miss you."

I hung up feeling more uncertain than ever. My husband had stood me up again, breaking his promise to visit me on location for the umpteenth time. He always found a reason why he couldn't come. I didn't expect him to follow me around the world, but I guess I secretly wished he would. His decision not to fly down came at a time when I already doubted his commitment to our marriage.

Thoughts of that tarty actress filled my head and, not privy to his comings and goings while I was out of town, my imagination conjured up the worst.

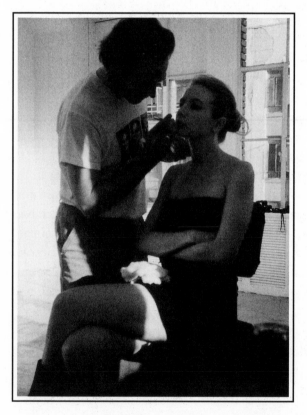

Makeup artist Jeff House paints my face,
Los Angeles, 1990.

49

Flesh Wounds

I spent my last night in Charlotte, North Carolina, with Vince and some friends. We left the *Bandit* set after wrap in search of a tattoo parlor. Vince was no stranger to ink. His back was covered with Egyptian artwork. I teased him that tattoos looked silly when they sagged and that at his ripe old age of thirty-three, he might want to consider another hobby. He gave me his best bitch look as we pulled into the parking lot of his favorite ink joint. My palms grew sweaty as I imagined the pecking of a tattoo needle digging into my skin. I loathed needles and was a tattoo virgin. Brook was amazed that I didn't have a single one. He himself sported a Japanese dragon he'd gotten years ago on his left arm.

I nearly chickened out as Brutus the tattoo artist showed me the sanitary needles he was removing from their protective sleeves. Gulp. Perhaps getting a tattoo was too permanent a statement. *Oh no, you don't. . . . You're not backing out now. I need this reminder.* I handed the artist an old crucifix I had bought from a beggar on the streets of Italy years before. I'd carried that crucifix in my pocket ever since. I thought of it as a symbol of strength, one I really needed at the moment. I felt weak, tempted by the nightclubs' offers of sex, drugs, and rock and roll. *How do people stay on the straight and narrow? How had I? Why had I all these years?*

Man, I knew the deal. I also remembered the price. At times it was just hard to stay present and sober in a world that could be so mean. *Doesn't everyone self-medicate in their own way?* I wasn't thinking about hard-core drugs at this point, just a few beers and a hot guy. I couldn't believe I was fantasizing about such things.

It was definitely time to go home.

The needle poked holes into my soft inner ankle, leaving behind a blue-gray cross. Brutus carved away, freehand, on my flesh. The slicing sensation brought me back to reality and I welcomed the pain. It slapped me right back in line.

I caught the red-eye home to Los Angeles around midnight.

It was ten in the morning on a cool October day when Mr. Steve greeted me as I walked in the door. He meowed at me and I meowed back.

"I missed you too, fella," I told him, stroking his soft fur. "Where's your daddy?"

He was all purrs as he wrapped himself around my bare legs, irritating the freshly carved tattoo on my left ankle. The house was quiet as I made my way inside. Hanging up my coat in the front closet, I continued down the hallway, setting my suitcases down beside the washing machine. I had weeks' worth of dirty laundry. And from the look of things, so did Brook. The house was a mess. He must be working long hours. I paged him, letting him know I was home.

I was loading dirty dishes in the dishwasher when I heard the front door open. Brook bounced into the kitchen and engulfed me in a bear hug, kissing me and telling me how sorry he was for not visiting me on location. "Yeah, that sucks," I replied, not letting him off the hook so easily.

"What's so important that kept you away from me? I thought we agreed I would take the job and you would support me by showing up? You know, I had a lot of volunteers willing to spend time with me," I teased, wanting to get a rise out of him.

His brow furrowed, clearly jealous, and he kissed me hard. "Don't fuck around, Traci."

As much as I wanted to drop the attitude, I couldn't quite do it. I backed off, taking in his sweet familiar smell. *How could I love someone and want to fight with him at the same time? I left—not him. Why am I pissed? Is it because I'm scared?* Both of our careers were going really well, so well we had little time for each other. I felt like I was missing out. . . . I felt like I was losing him. . . .

I settled onto the sofa in the living room, stubborn but willing to talk. We just stared at each other. He broke the silence by telling me he had big news. He'd been offered the resident prop master job on Barry Levinson's new television series *Homicide: Life on the Street.* It was a steady gig, which meant he'd have to relocate. It was filming in Baltimore. His mother was already set to run the casting department so it would be a family affair. "It's the break we've been waiting for, Traci," he said.

My head was spinning.

"It sounds like you've already made up your mind," I said quietly. "I think it's an amazing opportunity, but it's so far away from home. What about us?"

I tried to hide the tears that stung my eyes.

"Hey," he reminded me, "we always said, the first one of us to get a series, the other one would go."

"You want me to move to Baltimore?" I tried to imagine it. *What would I do for a living? I can't act in Baltimore.*

"Don't you get it?" he said. "That doesn't matter anymore. Quit your little hobby, work in a coffee shop or something. I'll buy you a house, we'll have a kid, it'll be great. Otherwise we'll have to do the distance for a while."

I was stunned by his choice of words. *"Quit my little hobby?" He thinks of my career as a "little hobby"?* I was fuming as I excused myself, needing some time to regain my composure. I really didn't want to say out loud what I was thinking at that moment: *My own husband doesn't take me seriously!?*

I returned to the living room ready to let him have it. He pulled me close, oblivious to how upset and insulted I felt about his decision to take the job no matter what. I felt abandoned. It hurt that he could walk away so quickly.

My anger turned to tears as he held me, and I couldn't say a word. But I got it. I knew I would do the same thing. Our work was number one for both of us and that admission to myself tore at me. Once again I wondered if seeing my name in lights was worth it.

Brook left for Baltimore a week later without me. I couldn't hold up my end of the bargain and go with him. I just didn't see myself working in a coffee shop and I certainly wasn't ready to be a mother. The choices I had weren't options. I couldn't live someone else's dream. I had my own. And ultimately I chose the same thing he did—a career. He said he understood, and although it took another six months for us to completely walk away from the marriage, I felt it had really ended before my trip to North Carolina.

I was heartbroken.

I filed for divorce that winter. Not only was I losing my husband but I was also losing a family. I hoped we'd all be friends again one day, but it would take some time for the wounds to heal.

50

A Spot of Tea

The months after Brook and I split up were rough. Every song on the radio made me weepy and every black Bronco truck that drove by had me craning my neck to see if it was him. I thought I heard his voice in crowds and saw his face in my dreams.

What had I done?

I had serious doubts about my choice to remain in Los Angeles on my own. I was depressed to think it might all be for nothing. Relentlessly, I searched for an opening, needing an emotional outlet that acting just wasn't giving me. I spent my free time writing in journals and pouring out my heart on the pages. I continued to take voice lessons, finding both a friend and mentor in my coach Robert Edwards. He encouraged me to search for a record deal, planting the initial seed in my head.

I met radio DJ Rodney Bingenheimer around this time, at a birthday party in the Hollywood Hills. He was a legendary presence in the rock-and-roll world, known for his bold tastes in music, and I told him of my aspirations as a singer-songwriter. At the time he seemed interested, but I didn't really think anything would come of it.

Weeks later I found myself at the offices of Gary Kurfirst, the man who managed my idol Debbie Harry! His independent label Radioactive Records was producing the soundtrack for a film called *Pet Cemetery 2*, and I was recommended by Rodney Bingenheimer to Gary's A&R person, Jeff Jacklin. Jeff hired me to record the track "Love Never Dies" and shortly thereafter I was signed to a development deal with Radioactive.

I worked closely with Jeff, a British A&R man named Brendan Burke, and an exceptionally enthusiastic young guy named Kent Belden, who was just starting out. Brendan was a pro, having been in the business for years, and he worked closely with the band Live. Kent was an eager twenty-two-year-old with a passion for all things Traci Lords. Together we defined my sound, one which would later earn me the title "Techno Queen" in the underground rave scene.

Radioactive arranged for me to fly to London in the spring of 1994 and put me up in a one-room flat above a coffee shop in Hampstead Heath. I was ready to begin work on my first record. I called my producer Tom Bailey, of Thompson Twins fame, and announced my arrival. I was a huge fan of his and remembered listening to his music when I was in school. I still had an old Thompson Twins T-shirt from a concert I'd gone to as a young girl, but decided to keep this information to myself, not knowing if he'd take it as a compliment. I couldn't believe the man I'd watched onstage as a screaming fourteen-year-old was now my producer!

Tom Bailey and Alannah Curry lived in a loft just outside London. Their recording studio was located up a set of winding narrow steps above their living quarters. It was an attic paradise. I tried to make small talk as we began to check sound levels, but I was so nervous that wit didn't come easily. I was intimidated to be working with one of my idols. Tom Bailey was a great singer and I felt completely inferior in his presence. I could not have felt more vulnerable standing there in the middle of the studio, mike in my hands, choking out the words to the first song. Tom understood and made light of my jitters, telling me he hated to sing these days.

"What?! Why? You're a genius singer," I blurted out, feeling like a geek as soon as the words came out of my mouth.

He just smiled. He was a gentle, soft-spoken person, his demeanor anything but threatening. He fixed me a cup of tea and suggested I give the closet a try. "It could make a bloody good recording booth." He was right, and by the end of the day I'd found my nerve, recording "I Want You" in the privacy of Tom Bailey's closet. One lone candle burned through the darkness of my cozy vocal paradise as I sang "It's four in the morning and I'm praying for rain."

We worked together on three songs, "I Want You," "Fly," and "Just Like Honey," which later was rerecorded by Keith Farley of Babble (Tom Bailey's new group) with a different set of lyrics. In the end it was called "Father's Field," the words I'd written in New Zealand a few years earlier, finally immortalized in song. *Was I revealing too much? Well, I could always insist that it not be used,* I thought, walking through the cool London night air as I shook off the day's adrenaline rush and prayed for a good night's sleep.

My album was coming together. The songs I'd recorded with Tom had a sexy ambient vibe. Now I wanted something with a harder edge to add another dimension. I was introduced to producer Ben Watkins, who was known for his aggressive jungle beats. He was a wild man and very passionate about his music. I told Ben I wanted to do a song that had elements of rock and roll but with a techno vibe and he ran with it, creating a slamming heavy metal guitar intro on an insanely hyper track.

I teamed up with an American singer named Wonder and together we created the lyrics to my first single, "Control": "You say you're lonely. You say you're blue. You lost your lover. Let me console you." Although it had a dominant-female vibe going on, I was still nursing a broken heart. I missed Brook deeply and poured my emotions into the lyrics I wrote and the words I sang.

Next, Ben and I worked on "Outlaw Lover." I spent days scouring through cowboy stories and watching westerns, trying to get the lingo down. It had a real camp element to it. I cast myself as a woman in a small town who had been wronged, and I tell my unfaithful lover, "You best be warned I'm a woman scorned," before shooting him dead.

We finished up and rested for a few days. I slept until noon and took long, steamy baths. I joined the locals for a spot of tea in the café downstairs and treated myself to a rare cigarette. I knew no one in London except my producers, but I enjoyed my isolation, grateful for the quiet.

The following week I met Mike Edwards, the handsome lead singer of the band Jesus Jones. He'd also become a respected London DJ, moving away from his pop success. He was a fixture in the underground scene and I was a fan. I had all his CDs back home and I looked to him for advice on the music industry. He ended up writing the music for a hauntingly beautiful song that I named "Distant Land." A songwriter named Blue and I wrote the lyrics. It was the only ballad I recorded, a sad tale of a woman waking up lost and not knowing where she is, searching for light in a distant land.

Mike and I recorded "Say Something" next, then finally a silly over-the-top song called "Okeydokey Doggy Daddy." It was a goof track we'd recorded while having drinks at the end of a recording session. Mike asked me to ad-lib some lines as I finished off my beer. Looking around the eggplant-purple studio I started to make comments on my surroundings. "Here in my purple room, I'd like to thank you all so much for this"— fake sob of joy—"Oscar!"

Hollywood was clearly on my mind.

It was time for me to go back to Los Angeles and face my life. I had finished recording my first album. And I felt like I'd accomplished something.

Maybe, just maybe, it was worth it after all.

In the recording studio with Chad Smith and Dave Navarro of the Red Hot Chili Peppers, Los Angeles, 1996, during a remix session for "Fallen Angel."

51

Pretty on the Inside

I returned to Los Angeles with a bounce in my stride. I knew I was on the right path. I wasn't just dreaming about recording a record anymore, I'd done it. As absurd as I knew they were, Brook's words had lingered in my mind. I had to prove to myself that he was really wrong. My career wasn't just a "hobby." I hadn't outlived my fifteen minutes of fame. I had the rough mixes of my songs in hand and they were the proof I needed to walk confidently into the new life I'd chosen.

The homey Studio City house I leased after I split with Brook was just as I'd left it—unpacked and unlived-in. The scent of mothballs and fresh cat shit hung in the air. Mr. Steve ignored me, pissed he'd been incarcerated at the kennel up the street while I was away. "Ah come on, buddy . . . I'm sorry I left ya. Can we be friends again?" He tore across the house, completely uninterested in my fickle brand of love. I guess it was time to pay for my neglect. There I was, a single woman with an angry cat and a house full of remnants of a failed marriage. If there was ever a time for "happy hour," it was now.

I dismissed the "happy" thought in favor of unpacking my life. As I emptied the dusty moving boxes in my new living room, I was confronted with skeletons of my married years. I

From a photo shoot for Radioactive Records.

voted against a trip down memory lane and shoved all the remaining traces of Brook away in a back closet, knowing full well that my baggage had just gotten heavier. *Man, how much baggage can one girl accumulate?*

I couldn't stand to be still for a moment. I didn't want to feel the loneliness that nagged at me, so I put my life in high gear. *Idle time is the devil's playground.* . . . I made the rounds, calling my manager and chatting up my agent. I was back and anxious to get cracking, and I needed the distraction of a busy schedule. Pouring my energy into my work, I was game to audition for any decent part that came my way.

I was thrilled to land a role on *Melrose Place* shortly after my return, cast as one of the followers of a cult leader who enticed resident *Melrose Place* star Laura Leighton to join our happy family. It was a wicked role and I was a secret fan of Darren Star, who was the creator of *Melrose Place*. My favorite character on the show was Sydney (Leighton) and it was the best of all possible worlds to book a job, actually like the show, and get to work with Laura. I thought she was great fun to watch and I eagerly waited for the scripts to arrive. Finally, a show my mother would have heard of, perhaps even liked—I couldn't wait to tell her.

As I settled into life as a single woman and prepared for my work on *Melrose Place* and the upcoming release of my first single, "Control," I started to enjoy myself.

I had met Roseanne Barr and Sandra Bernhard at a Grammy after-party the year before. They were hanging out in the VIP section of a hip La Cienega nightclub when I arrived with the gang from Radioactive Records. Roseanne introduced herself, generously saying she had a lot of respect for me. She said Hollywood was a tough place, especially for a woman with a past. I was taken off guard by her candor, amazed that she even knew who I was. She left me with a promise that if there was ever a role on her show that was right for me, it would be mine. Nearly a year had passed since that encounter and I was working on *Melrose Place* when the call came in. Roseanne had kept her promise and Juliet worked it all out. I would finish the five-episode story arc on *Melrose Place* and then start shooting a recurring role on *Roseanne*.

It was the first time in my life when I actually knew what my next gig would be.

We filmed *Melrose Place* on a soundstage deep in the Valley, just past Magic Mountain. As I soared along the 101 freeway to work, I listened to Courtney Love's band, Hole, tear through the air. *Pretty on the Inside* was my anthem record and I screamed every word to get psyched for the day.

I was halfway into filming the episode in which I destroy designer Jane's clothing line. I was running lines in my head as I pulled onto the stage lot and made my way to the makeup room. Heather Locklear was already there looking perfect. She was pleasant as always and her friendliness was contagious. I respected her. She was one of those people who always made you feel welcome but still managed to keep you at a safe distance. She had an

With costar Laura Leighton during my stint on *Melrose Place*.

impeccable reputation, everyone loved her, and she was the ideal role model, so I studied her set etiquette to see what I could learn.

The women of *Melrose Place* all got along fabulously. At least that's how it looked to me. Many of the actresses had already done their share of prime-time television and were completely at ease in the frantic world of makeup, hair, wardrobe, press, and filming that they lived in. I've always found it unnerving to enter a production when it is already in full swing, whether it's a film that has started shooting weeks earlier than your character's start date or a group of people who've been working together for a few years on a series. When the principals have already formed relationships, you are clearly the new kid on the block. It's like jumping into the rapids and swimming for your life. There's a real rush involved but also a genuine chance of drowning.

Juliet came to the set a lot. I was grateful to have her there and relieved to encounter a truly kind person in Laura Leighton. She was open and warm, and made me feel welcome in her domain. I got no attitude from her or anyone else on the set.

I fell into the groove of weekly television series as my five-episode arc continued. I wouldn't have minded sticking around longer. I realized then that being a regular must be the hardest job in show business. The hours are brutal and the workload fierce. But it's also the steadiest gig an actor can get and the thought of that security was very appealing to me.

I wondered if Brook thought the same thing about his steady *Homicide* gig. Did he think of me as often as I still thought of him? It had been months since we'd spoken and I hated not knowing where he was or what he was doing. Was he happy with his choice? Was I really happy with mine? Why couldn't I have my cake and eat it too? There were plenty of happily married actresses working in Hollywood—weren't there? In that moment, I couldn't think of one.

My experience on the set of *Roseanne* was even more frantic than filming *Melrose Place*. Half-hour comedy, as I had discovered years earlier on *Married with Children*, was all about energy and pace. And these people had it. Every morning I would arrive for work and prepare myself for the first race of the day, always waiting for the arrival of cast member John Goodman, Roseanne's husband, Dan, on the series. I thought he was the coolest. We goofed off a lot together, racing with our shoelaces tied together from the cast parking lot toward the working stage. Goodman always dusted me, easily zooming up the hill and crossing the finish line first. I don't know how he did it, but I was sure he must have had motorized shoes. He gloated, his six-foot-something beefy frame shaking with laughter. "Better luck next time, kid," he'd say with a satisfied smile, and be gone, leaving me at my trailer screaming, "I demand a rematch, Goodman!"

I spent the first morning in a cast read-through on the *Roseanne* stage sitting around a long wooden table where I traded lines with Roseanne Barr and Laurie Metcalf, two unbelievably talented comedians. I was in awe of their level of skill and terrified I wouldn't be able to hold my own with such pros. *How did they get so good? Were they just born funny?* I called Juliet looking for advice, and she led me to the door of acting coach Howard Fine.

Howard was one of the hottest acting coaches in Hollywood, known for his direct approach to the craft. In short, he told it like it was without the sugar coating. I know that sounds simple, but believe me, in a town where people are afraid to offend celebrities, the truth is not always easy to come by. He had good taste in actors, chose his students carefully, and always had a way of pulling the best out of everyone. He became a huge influence on my work.

By the middle of December I felt wiped out. I'd been doing double duty finishing up the last episode of *Melrose Place* and working on *Roseanne*. Completely consumed with my career, I was obsessed to the point that work started to enter my sleep.

I had nightmares about giving interviews for my upcoming single, "Control." I knew I had to promote my album, but that meant doing press.

I was prepared for the worst.

Weren't there any honest journalists out there?

I found one in writer Chris Heath.

I was amazed to learn that Juliet had nabbed me the much coveted cover of *Details* magazine. I'd done a fashion layout there a couple of years earlier and had developed a great working relationship with the *Details* team. World-famous photographer Albert Watson was hired to shoot me and I was thrilled at the prospect of working with him again. Excited by the visibility such a high-profile cover would give me, I was still concerned about what the headline would be. My nerves prompted me to check out Chris Heath's previous features and I was impressed to discover that he seemed like a reasonable human being. Maybe there was hope after all.

As the holidays approached, life slowed down and I battled the blues—bah, humbug. I saw families all around me, choosing trees, wrapping gifts, and loving each other. I thought of Christmases gone by: Brook's family, decorating the tree, Patio with a

Another shot taken for Radioactive Records.

big red bow around her neck drinking my father-in-law's eggnog.

Life sucked, but I had a party to go to.

Howard Fine's annual Christmas party was a must-appear, so I searched my closet for a festive frock. Pounds seem to melt off me when I'm working hard, and I settled on an ill-fitting long slinky red dress. *Man . . . I'm skin and bones. . . . Oh well, no time to be fussy.* I picked up my date, Juliet, at her Hollywood home and off we went to the ball.

Howard's studio was packed to the gills with actors. I recognized Emily Lloyd and the woman she was talking to, Lara Flynn Boyle. With their designer dresses and Colgate smiles, they seemed right at home on the balcony, entertaining an eager-looking group of men. I felt out of place and uncomfortable in this oh-so-Hollywood crowd. *What am I doing here?*

A cool December breeze carried a waft of cigarette smoke across the room; although I was only an occasional smoker, a cigarette sounded real good.

Abandoning Juliet and dinner in favor of someone who was "holding," I spied a dark-haired man smoking in the center of the room, seemingly unaware or unconcerned about the "No Smoking" signs posted nearby. I said hello, bummed a smoke, thanked him, and began looking for an exit. He stopped me.

"Where are my manners?" he said with a New York accent, offering me a light. "I'm John Enos."

As we chatted casually, I became aware of considerable gossip and snickering going on around us.

Emily Lloyd craned her neck to look at us and I got annoyed. At the time I didn't know she and John were friends. I just thought she was being catty, and wondered if this guy was her boyfriend. Or was it about me?

I managed to smile as the party photographer snapped a photo of John and me together, then I flicked my cigarette away and excused myself, fed up with the crowd. As I made my way toward Juliet, John stopped me and thrust his phone number into my hand. *Is he hitting on me?*

"Ah . . . umm . . . thanks," I managed.

"Give me a call, let's have coffee," he said, moving off into the crowd as coolly as Elvis.

Eagle-eyed Juliet witnessed this exchange and teased me accordingly. "So, you have to bum a smoke off the best-looking guy here, huh?"

I looked at Enos holding court across the room. The thought had never even occurred to me. Yep—she was right. He was a looker. But I wasn't in the mood for romance. The holiday season had soured my libido. Maybe I'd call him later. . . . Juliet and I slipped out the back and drove home talking shop.

Though I dreaded the holidays, I was excited about the new year. I was all over the television and had a good feeling about the upcoming *Details* cover. "Control" was creating a buzz in the underground dance world and my record company was anticipating a hit.

On the outside, it seemed I was on a roll. I wish I could have felt pretty on the inside.

52

Control

I endured the holidays with all the gusto of a cranky Scrooge. While I had my own family who still resided in the Redondo Beach area, it just wasn't the same without Pat and the Baltimore gang.

In more recent years my family and I had grown closer but there was still some distance in those relationships. We all had our own lives, dreams, and pasts we wanted to forget—maybe me most of all.

Mr. Steve and I welcomed in New Year's together. My pal Vince, the makeup artist from North Carolina, had moved to Los Angeles, so we hung out together shooting pool, playing the jukebox, and tossing back beers. It was a far cry from the glamorous life people thought celebrities had, but it was always amusing.

By mid-January, everything was moving at superhuman speed. "Control" climbed into the number two spot on the Billboard dance charts and it remained there for two weeks, creating enough buzz to generate real excitement in my camp. Everyone was telling me it was my time, and with my face splashed across the covers of magazines such as *Details, Surface,* and *BAM,* it seemed they were right. The folks at Radioactive

Records worked their tails off riding the hype, planning the next move. I shot a music video, gave countless interviews, and appeared at parties all over town, talking up the release of my upcoming album *1000 Fires*.

But riding the wave took a lot out of me.

Weeks later, on a quiet February morning, I sat perfectly still in my Studio City backyard. I was momentarily free of my thoughts, soaking in the sun and enjoying a moment to myself. I'd been caught up in a whirl of photo shoots and press events that had left me sleep deprived and weak. Now, I watched my cat scratch himself on the warm cement, his long white fur picking up leaves as he wiggled. Unruly weeds had taken over my once immaculate garden turning it into an urban jungle.

I swallowed the last of my muddy cup of coffee and lit the first cigarette of the day. It was time to get myself together. Collecting Mr. Steve, I returned him to the confines of the house. I felt guilty leaving him alone so often but duty called.

Grabbing a stack of vinyl records, I walked out of my house to the garage. My eyes adjusted to the dark space as I settled in for an afternoon of vinyl surfing. I had transformed my garage into a home studio, complete with mikes, recording equipment, and a top-of-the-line set of turntables. An old couch sat in the corner and the walls were lined with underground techno posters. With the exception of Moby, most of the artists I was familiar with were from the United Kingdom and Europe, where techno was all the rage.

Following the success of "Control," I had a brainstorming session with the Radioactive gang and we'd decided that the best way to promote a bandless solo singer with an album filled with computer-generated sounds was for me to perform as a DJ. The world of spinstress was completely foreign to me. But at a time when techno artists were snubbed in mainstream music in America, and live techno shows were unheard of, it was as credible an option as any to promote my album.

Stretching my body over the coffin (the turntable bed that DJs use), I blew the dust from the decks, determined to master the art of DJ-ing in a few short weeks (yeah right!). Under the wing of DJ Dawna Montel, whom I'd recently been introduced to by my record company, I fell into the groove. It helped that I have eclectic taste in music and genuinely liked spinning.

As I practiced beat mixing in my dusty garage, my eyes met those of DJ Paul Oakenfold, his face looking down into mine from the autographed record hanging above the turntables. He was a god in the techno world and I kept him hanging around for inspiration. I'd met him with Brendan Burke months earlier in London, where he was DJ-ing at a club. Brendan and I were there doing initial publicity for the album and we were looking for a way into Mr. Oakenfold's very private world. Everyone on the club circuit knew that if Oakenfold played your record, you were as good as guaranteed a spot on the dance charts. He was a one-man hit maker, and I was banking on him liking what he heard.

At the Grammy Awards with Lady Kier and Radioactive Records president Gary Kurfirst.

Brendan and I had been praying for a shot at him all night. Finally the bouncers had disappeared and we wasted no time going into action. Paul got quite a shock as I tumbled over the top of the partition and into the corner booth where he was mixing. I was a sprawling heap of platinum blonde hair as I tumbled into his private DJ booth, and I had to act fast before Brendan and I were thrown out of the club.

The tiny booth was dark. His back was to me and he clearly had no idea I was there. Gently, I tapped him on the shoulder, which completely freaked him out. He nearly jumped out of his skin as he looked from me to the locked partition door with the incredibly small open space at the top.

"I'm so sorry I startled you, Mr. Oakenfold."

He had one earphone on and one off as he attempted to mix a record.

"What? How did you?"

He wiped his mop of curly dark hair out of his eyes to get a better look at me, probably wondering who the hell I was. I talked a mile a minute, thrusting the "white label" vinyl record toward him. (A "white label" is a record company's very limited pressing of a vinyl record with no name or title on it which is handed out to DJs so they'll play it and start a buzz happening.)

"I'm really sorry to drop in on you like this," I said sincerely. "I'm Traci Lords, and I'm a huge fan. Could I please give you my new record to listen to?"

The club went silent as the previous record finished.

Paul looked horrified as he frantically allowed an ambient track to slowly fill the air. I could hear the crowd of dancing bodies scream in appreciation, thinking he had chosen a new groove. My face was hot. Oh my God! I'd made Paul Oakenfold miss his mix! I stood there frozen, not breathing, as I waited for him to strangle me. Instead, he took his phones off, turned around, and casually said, "Thanks for the record but you better go now. Here—this is my new one. Cheers."

His eyes looked down at me now as I peeled the plastic off a new record by "Wink."

Remembering how cool he'd been, I smiled to myself. Paul was the first major DJ to play "Control," and he even added it to his favorite pick of the week list. It was a major score for me. *All hail Paul Oakenfold!*

After remembering that night, I realized my DJ partner Dawna had already called twice this morning, wanting to know what I thought of the new records we'd picked up. I pulled the headphones on and let the music transport me. *Ohhhhh, I like it . . . I really like* it*!* I puffed on my smoke and practiced mixing into an old Oakenfold track, feeling alive again.

I was counting the days I had left to prepare for the road.

Perry Farrell of Jane's Addiction (and later Porno for Pyros) fame booked me to perform as a DJ on the after-hours Lollapalooza tour called "Enit," and I felt the pressure to ace the gig. People like to talk and I was sensitive to the snide gossip in the music rags. The headlines screamed "Porno for Perry" and implied our "friendship" was responsible for my hiring. I'd met Perry shortly after returning from work in London. We hooked up in Los Angeles. We'd spent the night club-hopping with friends. The group of us—about four guys and three girls— ended up in the pool at his house somewhere in Venice for a midnight swim. We shared a sweet, somewhat drunk kiss good night and then went back to our very separate lives, talking once in a while on the phone. He ultimately became one of my greatest supporters in the underground scene.

I opened three weeks later for My Life with the Thrill Kill Cult, a kooky shock-rock band that was the opening act for the king of techno himself—Moby. Once the rock and rollers had finished on the main stage, day gave way to night, and Dawna and I downed a shot of Jägermeister before hitting the tables. At six feet tall, Dawna wore the pants on our team—literally. She was as much my bodyguard as she was my partner. She tossed many a starstruck intruder from our stage.

It was hard keeping my vices in check while running in a world without limits, but I managed. The temptation was fierce, and I took the edge off with coffee, nicotine, and the mandatory prestage cocktail. The eyeballs that peered at us as we played our set both inspired and intimidated me. Some moments I was completely at ease onstage controlling crowds of humans with a flick of a record. We set the mood; we ruled the club. But at other times I was hit with such jitters that I had to force myself to go on. It was then that I would hide behind dark bug-eyed sunglasses with arms that lit up around my ears.

During the "Enit" tour I discovered the rush of playing for a crowd. They were the best monitor, always letting us know where we were at. We'd go on around 11 P.M. when the crowds were a mixture of Lollapalooza rock and Ecstasy-trippin' club kids. They came from all walks of life. Some weren't even old enough to order a drink. There were flamboyant drag queens, computer geeks, and gangs of Mötley Crüe–looking fans.

When we were good, the electricity in the room raised us up even higher. But when we were off we died a slow death in front of a heckling crowd. We played hard-core techno records like Southside Reverb, Hardkiss, and anything from Juno Reactor. We'd make them sweat, then let 'em down easy, mixing in some trippy slow ambient tunes. I found out how many fans I had in those days and I was floored to discover what a broad base it was. Sure, I had the porn fans, but I also had the television fans, the John Waters fans, and the club kids who knew nothing about me except that I was the singer of the "Control" song. "Control" eventually went double platinum and was added to the film soundrack for *Mortal Kombat*. There were genuine fans everywhere we traveled in this all-new rave scene. It was good to know. And good to feel.

I returned from the "Enit" tour to film an appearance in the movie *Virtuosity* with Denzel Washington and Russell Crowe. It seemed Hollywood had noticed the hype. Director Brett Leonard was a fan of techno music and offered me the role of a nightclub singer in his new film. I performed my second single,

"Fallen Angel," in the movie. Then I was sent back to London to film a video to accompany the song's release. My album, *1000 Fires*, was taking off and I certainly felt the heat.

When I arrived home from London to a much needed rest, my mail was piled high on the top of the Japanese dining room table I'd recently purchased to celebrate my success. I sighed deeply. I'd wanted that table for years. I'd first seen it in the window of an Asian furniture store on Ventura Boulevard, right after Brook and I moved to Sherman Oaks, and remember pulling over and racing into the store to check it out. I was disappointed to learn it cost more than five thousand dollars! I didn't have five grand to blow on a new dining room table at the time, so I used to just drive by, visit it once a week, and imagine serving fabulous meals on it.

I stroked the table now sitting in my dining room covered with mail, not food. Weird. . . . I now had the money, the fame; I even had the table of my dreams. But I had no one I felt like cooking for. Was this the trade-off?

53

Broken China

John Enos was the kind of guy my mother should have warned me about. This six-foot-three Italian bad boy had blazing green eyes, dark chocolate-brown hair, and an appetite for destruction. He should have come with a "Proceed at Your Own Risk" sign. He was a bull in a china shop, a walk on the wild side, a testosterone-driven madman. He drove Harley-Davidson motorcycles, enjoyed a good barroom brawl, and drank Jack and Cokes like water.

He was as far away from the Brooks of the world as one could get, and at the time that's exactly what I was looking for.

John was no stranger to life in the fast lane. He'd seen it all. He was an ex-model/actor who had appeared on the pages of *Vogue* and traveled the world as one of the "beautiful people." He'd wined and dined with the best of them. He walked the walk and knew all the shortcuts. He'd had his share of famous girlfriends, the most recent being Madonna, and needless to say my frantic schedule and budding music career were nothing compared with hers. It didn't faze him.

With my single topping out at number two on the charts, my video added to Les Garland's The Box (an interactive version of MTV), and a new guy in my life, I had no time to spare. I traveled all over the United States, the United Kingdom, and Germany promoting my music career.

For two years John and I dated and lived in a world of dinners, parties, designer clothes, and trips to Miami. I felt like I was at the hub of everything exciting that was going on in Hollywood. And it was fun. But after a while, it left me longing for a hot bath and a clear head. I grew sick of the rumors, sick of champagne and caviar, and just wanted a quieter life. In spite of

With John Enos.

all my experiences, at heart I was really a small-town girl who wanted simple things—a fireplace and a home-cooked meal. Enos didn't have those things to offer, and although I knew it, I hoped it would change.

It was during this period that I was cast in the Wesley Snipes movie *Blade*.

Even before John and I moved in together I knew it wasn't right, but I did it anyway. Why did I do it? Because I *reallllllllly* wanted it to work. I wanted to be in love again, get a house, get married, have kids, recapture the dream I'd given up years before. But Johnny was no Brook and you can never go backward, only forward, and I was hanging on to the past.

As I unpacked the first moving boxes, I found myself tempted to reload the truck and make a break for it. That little voice inside my head screamed *run!* But I didn't listen. Instead I took a deep breath and convinced myself I'd made the right decision. Taking a seat in the sun in the backyard, I twisted my hair into a knot and asked myself the big question: Do I love him? And the answer was yes. I did. But was I really over my marriage? *Should I tell John I need time? He was due to arrive with all his worldly possessions any minute and move into this house with me. How do I tell him I still harbor feelings for my ex-husband? Was I just nervous about making a commitment? Oh man . . . oh man . . . oh man. . . .*

I sat there staring out into our backyard stroking Mr. Steve's furry belly. He was such a good listener. "You like it here, buddy?" He yawned lazily, bored with my head trips. *I'm just being silly. Look at this place. It's all good. Don't worry about it, girl.*

It was a great old Spanish-style house. The rosebushes that lined the driveway reminded me of Granny Harris's house (minus the ugly parts). I'd come a long way from those bloody sidewalks. . . . Searching the sky, I wondered if my great-granny was watching me now from heaven.

John and I moved in together that afternoon. He arrived with a smile on his face and his dogs at his heels. Yes, that's right—*dogs!* Enzo and Lucy were to Johnny what Mr. Steve was to me—buddies. Although I wasn't a dog person and the idea of

Taking a break, Malibu, California, 1997.

A quiet
moment with Mr. Steve.

having two pit bulls around made me nervous, I'd spent a lot of time with his dogs and really liked them. Johnny and I agreed the dogs would stay outside, where they had an enormous backyard to run in. He assured me the only real problem with our animals coexisting was in my head. But just to be on the safe side, he promised the house would be a dog-free zone. I sealed up the doggy door and began to relax, giving Mr. Steve full run of the house.

My head was filled with thoughts about my next album when the opportunity came up for me to audition for a regular role on the NBC series *Profiler* for producers Kim Moses and Ian Sanders. Ultimately, I won the role of the resident psycho Jill. It was an incredible moment. I was now a series regular! My agent, Stephen LaManna, and Juliet and I were thanking our lucky stars. It was an undeniable victory. All the pieces of my career were falling perfectly into place.

I reported for work on *Profiler* two weeks later and came home that afternoon to find my beautiful living room filled with congratulatory flowers, cards, and gift baskets from my agents, friends, and the folks at NBC. I was floating on air. I settled into the sofa to read the cards.

My handsome boyfriend walked in the door a few minutes later, laughing that with all the flowers around the house looked like a morgue. He just stood there in the doorway staring at me for a moment. Then he tossed me a little red box, which nearly bonked me in the face. *Hey!* I totally didn't get it. Then I opened the box to find a stunning diamond the size of Texas winking at me. I was speechless.

"Well . . . will you?" he asked as casually as if he was asking me to dinner.

He kissed me, not waiting for a response, and placed the ring on my finger. "I love you, baby." And in that moment my doubts gave way to the fairy-tale dream.

"I love you too," I said, kissing him back.

A month later, it fell apart.

I got home late one evening from work on the *Profiler* set to find the dogs running free in the house. I called for Johnny, praying Mr. Steve was okay.

I found my cat's mauled carcass on the back steps of our house. He'd been dragged out into the yard and torn apart by the dogs. I became hysterical. *What if that had been our kid?! What am I doing? How could I be with a man who's so irresponsible? What the hell am I thinking!!??*

I was stunned. Sobbing hysterically I called Vince, who now lived nearby. I told him what had happened and he came right over. We wrapped Mr. Steve up in my favorite Dr. Seuss bathrobe and called the pet cemetery. John walked through the front door and found me with my dead cat in my arms. Honestly, it wouldn't have mattered how many times he said he was sorry or how much he wished he could take it back. But the fact that he didn't say those things until much later only pushed me over the edge. He'd fucked up big time and confirmed all my worst fears about him.

I ended the relationship that night. His apologies met deaf ears as he offered to buy me a new cat. He really didn't get it and I felt like a moron for wasting my time with someone so insensitive. My cat had died a hideous death, and the fact that John didn't take responsibility for what his dogs had done was inexcusable. But it was more than that. It opened a Pandora's box. I'd known life with him wouldn't be as quiet as I might have dreamed and I knew he wasn't perfect, but I really thought I could trust him. And while I may have overlooked the other things, I couldn't ignore this one. I buried myself in my work.

I was in the mood to play a serial killer. . . .

54

The Onion Effect

My life as a steadily employed single woman left me with little time to contemplate the breakup with Enos. As casually as he'd arrived in my life two years earlier, he'd disappeared from it now. My world was mine again and it was a kinder, gentler place. I set the pace, made the rules, and chose my playmates much more carefully after that.

Unlike in times past, I wasn't looking to forget my problems. I was just giving myself some room to breathe and a stricter set of guidelines to work from. I was done with bad boys and said good-bye to the fast crowd I'd been hanging with. I kept my head down, avoided my old haunts, and plowed straight ahead.

Enjoying the harsh pace series regulars are expected to perform at, I found the nonstop schedule invigorating. In the mornings I did pilates in a small West Hollwood studio. The Zen-like atmosphere grounded me and put me in the right state of mind for work. I went on a major health kick, determined to give up smoking once and for all. Typical Traci—all or nothing, hot or cold. *But would I ever master that balance thing?*

I would leave the workout space with the remnants of my former nicotine vice pouring out of my skin and head home to Casa Martel to grab a quick shower before work. The *Profiler* stage was only a hop, skip, and a jump away, and I had the schedule wired. I arrived on the set each day with just enough time for a hazelnut latte and a quick chat with costar Dennis Christopher before going into makeup. We had already established a rapport, having worked together years before on the film *Circuitry Man II*. I was thrilled when I learned he was playing the mysterious Jack. He was a gracious actor, completely confident in his work, unafraid to do the dance.

The first episode showed Jack collecting me from a woman's prison and then transforming me into a look-alike of female lead Ally Walker's character, Sam, with whom he was obsessed. Once the makeup department had finished with me, I bore a haunting resemblance to the actress. Walking onto the set the first time, I was greeted by producer Ian Sanders with a "Good morning, Ally," as the makeup people cheered behind me. Success!

Ian Sanders and Kim Moses had championed my casting in this role and I was indebted to them. They are that rare breed of producers who actually like actors, and I was excited to hear that Ian was directing my first episode, my respect for him driving me to work even harder.

I spent the better part of that year performing bizarre killings at the request of my master, Jack. I studied all the bones in the human body, and learned the quickest way to murder someone. My homework was a bit creepy—the hanging charts of body parts in my home were a major deterrent for potential dates. It was not uncommon for me to drive home from a late-night shoot covered in fake blood, and I often wondered how I would explain myself if I was ever pulled over by the police. . . .

I began doing double publicity duty for *Profiler* and the soon-to-be-released *Blade*, the Wesley Snipes film I'd shot the previous summer. Juliet and I traveled to New York to attend the film's world premiere. I was flattered to be invited as I took my place among *Blade* stars Snipes and Stephen Dorff. I walked on the red carpet wearing a gorgeous midnight blue silk gown. I felt more confident than ever.

Returning to Los Angeles to finish my stint on *Profiler,* I was sad to leave my pals behind but definitely ready to put down my weapons. I had no idea what was next but had the urge to do a nice light comedy!

I spent my suddenly free days digging around in my rose garden. I talked to the flowers, fed the hummingbirds, and wandered down the street for early dinners with my buddy John Tierney, who owned the Hollywood hot spot Muse. John was like a brother to me and we often shared tales of our very different life experiences over delicious meals at his restaurant. I was, however, a bit baffled by his presence in my life, and during one of these dinners I asked him right out if he thought it was odd we were friends. "I mean, what's in it for you?" I asked.

He set his drink down, looked me in the eye, and said, "I can't believe you still don't get what an amazing person you are. I'm in awe of you. You remind me that if you could rise above the obstacles in your life, then I certainly have nothing to bitch about."

I was stunned: someone could relate to my struggle.

I left the restaurant deep in thought. Tierney's words had really hit me. I was shedding another layer. I was like an onion with layer after layer of life slowly being revealed.

Blade opened to sensational business. It was the number one movie in America. My agents were thrilled and so was I. *Holy cow! Sanity* and *a film career?*

As vampire Raquel in <u>Blade</u>.

Enjoying my killing spree in the role of Jill
on the set of <u>Profiler</u>.

55

Bullet Proof Soul

My blue-and-white ribbed Nike slip-on tennis shoes sloshed along the slick pavement. I felt my heart racing as I sprinted the final mile. The drizzling rain freckled my face and I grit my teeth, swallowing the burn in my side as I pounded the joggers' path toward Yale Town in Vancouver, British Columbia.

I doubled over to catch my breath, exhilarated from the five-mile run to Stanley Park. Soaked to the bone, I walked in little circles while watching the morning's first water taxi float by.

It was an Ansel Adams–looking day. The sky was painted with gray swipes against the fluffy white cauliflower clouds. I closed my eyes and breathed in the glorious moment, stretching my quads across the street from the high-rise I currently called home in what was by now pouring rain. My G-shock watch read 5:05 A.M. *I'd better get a move on.* I headed for my new Vancouver digs as Sade's "Bullet Proof Soul" pumped through my Walkman.

I'd been cast in the Larry Sugar–Chris Brancato–Francis Ford Coppola series *First Wave* in the role of Jordan Radcliffe, an heiress whose privileged life is destroyed by her parents' murder. She learns that an alien force is responsible for the killings and, using her considerable fortune, she starts an underground militia to fight the invasion. It was exactly the kind of role I excel in—the feisty underdog. She was a kick-ass, whip-smart Sigourney-Weaver-in-*Aliens*-meets-Linda-Hamilton-in-*Terminator* kind of woman and I loved playing her. Only weeks into my new Canadian lifestyle, I had zero homesickness, and enjoyed a freedom and peace of mind that I had never experienced before.

I welcomed the change of scenery Canada afforded me. I felt energized and only missed the sweet felines I'd recently adopted named Malickai and Pea, whom I'd left in my sister's care. One thing was certain in my family—we all had an absolute love for cats.

At 5:17 I crossed the street and punched in the security code for 239 Drake Street. Getting to my rooftop apartment, I stripped off my wet clothes and welcomed a hot shower, babbling out loud to myself as I practiced the day's dialogue. I dried and dressed quickly, pulling a "Vancouver Canucks" sweatshirt over my newly scarlet hair.

I loved it here in my rooftop paradise. Producer Larry Sugar had hooked me up with a real-estate agent who specialized in finding housing for visiting actors after I had mentioned that living in a hotel for an extended period of time just wasn't working for me. He went out of his way to please me and I rewarded him with home-baked chocolate cakes.

My driver arrived promptly at 5:45 A.M. We collected our preordered Starbucks coffee on the way to the set and Roger dropped me off in front of my dressing room a few minutes later. There I cranked the stereo, singing "Superlove" along with Macy Gray—"We are the genius of love, feel like an ex–X-rated movie star, it's the way you love me down, the way you love me down"—as I changed into Jordan's skintight black leather pants.

Checking my leather-covered bottom in the mirror, I approved of *First Wave* costume designer Vicky Mulholland's choice of combat gear—*not bad, lady*—and headed off to the makeup department to see the paint slappers. *Helloooooooooooooooo*, I kissed Donna Stocker, the head of the makeup department, on the nose and plopped down into the hair chair, where my unruly locks would be beaten into submission by

Maui, 2000.

Danna Rutherford, aka Danna Danna Banana, Fe Fi Fo Fanna, Danna. . . .

Six forty-five A.M. I was wide awake as episode director Ken Geraldi bounced into the makeup trailer, saying "Hello, ladies!" I was always thrilled to see Ken. He was my favorite director on *First Wave*, a real goofball whom everyone loved. His silly nature and self-deprecating humor always kept the set atmosphere light. We'd hit it off immediately and took turns playing jokes on each other. He was a down-to-earth guy with an impeccable eye for detail. He didn't pussyfoot around actors. He went right to the heart of what he wanted. After a take I could look at him from across the room and know what he wanted done differently just by the way he walked toward me. It was kind of like Mind Reading 101, and I loved doing that dance with him.

Series creator Chris Brancato took my character, Jordan, through some serious battles throughout the third season of *First Wave*. Jordan immediately clashed with Cade Foster, played by actor Sebastian Spence, and their struggle for power eventually led to a joining of forces as they fought to save the world from the aliens known as "the Gua."

It was a physically demanding role. Jordan was the jock of the show, which meant I suffered many a broken nail! And while Spence was nursing a back injury, I was the one who had to do all the running, jumping, and scaling of buildings. But I wasn't complaining. Playing with the stunt guys, I became fascinated with Ninjitsu (a style of martial arts) and started training with a Ninjitsu master Donald Munro. He worked in Larry Sugar's production office so word of my victories spread fast. Donald taught me how to throw a two-hundred-pound man. I was very good at it and kept a mental list of future potential victims. By the end of the season I had graduated to a brown belt.

Spence and I had chemistry on-screen and Brancato took full advantage of it, always putting Jordan and Cade nose-to-nose without letting them touch, teasing the audience for a full season. My on-screen relationship with Spence was the closest to a man I'd let myself be in months. I was single and intentionally dateless, having grown leery of all those possessing a penis. I'd become very *Sex in the City*, enjoying months of girl talk and cosmopolitans with my makeup and hair team coworkers, Donna Stocker and Danna Rutherford. We spent many long days on the set together and had become close friends. It was just me and the six-foot Canadian blond girls. They became my designated bodyguards, and the "Green Machine," aka manager Juliet Green, was very happy with the merger.

Juliet checked in on me often, and we spent most weekends on the phone gossiping about work. We'd become very close, particularly over the past year, and she was the one person I missed most besides my buddy John Tierney. I often called John from my living room as I'd watch the Vancouver rowing team stroke by my window. Usually they were shirtless, and man—the arms on those men!

Now I was calling John to let him know that I had a three-day break coming up and I was heading to L.A. We made plans for a dinner date that Saturday at Muse. I was going home for the weekend! I was going to play with the kitties! Yay! I did a jig in the living room, waving to the Peeping Tom across the way who was watching me dance in my apron. Then I remembered Larry Sugar's birthday cake in the oven. *Yikes!* I saved it just in time from a bitter fate. Frosting the devilish morsel carefully, I placed it in the fridge for delivery tomorrow, before my escape.

Packing my weekend bag, I jumped into bed and fantasized about catching up with John and driving down Pacific Coast Highway in my black convertible. Eventually, my excitement gave way to sleep as I drifted off blissfully.

Work sped by the next day. After lunch I serenaded my boss. Placing the sinful cake in front of him, Danna and I sang him a "Happy Birthday, Sugar Baby" song and then planted kisses on his face before I scrambled for the airport to catch a flight back to Los Angeles.

I walked into Muse several hours later. It was lipstick lesbian night and I raised many a prettily tweezed eyebrow with my body-worshiping Dolce and Gabbana dress and sexy Gucci high-heeled sandals. John greeted me at the door with a good squeeze hello and whistled as I gave my best diva strut toward our usual table.

He ordered us a beautiful bottle of Caymus and I purred like a happy cat when the waitress placed two ounces of beluga caviar in front of me. John always ordered for me, knowing exactly what I liked. We clinked glasses before he darted off to the kitchen to speak with the chef, and I sank back comfortably into the soft leather booth.

I watched the ladies at the bar competing for one another's attention and then momentarily locked eyes with Jeff, the lone male bartender across the room. He smiled and I smiled back, taking him in. I remembered him well — he'd poured me several martinis over the years. Tonight he had his hands full, surrounded by a heck of a lot of estrogen, and I laughed to myself. . . .

Over an amazing dinner of salmon and mashed potatoes, John and I swapped stories about his love life and my Canadian adventures. The restaurant was packed, though, so he often had to excuse himself to tend to business. I didn't mind. Sitting contentedly at the candlelit table listening to Barry White croon, I was just glad to be in the company of friends.

Jeff took a break and slid into the booth beside me. Smiling warmly, he offered me another drink and we chatted until John Tierney returned, teasing me about how I'd replaced him so quickly. "Not on your life, honey," I said, excusing myself to the ladies' room and leaving the boys standing by the table. I looked over my shoulder and caught them watching me.

I felt beautiful.

Forty-five minutes later John and I called it a night. We made our way toward the front door and collided with Jeff on the way out. He offered me an arm. *Man, was he gorgeous.* I looped my arm through his and John's, and off we went to collect our cars from the valet. I gave Jeff a kiss on the cheek good night and turned my attention toward John, hugging him extra tight. "Thank you for an amazing evening," I said. "I'll see you soon, okay?" He grinned, peeling out in his Porsche.

I said good night to Jeff again and he pulled me close into a hug. Then he gave me a nice kiss, smack-dab on the lips. *Whoa,* I felt dizzy. I broke the moment, backing off.

"Not bad," I said coolly, even though I was screaming on the inside. He laughed, his whole face lighting up. Holy cow—blazing green eyes!

He kissed me again . . . deeper. . . . *Wow!*

"Ahh, it could use some work," I quipped, leaving him standing alone on the sidewalk grinning like a Cheshire cat. Every hair on my body was standing up. I wasn't ready for this.

56

A New Wave

My weekend jaunt to Los Angeles had been the perfect blend of good food and old friends, Jeff's final kiss being the icing on the cake. I returned to work in Canada with a spring in my step and a lingering feeling about a certain bartender. Did he think I was a tease? I was a serial monogamist who seemed to have an undesirable talent for attracting bad relationships and I just didn't want to do that again.

As I sat in my trailer on the set of *First Wave*, engrossed in the upcoming week's script, I gasped in mock horror when I learned my character would be possessed by the alien Antichrist Mabus! What fun! Oh goody . . . oh goody . . . oh boy! I called Chris Brancato, thrilled with the evil plot he had conjured up. My imagination ran wild as I fantasized about tormenting my fellow cast members—*I would enjoy this!* Brancato encouraged me to unleash my wrath on the unsuspecting alien fighters. Man, I loved my job!

Brancato called me from Los Angeles the following week, having just gotten in the first Jordan/Mabus dailies. He applauded my performance and teasingly announced, "You're a great villain. I should have made you a bitch a long time ago!"

"Hey!" I feigned indignation, clearly pleased to have my

work praised by the producer. He filled me in on my character's story line for the remaining episodes and told me of his plan to have Jordan/Mabus seduce Cade Foster in a coupling that would result in Jordan becoming pregnant with his child.

Holy cow! I was going to be a pregnant alien Antichrist!

Days later, costar Sebastian Spence and I climbed onto a round bed, nearly naked, but not quite, to film a very PG-rated, TV-friendly love scene. We treated it like any other scene, but for me, as tame as it was and as smoothly as it went, it was a big deal. I wondered if the scene was really necessary. *Or was it about getting Traci Lords to do a love scene?* Any other actress would have concerns about that kind of scene, but no other actress would have had mine. Was I being overly cautious because of my past? Was every screen kiss today magnified because of it? Did my sexuality have extra weight because of the porn queen title?

Did I still have something to prove?

As the final season of *First Wave* came to an end, so did my time in Canada. During that year I'd found the balance that had eluded me my entire life. I don't know why it took moving away from everyone to discover that missing piece of myself, or if that's really why or what happened, but I do know that I returned to Los Angeles one layer thinner, stripped of what remained of my own judgment about myself.

It was during those days that I realized there was nothing screwed up or missing or wrong about me. I was just a work in progress, like everyone else, and in truth I was as shockingly normal as they came. I'd just had an extraordinary journey.

57

Jeff

On December 23, 2000, I walked into Muse and took a seat at the bar. My pal Tierney had some lingering business to finish up and left me in Jeff's very capable hands. I hadn't seen him or spoken to him since our kiss, but I'd thought about him often.

With my best Ohio twang, I teased, "How'd a nice western boy like you end up in a place like this?"

"This is fer mad money, honey," he answered back in a thick Colorado accent. "You should see what I do fer real kicks!"

I was intrigued to learn bartending was an amusing night out for this man named Jeff. His day job was far more intense: he was a union ironworker. *How sexy!*

"A union ironworker working nights in an oh-so-Hollywood bar?! Really now—that's a new one," I said, almost spitting my olives across the room, my head filled with images of him in a hard hat and a faded pair of Levi's 501s. *Oh my goodness.*

I nearly slid off my seat as I threw back the rest of my martini, grateful Tierney had come to save me from myself. *Down, girl!*

I started dating Jeff in February 2001. Apparently, I was the only one who hadn't noticed the crush he'd been nursing on me for the past *seven years*! He said he was a patient man, and over the next several months, I found out how true that really was. But I was cautious going into this relationship, testing him often, wanting proof that he wasn't going to hold my life against me as so many others had.

Looking back today I realize I had never really gotten over Brook. *Was it possible that I'd been in love with him all along?* For years I was convinced he was "the one who got away," and during my time in Canada, I'd decided to do something about that. I'd reconnected with Brook, revisiting those feelings and finally putting them to rest. Ironically, I discovered I'd been hooked on the *idea* of him as the husband and family man but not really on *him,* and while I was glad we could remain friends, thankfully, his ghosts had finally left the building. My heart had a vacancy, but squatters were not welcome, and I spent the next few months scrutinizing potential resident Jeffery Lee.

At the very least, our relationship had seven years of history behind it. Jeff and I had shared many a late-night chat at Muse about everything from boyfriends to jobs to sex, and we already had an ease with each other that was rare. It also helped that there was a lot I didn't have to walk him through. He got life. He was a grown-up. His thirty-eight years on this planet had left him with his own battle wounds. He was a fighter and I appreciated that. I saw a kindred spirit in him.

Our relationship blossomed. We wasted no time on the petty stuff new couples sometimes struggle with. He wasn't interested in how many lovers I'd had, or who was the best, or any of that kind of meaningless ego stuff. He was secure in himself, smart and sensitive, and I was impressed.

One evening at dinner in a romantic restaurant in the Hollywood Hills, the heel of my brand-new Gucci shoe broke. While I was glad to be sitting when it occurred, I was mortified at the thought of how I would leave the restaurant with a crippled shoe, in a town where image is everything. I whispered my dilemma to my handsome date and he just smiled, telling me to pass the shoe under the table to him. Hiding it beneath his jacket, he excused himself to the men's room. What was he going to do? Did he have a miniature welding machine in his pocket?

He returned to the table and discreetly slipped the repaired shoe back on my foot. We finished our meal and managed to make it out the front door and into the cool spring air before the heel snapped off again. I laughed, grateful for the rig job at least, and leaned on him to steady myself. Jeff was the kind of man a girl could lean on and a woman could trust.

Six months later, we strolled arm in arm down a wooden pier in Moorea, Tahiti, a bottle of our favorite red wine in hand. We cozied up on the edge of the pier and looked out over the pristine turquoise water with not another soul in sight. Speak-

Me and Jeff in Los Angeles, 2002.

ing softly, our sarongs dancing in the tropical air, we sipped our vino and rested in each other's arms.

A brilliant sunset of orange and yellow painted the sky, and Jeff's fingers slowly ran through my hair. The sun was so warm and his skin was so hot. I wanted him to kiss me, and I wasn't afraid of what would happen next. . . . I was that little girl again . . . ten years old in the field . . . but everything was different — I was wiser and those wounds were badges of courage.

He sees me, I thought, *he really sees me.*

And here I am.

"Will you marry me?" he whispered in my ear.

I guess that broken Gucci slipper was an omen, because Jeff turned out to be the prince of princes. I'd given up looking for Mr. Right. He'd been right under my nose all along.

On a glorious February morning in 2002 I drove up Pacific Coast Highway listening to U2 sing "Beautiful Day" and feeling like it truly was. My long red hair danced in the wind and my cell phone rang every so often, bringing me greetings and well wishes from my best friends Juliet, Donna, and Danna.

I arrived at the private beach club just before noon and greeted the waiting staff. My dressing room was already filled with my giddy friends, and my hairdresser Reny whisked me into a chair and started combing out my windblown locks. I sipped a Starbucks latte and watched the waves crash through the big glass window overlooking the sea. People were rushing around outside. The scent of gardenias hung in the air, and the unseasonably warm February breeze sent iridescent teal green tablecloths dancing.

Fishnets decorated the buffet tables and caterers bustled in the back kitchen. The whole place buzzed with excitement as guests began to arrive. Donna did my makeup and Reny pulled up my hair into a cascading mass of curls. Juliet and Danna helped me slip into my gown and John Tierney practiced the "butchest" way to hold the bridal bouquet, taking his role as "best thing" very seriously.

With Canadian gal pal Danna, July 2000.

With John Tierney at a Hollywood Bowl concert, July 2000.

*My soul sister Juliet and me on my wedding day,
Malibu, California, 2002.*

Jeff and I were married quietly on that afternoon, over-looking the ocean in Malibu, California. We were surrounded by the most important people in our lives.

My mother was one of them.

Me and Jeff.

58

Underneath It All

I have spent the last twenty years of my life trying to figure out who I am, what I stand for, and what my journey here on earth is all about.

I've always believed that celebrities are given a platform, a stage, that enables them to comment on things in a very public way. Whether they choose to do so or actually have anything to say is another story. I for one have always been a bit reluctant to speak out on certain subjects, mainly because words have a way of getting tangled up. After having several articles come out filled with half-truths, untruths, and various other slants, I chose silence as a defense.

Writing this book has broken that silence. It terrifies me on one level, to give my innermost thoughts to whoever chooses to read them, but it gives me great satisfaction to know that I finally got to tell my side of the story, after years of being terribly misunderstood.

I talked about the onion effect earlier and once again I find myself surrounded by peelings. My quest for balance still continues after all these years, but I look at life differently now. I don't believe things are black or white anymore. I see the gray area. I carry with me the scars of my battles, but my heart has healed a great deal.

While I now have a caring relationship with my mother and sisters, I've accepted the fact that that will never be the case with my father.

The hardest person for me to forgive has been me. I thought for such a long time that I was just a bad girl, and what happened to me was simply all my fault. Working those issues out in front of the camera, first in porn, then later in mainstream Hollywood, was hell. Today I feel about porn as I feel about an episode of *Jerry Springer:* I just can't stomach it.

Today porn is everywhere I look. I find it in the junk mail folder on my computer, it peers at me from local magazine racks, and sits blatantly in the window of the liquor store where I buy my wine. Porn stars play themselves on television shows, appear on billboards, and give interviews about how "liberating" porn is for women. Well, I believe it's anything but. It annoys me that I can't block out these unwanted intrusions in my life. I find the junk mail insulting, the box covers inappropriate (in a public place), and the women who claim porn is liberating, irresponsible.

It disturbs me deeply to think some young girl could hear what these women say, find out about my start in porn, and think that is a viable path to success. While I am opposed to government censorship, I can't help but wonder where it will stop. When is sex no longer sexy? I have struggled with that question in both my career and personal life. And I have come to the conclusion that, while I find sexuality and eroticism as healthy as laughter and as nourishing as good food, I believe hard-core porn is desensitizing to the viewer and that it objectifies its performers. I am speaking from personal experience when I tell you that while many porn stars may look pretty on the outside, I have never met one who wasn't damaged by a business that makes it impossible to think of its "stars" as human at all.

I hate that I'm the poster child for a business I loathe. I'm constantly reminded all these years later that I was a teenage porn star by people from all walks of life, people who are either ignorant of the fact that I was just a kid when I made those movies twenty years ago or who just refuse to see me in any other way. I find it infuriating at times and just plain simple in others. All I can say is, it keeps me humble!

Growing beyond the porn queen image has been a daunting task in Hollywood. There were those who accepted me, gave me a chance, and to them I will be forever grateful. And then there were the others: the producer who got cold feet and fired me the day before I was to start work because he was afraid I would "taint" his project; the network exec who had my role cut because he didn't think I belonged on his network (though he's known to have a large collection of my bootleg tapes). I could go on and on, but I won't. They say if something doesn't kill you it makes you stronger. And in my case it's true.

I think about how close I came to becoming another statistic and it chills me. I was another runaway, another molested child, another victim of sexual predators. But underneath it all I was a survivor. I chose to write this book for that very reason.

The beginning of my happy ending.

Photograph Credits

Photographs on pages 2, 4, 6 *(top)*, and 14 by Mike Ruiz. Copyright Divine Entertainment. All rights reserved.

Photographs on pages 3, 12 *(bottom)*, and 13 by Sam Maxwell. Copyright Divine Entertainment. All rights reserved.

Photograph on page 5 *(top)* by Albert Sanchez. Copyright Divine Entertainment. All rights reserved.

Photograph on page 5 *(bottom)* by Michelle Laurita. Copyright Divine Entertainment. All rights reserved.

Photographs on pages 8–9 and 16 by Jaques Bettinber. Copyright Divine Entertainment. All rights reserved.

Photographs on page 10 by Gilles Toucas. Copyright Divine Entertainment. All rights reserved.

Photographs on pages 11, 12 *(top)*, and 15 copyright Albert Watson. All rights reserved.